PHILIP'S COUNTY GU

CW01618849

HAMPSHIRE

GENERAL EDITOR
ROBIN DEWHURST

WRITERS

Chris Barrett

Russell Chamberlin

Ron Coates

David Souden

Richard Tames

All rights reserved. Apart from any fair dealing for the purpose of private study, research, criticism or review, as permitted under the Copyright Designs and Patents Act, 1988, no part of this publication may be reproduced, stored in a retrieval system, or transmitted in any form or by any means, electronic, electrical, chemical, mechanical, optical, photocopying, recording, or otherwise, without prior written permission. All enquiries should be addressed to the Publishers.

British Library Cataloguing in Publication Data

Dewhurst, Robin
Hampshire. – (Philip's County Guides)
I. Title II. Series
914.22704

ISBN 0–540–01275–0

Text and maps © George Philip 1993
Series Editor: Theresa Wright
Design: Peter Burt
Page design: Keith Williams

First published by George Philip Limited,
Michelin House, 81 Fulham Road, London SW3 6RB

Mapping based upon Ordnance Survey maps with the permission of the Controller of Her Majesty's Stationery Office
© Crown copyright

Printed in Hong Kong

ALSO AVAILABLE
East Sussex
Surrey
West Sussex

ACKNOWLEDGEMENTS
The publishers would like to thank the following for their advice and assistance during the preparation of this book:
East Hampshire Council
Fareham Council
Havant Council
Portsmouth City Council
Southern Tourist Board

FURTHER READING

John Barton *Hidden Hampshire* (Countryside Books, 1989)
Tony Brode *The Hampshire Village Book* (Countryside Books, 1980)
The New Hampshire Village Book, compiled by Hampshire Federation of Women's Institutes (Countryside Books, 1990)
N. Pevsner and D. Lloyd *The Buildings of England: Hampshire* (Penguin, 1967)

PICTURE SOURCES
John Bethell pp.23, 43, 71, 79, 93, 100, 115, 123
Derek Forss pp.57, 64, 108, 130
Skyscan pp.34, 50, 86

CONTENTS

INTRODUCTION

If you go in search of England – almost any England – then you are likely to find it in Hampshire. This is a county of high, rolling downlands and deep forests, of still, green water meadows and sparkling trout streams, of orderly Georgian market towns and secluded villages, complete with Norman churches, thatched cottages, rampant clematis and stately dahlias. This is where London overspills into a cluttered mix of semi-industrial suburbia, interspersed with heaths and woods. It is also a county of the coast: busy ports, seaside resorts, fashionable residential marinas, monotonous housing estates and lonely mudflats that glisten stickily at low tide.

There is history in abundance. Stand in the cathedral city of Winchester and you are in the ancient heart of England, metaphysically if not geographically. Here the country was founded, kings were baptized, crowned and buried, and the Domesday Book was compiled. The Romans built a port at Southampton and Nelson sailed from Portsmouth, where the masts and rigging of his flagship, the Victory, provide a background of delicate tracery to the menacing grey bulks of today's warships.

LANDSCAPE

Hampshire is the third most densely wooded county in England, yet the most striking first impression is likely to be the smooth and swelling curves of the chalk downlands that roll in a broad central belt right across the county. In prehistoric times, trees grew on the chalk but through the ages farmers cleared the forests for grazing sheep and cattle. Water-meadows created from river valleys during the 17th century provided richer grazing and gradually the downs were transformed into the vast open fields you see now, intensively ploughed and fertilized for the summer carpeting of cereal crops and oil seed rape, with its disturbing, discordant glare.

The high chalklands are bare and bereft of trees and buildings. In total contrast below lies a surprisingly luxuriant countryside of well wooded valleys, tranquil water meadows and unspoiled villages of thatch, wood, stone and brick. Largely from the 16th to 18th centuries, their setting among fields and woods compose the calendar version of rural England. Here, you find the county's great trout rivers, the Test and the Itchen, and the drowsy rural charm of the Meon.

Chalk rises to the spiny ridge of Ports Down hill overlooking Portsmouth, but elsewhere in the county, gravels, sands and clays predominate, producing poor soil. The 145 square miles of New Forest was created as a royal hunting preserve by William the Conqueror in 1079. With native oak and beech, among other older trees, it is now one of the finest relics of undisturbed deciduous forest remaining in western Europe, the oldest and largest of the great English royal forests and still looking much the same as it did in William's day. Almost half the area is grassland or heathery heath, often quite high and windswept; other parts are marshy, thick with bracken and moss, overhung with alders, while elsewhere peaty streams trickle through dappled glades. Ponies roam freely and so do the deer, many of them direct descendants of those the Normans hunted so keenly.

Other forests, also once royal hunting grounds, remain, though reduced in size. Alice Holt Forest, bisected by the busy A325 south of Farnham, was once part of a Saxon forest; some 2000 acres remain. Only a fragment is left of the original medieval Forest of Bere near Wickham, which stretched from Romsey to the Sussex border, but oak, beech and chestnut survive. The Queen Elizabeth Country Park, south of Petersfield, is rather different. The recent planting of trees, mainly beech, has returned a section of the chalk downs to their original forested condition. Now you can experience the 'before and 'after' by walking through the wooded hillsides and across to the open green-shaven summit of Butser Hill. At 887ft, it is one of Hampshire's highest points, with superb views across countryside and water to the distant Isle of Wight.

In the north-east, the terrain is largely sandy heathland, sprinkled with pine and birch, ground which in the Aldershot area, for instance, has proved ideal for military training. East Hampshire offers a contrasting mix of downlands, heathlands and woodlands. An outstanding feature is The Hangers, a long line of steeply wooded hills that follows an escarpment from Petersfield to Alton. The outstanding scenery has prompted such descriptions as 'Little Switzerland' and 'The Hampshire Alps'

By comparison, Hampshire's serrated coast is generally unspectacular, though the view from Ports Down is exhilarating, a vast panoramic vista that stretches from the Solent to Sussex and across Portsmouth to the Isle of Wight. Far below, toy ships trace wispy wakes as they head out to all parts of the world. But at sea level, the scenery is unexceptional; no high cliffs to break the monotony of ribbon development for much of the coast and, with the exception of Hayling Island, beaches are pebble or shingle. The rise in sea level, coupled with erosion, created the Solent, Southampton Water, the Hamble and Beaulieu estuaries and Portsmouth and Langstone harbours. Sheltered estuaries provide a safe haven for many water sports, and creeks, salt marshes and tidal mud flats offer a sanctuary for a rich and varied wildlife. The coast is dominated by Southampton and Portsmouth, now virtually joined together through a series of built-up conurbations, though you can still find unexpectedly rural pockets.

EARLY HISTORY

Of some 450 scheduled ancient monuments in Hampshire, the oldest are the earthen long barrows of the Neolithic period. About 40 of these survive, mainly on the downs, and visible from long distances. The most numerous prehistoric sites, though, are the Bronze Age round barrows; over 200 exist on the downs, in the north-east and the New Forest. Of the estimated 30 Iron Age forts, the best known and most visited is Danebury Hill, which has been extensively excavated and gives a remarkable insight into the life of those times; it was occupied from around 550 BC to 100 BC. Another hill fort, Old Winchester Hill, is also a nature reserve, rich in flora and fauna. It provides an excellent opportunity to see how a large area of chalk downland looked before it was put under the plough. Beech, yew and juniper grow here, along with chalkland scrub, all of which attract many species of butterflies and birds. This outstanding natural botanical site has been singled out for special protection by the Council of Europe.

Visual evidence of the Roman colonization of Hampshire is patchy. Vespasian captured the Isle of Wight in AD 43 and quickly 'romanized' the county. The Romans crossed the River Itchen by a prehistoric ford and built a walled city called Venta Belgarum. Some 6000 people lived in the regional capital but little has survived because modern Winchester is built on top. Of the other main town, Silchester, or Calleva Atrebatum, like Winchester a late Iron Age tribal centre, only some of the town wall and amphitheatre remain. At Rockbourne a villa has been excavated, and pottery was produced in the Alice Holt Forest. On the coast, Bitterne was Southampton's predecessor and first port. But by far the most impressive relic is Portchester Castle, overlooking Portsmouth Harbour and built sometime after AD 286, possibly as a fleet base for clearing Saxon pirates from the Channel. Inside the original Roman fort, which occupies more than eight acres, is a medieval castle.

SAXONS AND NORMANS

The name 'Hampshire' is of Anglo-Saxon derivation, from Hamtunscir, the 'shire of Hamtun', the district governed from Southampton which eventually became the county of today. The kings of the West Saxons created Wessex and Winchester became the capital, where an early cathedral was built. The Saxon hero was King Alfred the Great (849–99), who drove back the invading Danes and rebuilt the town. Today's basic framework of central streets follows the Saxon pattern. King Alfred is regarded as the founder of the kingdom and his descendants became the first kings of England. A little of the Saxon period remains in Winchester; other tangible legacies are to be found in a few churches, among them those at Breamore, Boarhunt, Corhampton and Titchfield.

The Norman and medieval heritage is far greater, particularly in Winchester, where the magnificent cathedral, the longest in Europe, is just one of several outstanding attractions. Dozens of small village churches retain strong evidence of their Norman origin, despite later additions and alterations: among the more authentic are those at East Meon, Portchester, Romsey, isolated little Idsworth near Rowlands Castle, Colemore and Bighton, to single out a handful. Whatever their age, village churches should not be overlooked in favour of more grandiose historic buildings for often they provide a revealing insight into local social history.

MEDIEVAL HAMPSHIRE

The 12th and 13th centuries were a time of growth. New towns, such as Portsmouth and Lymington, were created; abbeys and palaces built (Beaulieu and Bishop's Waltham, both in ruins); and castles established (Portchester and Southampton, where impressive fortifications remain). Hampshire's fortunes waxed and waned down the centuries. The wool trade brought prosperity for a spell; Alresford had one of the busiest wool markets in England and Romsey specialized in cloth production. There was naval boat-building at Southampton, Bursledon and Bucklers Hard. Portsmouth grew as the navy expanded.

The Black Death decimated the population and villages declined or were abandoned. Ironically, this may have saved many of Hampshire's woodlands from further devastation by farmers eager to create yet more fields for crops and animals. Trees were further spared much later when ship building turned from timber to iron. Winchester eventually lost its power and position to become one of England's most attractive small county towns.

DEFENCE

From Tudor times on, there was an immense amount of new military building. Henry VIII secured the Solent with Hurst Castle, Southampton Water with Calshot and Portsmouth with Southsea. Much later, during the 18th- and 19th-century threat from France, elaborate defences were constructed in Portsmouth, Gosport, the Solent generally and high up on Ports Down. Many of these impressive military fortifications can be visited, including Spitbank Fort, one of four massive sea forts built between Portsmouth and the Isle of Wight. Aldershot became the first military town in Britain since Roman times when the government purchased 10,000 acres in 1854 for army training; it is now the official home of the British Army.

During the 17th-century Civil War, Hampshire was sandwiched between the Parliament-controlled south-east and the Royalist west country. In Portsmouth, the Navy sided with Parliament while the Governor declared for King Charles, temporarily holding the town for the crown. After a naval blockade and the capture of Southsea Castle, the town fell. Royalists and Roundheads fought a decisive battle at Cheriton in March, 1644, which the Parliamentarians won, putting the king on the defensive. The defeated army retreated to fortified Basing House, the home of the Marquess of Winchester, which had already been the scene of a previous siege and was subject to yet another before being stormed and captured by Oliver Cromwell and later destroyed. You can visit the ruins of Basing House and inspect a small monument to the Battle of Cheriton.

Hampshire has always been inextricably tied up with defence, and its history can be appreciated in coastal fortifications and in army, air and naval museums throughout the country. Aldershot has six military museums alone and Winchester a further five. In Portsmouth is concentrated a wealth of naval heritage with an impressive number of world class exhibits. You can, for instance, trace the story of the warship through Henry VIII's great flagship, the *Mary Rose*, Nelson's HMS *Victory* and the meticulously restored HMS *Warrior*, Britain's first iron-hulled armoured ship. On Southsea front, the D-Day Museum tells the story of the Normandy landings through the remarkable 272 ft long Overlord Embroidery. And all along the coast are an astonishing number of castles and forts, from Roman Portchester to the massive blockhouse fortresses on Ports Down, built in mid Victorian times.

Quite apart from the museums, there are military mementoes in more domestic, though impressively grand settings. Stratfield Saye House, near Basingstoke, was given to the Duke of Wellington after the Battle of Waterloo. Broadlands, at Romsey, was once the home of Lord Palmerston (the Victorian prime minister who ordered the construction of the forts on Ports Down) and later of Earl Mountbatten of Burma, and has displays devoted to both men.

TOWN AND VILLAGE

The arrival of the first railway line from London to Southampton in 1840 opened up the county. Southampton briefly became a resort before developing into Britain's premier passenger port, Southsea developed as a Victorian seaside resort and Portsmouth's dockyard continued to expand. Hampshire saw an immense building boom in the Victorian era, only exceeded in the period following World War II. Industrial and commercial expansion has taken place along the coast from Portsmouth to Southampton and in the London overspill towns of Basingstoke and Andover, enlarged out of all recognition.

For many, the magnet of Hampshire remains its glorious countryside, its orderly, predominantly Georgian market towns and the number of unspoiled villages with their vernacular architecture. Yet as the county lies outside the main limestone belt, a major deficiency has been quality building material. In medieval times, stone for major works such as Winchester Cathedral and Portchester Castle was imported from the Isle of Wight and Caen, in Normandy. The re-use of this stone was common. Many cottages and some earlier churches are built of flint, the stone knapped for facings. Occasionally, you can find the characteristic 'Hampshire Nails', small studs of local ironstone set into the joints.

Timber-framed buildings can be seen throughout the county, infilled with stone, brick or rough cast coarse plaster, and often thatched. An outstanding thatchless example of timber framing is the Tudor House in Southampton, now a museum. Oak was used frequently until the late 18th century as the supply remained plentiful in Hampshire, though legislation controlling its use had been introduced during the reign of Elizabeth I. In east Hampshire villages, the pale, soft malmstone, quarried locally, is a common sight. Brick became fashionable in the 18th century and Hampshire clay was particularly productive in the making of different coloured bricks, predominantly red or yellow. Fine examples of Georgian brick building can be found in Odiham, New Alresford, Wickham, Fareham and Lymington.

HOUSES AND GARDENS

Hampshire has no nationally famous stately homes, but some imposing country mansions. Arguably the most impressive is The Vyne, a Tudor mansion built for the Lord Chamberlain to Henry VIII. Highclere Castle is not a castle at all but a Victorian extravaganza, the home of the Earl and Countess of Caernarvon. Also Victorian is Rotherfield Park at East Tisted. The interior is authentic aristocratic mid to late Victorian.

Hampshire's gardens are another feature not to be missed. Exbury, in the New Forest, has a profusion of outstanding rhododendron and azaleas, the largest collection in the county. At Hillier Gardens and Arboretum, near Romsey, some 36,000 plants from all over the world grow in grounds of 160 acres. Mottisfont, also near Romsey, has one of the finest rose displays in Britain. There are some specialist gardens, too: a 17th-century Physic Garden in Petersfield, a Tudor Garden in Southampton and a medieval garden in Winchester.

LITERARY HAMPSHIRE

Ghosts of a gentle past also inhabit Hampshire. The literary giant is Jane Austen, who spent most of her life in the county and wrote her six famous novels here. As you travel around you'll find spots associated with her: Steventon, where she was born, Ibthorpe, where she stayed, Chawton, where she wrote several books and Winchester, where she is buried. A steady pilgrim of admirers make their way to her old home in the village of Chawton, which is now a museum dedicated to her life.

Other writers are associated with Hampshire and you could quite easily construct your own literary tour. Charles Dickens (1812–70) was born in Portsmouth and his birthplace is open to the public. Charles Kingsley (1819–75), rector of Eversley for 30 years, is best known for *The Water Babies* and *Westward Ho!*. He used to fish the River Itchen and is buried in the churchyard at Eversley. Izaak Walton (1593–1683), author of *The Compleat Angler*, retired to the 'silver streams' of the Meon at Droxford. The classic book *Children of the New Forest* was written by Captain Frederick Marryat (1792–1848); he lived in New Milton at Chewton Glen, now a luxury hotel. A highly productive and popular Victorian writer, Charlotte Yonge (1823–1901) wrote more than 150 books and lived at Otterborne all her life. The poet Edward Thomas (1878–1917) was inspired by the countryside around Steep, where he lived for ten years.

The radical journalist and social reformer William Cobbett (1763–1835) for many years farmed at Botleys. 'The most delightful village in the world,' he called it. He also liked Hurstbourne Tarrant, where he stopped often when writing his *Rural Rides*. But pride of place has to go to the naturalist, Gilbert White (1720–93), a scholarly clergyman who lived in Selborne all his life and was curate several times but never vicar. He wrote *The Natural History and Antiquities of Selborne*, based on 40 years' observation of the local flora and fauna, which became a classic and put the little village on the world map. His home, The Wakes, is now a museum.

WILDLIFE

Much of Hampshire is rich in flora and fauna, although hedgerows in many parts have suffered from intensive farming. Among woodlands, the New Forest has by far the greatest variety, with hundreds of species of wild flowers and plenty of birds whose natural habitat is the older, undisturbed woodlands. The most common, and prettiest, of the four species of deer is the Fallow deer; others are Red, Roe and the Japanese Sika, generally spotted in the south of the Forest. Car parks are located throughout the forest and the best way to explore is on foot. Guided walks are organised from several centres or even on horseback, but if you are feeling lazy, wagon rides are available. Virtually all the forest is freely open to the public, but the millions of visitors each year emphasize tourism's eternal dilemma: how to preserve the attractions that mass holidaymaking can so easily destroy. Special laws protect this unique area of Britain. Forest roads, for instance, are fenced or ditched, cars are confined to car parks and a low speed limit, the roaming ponies must not be fed, fires cannot be lit and camping is restricted to official sites. The mandatory starting point to any visit is the Museum and Visitor Centre in Lyndhurst, where you can learn all about the forest's history, tradition and wildlife.

Sheltered parts of the coast and the somewhat forlorn mudflats of Langstone and Portsmouth harbours attract wildfowl and seabirds of all types. But a word of warning: the best time to go is in winter. Around the salt marshes of Lymington you have a better chance of seeing sea birds nesting in spring and early summer.

Wherever you are in the county, by far the easiest way of experiencing wildlife is in Hampshire's many Nature Reserves and Country Parks. As an example, Lepe Country Park, on the Solent near the New Forest, is rich in a variety of natural habitats. You may find Brent geese and curlew on mudflats, redshank and kingfisher on freshwater ponds, turnstone, a patterned shore bird, on a pebble beach, wild flowers on a farmland meadow and so on.

WALKING

Quite apart from the New Forest, Hampshire's varied terrain provides excellent walking elsewhere. Footpaths along the banks of the two celebrated chalk fishing rivers, the Test and the Itchen, are unfortunately limited; the Test's beauty spots can be most easily appreciated from its many bridges. There is, though, the Test Way long-distance footpath, which follows the valley and chalk downs for nearly fifty miles from Totton across the Berkshire border to Inkpen Beacon. Another long distance footpath, the seventy-mile Wayfarers Walk, cuts right across Hampshire from Emsworth on the coast, again ending up at Inkpen. The Solent Way hugs much of the coast for sixty miles from Milford on Sea to Emsworth while the Clarendon Way links Winchester and Salisbury, passing through superb countryside. Possibly the most scenic of all is the Hangers Way, 17 miles in all from Petersfield to Alton. The South Downs Way from Eastbourne now extends to Winchester.

SPORT AND LEISURE

If you find walking a shade too energetic, you may prefer Southern England's longest preserved steam railway, which runs ten miles between Alresford and Alton, the round trip taking about 90 minutes. The Watercress Line, so called because of Alresford's cress industry, puffs nostalgically out of the past, with all the fittings and fixtures of those times – engines, carriages, stations and cream teas. The line, which originally extended to Winchester, was opened in 1865 and closed, under strong protest, in 1973. Four years later, it re-opened and is now one of Hampshire's major tourist attractions. Another leisurely trip is by narrow boat along part of the restored Basingstoke Canal, which opened in 1794, hardly ever made a profit and finally closed earlier this century. Originally it ran from Basingstoke to Weybridge in Surrey. The trip lasts about 2½ hours and the boat sails from Odiham.

Hampshire's coast, though scenically often on the dull side, does offer a wide range of leisure pursuits. The best beaches are on Hayling Island, where some four miles of shingle runs along its southern shore. West Beach has the much coveted and strictly administered EC Blue Flag awarded for, among things, the purity of water. Southsea, although part of Portsmouth, has a character of its own as a traditional style of resort with two piers, a carefully kept seaside common and a long shingle beach that is safe for swimming. This can fly the blue and yellow flag of the Tidy Britain Group's Seaside Award, only marginally less strict than the EC Blue Flag. Portsmouth and Southsea's combination of conventional resort activities and historic naval heritage with several outstanding museums makes it a unique holiday destination. There are two small resorts on the west Hampshire coast, Milford on Sea and Barton on Sea, with beaches of pebble and shingle.

Despite its popularity as a yachting centre, the Beaulieu river estuary remains a peaceful rural retreat with a delightful riverside footpath between Beaulieu and Bucklers Hard. Hamble, on Southampton Water, is one of the most concentrated sailing centres in Britain with several marinas and boats for hire. Just about every type of water sport is available all along the coast and there are several centres offering activity courses.

As in most of Britain, local specialities and old traditions have largely died out in Hampshire. You'll have to look long and hard to find Hampshire Haslet, a baked mixture of minced pork, bread and spices, though a butcher in Lyndhurst provides first class venison pies, pâtés and sausages. Hampshire Hog is a dish of the past yet the expression lingers on. It was the farm workers' staple meal, named for the pork and apple that made it, not the way he ate it. If you're lucky, you might still find Gingerbread Husbands, dough in the shape of a man, at some of the old established fairs. Elizabeth I, whose obsession for things sweet turned her teeth black, claimed the best honey came from Hampshire; you can buy it now from farms and cottages throughout the county.The queen would still approve of the quality. Local beers are brewed and there are several vineyards.

But tradition permeates Hampshire in other ways, in the old parts of some of Britain's oldest towns, in the wealth of historic detail and in a rural landscape that our ancestors would still recognize. And it is in the quiet hidden villages, protected by narrow lanes away from the modern motorways, where you find the true heart of Hampshire still beats strongly.

ROBIN DEWHURST
BURITON, 1992

LISTINGS & SYMBOLS

LISTINGS

The A–Z of Towns & Villages lists all settlements as well as some other places (e.g. Hayling Island, The New Forest) which do not fall into the categories covered by the Days Out listings.

Cross references to entries in the A–Z are given in SMALL CAPITALS. Cross references to the Days Out section are given in the form 'see p. ...'. **Bold type** is used to highlight important buildings or other features, but does not imply that they are open, or even accessible, to the public.

Details of access and telephone numbers have been provided wherever possible. While every effort has been made to ensure these are up to date, they are subject to change. If you are planning a special trip to visit one of the places listed, it is best to check with the local tourist office in advance.

STAR RATINGS

All entries, and sub-entries within the A–Z, have been rated from 0–3 stars as follows:

★★★	major attraction
★★	general interest
★	local or specialist interest

SYMBOLS

Days Out

- Admission fee
- Refreshments
- Shop
- Guided tours
- Disabled access
- Mother and baby facilities
- No dogs
- Information centre

A–Z of Towns & Villages

- Church
- Castle
- Historic building
- Museum
- Monument
- Viewpoint
- Park or open space
- Pond, river or lake
- Pub or inn
- Information centre
- Archaeological site

HISTORIC HOUSES

AVINGTON PARK
Map p.150, E1
4 miles NE of Winchester off the B3047

Even the curmudgeonly William Cobbett, the 19th-century author of *Rural Rides*, thought this 'one of the very prettiest spots in the world'. The house's 17th-century core (where Charles II stayed with Nell Gwynn) is faced with a huge Tuscan portico of wood (*c.*1710), possibly by John James. The ballroom has a 17th-century painted ceiling depicting the four seasons and attendant muses which may be by Verrio; the gilding is 18th-century.

The brick church near the house is a Georgian gem. Raised between 1768 and 1771, it contains a barrel-organ which played 31 tunes, a 'Vinegar Bible ' of 1717 (so called because of the famous misprint for 'Vineyard') and a monument to John Shelley (d. 1866), elder brother of the poet, who owned the house. The mahogany furnishings are said to have been made from the timbers of an Armada galleon. They include a three-decker pulpit and a squire's pew big enough to hold an entire Sunday-school class.

May–Sept, Sun and BH Mons 2.30–5.30pm; other days by appointment all year. Tel: (0962) 779260.

BEAULIEU PALACE HOUSE AND ABBEY * * *
Map p.136, C4
5 miles E of Brockenhurst on the B3055

(ground floor)

Of the great Cistercian monastery founded by King John, only the refectory and the gatehouse survive, as well as parts of the cloister and monks' dormitory. The refectory has become the parish church; the gatehouse became the home of the line of Wriothesleys and Montagus who have owned Beaulieu since the Dissolution.

The gatehouse building was enlarged in the 1870s as a comfortable Victorian family home; the main downstairs rooms still have the vaulting of the gateways to the abbey precinct. The house boasts a distinguished set of family portraits from the mid 16th century right up to the present day.

The National Motor Museum is Beaulieu's principal attraction. Motor cars from the earliest to the newest, and from the fastest to the swankiest, are displayed in a huge hall divided into two levels.

The peaceful abbey ruins are in the furthest corner; the ground floor of the dormitory contains an extensive and well-organized exhibition on the monastic life.

Easter–Oct, daily 10am–6pm; Oct–Easter, daily 10am–5pm. Tel: (0590) 612345.

BREAMORE HOUSE * * *
Map p.141, C3
2½ miles N of Fordingbridge off the A338

The main fabric of Breamore House is Elizabethan, built in brick in the characteristic 'E' shape. The Hulse family have lived there since the 1740s, and most of the fine furnishings are the result of their collecting and advantageous marriages. Tours of the house take in the Great Hall with its original fireplaces, the dining and drawing rooms, and many bedrooms, some with very early needlework on the bed hangings, as well as the Victorian kitchen.

The former stable-block now houses a carriage museum, while a farmyard near the entrance gates has been turned into an absorbing countryside museum.

Apr, Tues, Wed and Sun; May–July and Sept, Tues–Thur, Sat–Sun; Aug, daily 2–5.30pm. Tel: (0725) 22468.

BROADLANDS * *
Map p.143, C2
Just outside Romsey off the A31

An 18th-century yellow-brick house set in grounds landscaped by Lancelot 'Capability' Brown, Broadlands attracts many visitors as the home of the late Earl Mountbatten of Burma. Vestiges of the original 17th-century house, especially some panelled rooms, remain inside.

The glories of the interior include classical sculpture brought back from the Grand Tour in 1765, original 18th-century furniture in many of the state rooms and, above all, the Saloon with its white and gold plaster ceiling.

The life of the Victorian Prime Minister, 3rd Viscount Palmerston (1784–1865) is remembered in a room inside the house; and the 17th-century stable-block houses a permanent exhibition on Lord Mountbatten.
Apr–Sept, daily exc. Fri 10am–4pm; also Fri in Aug. Tel: (0794) 516878.

THE GRANGE, NORTHINGTON *

Map p.150, D2
7 miles NE of Winchester off the B3046

Experts have dubbed this 'the most important neo-classical country house in Europe' . The core was a three-storied late 17th-century gentleman's residence, itself elegant enough to have been leased by the Prince Regent. In 1804 Henry Drummond asked the 26-year-old William Wilkins, future architect of the National Gallery, to restyle it. Wilkins took as his model the well-preserved Temple of Theseus in Athens. The dominant feature is what Professor Pevsner has called 'a Parthenon portico of tremendous pathos', with massive Doric columns six wide and two deep. The banker Alexander Baring added an orangery (formerly adjoining the house and now being restored) whose revolutionary cast-iron and glass construction is modestly screened by an Ionic portico. In its heyday The Grange provided an imposing setting for the house parties of Lady Ashburton, a literary hostess of ruthless fickleness.

Still a grand residence in the 1930s, the Grange was a wreck when the Department of the Environment took it over in 1975. The interior has been gutted (it is not accessible to the public) and the handsome 17th-century brick west front exposed; the landscaped park remains, though the approach road across it is execrable and should not be attempted in poor light. An excellent set of display panels traces the history of the house.

HIGHCLERE CASTLE **

Map p.154, C2
1 mile SE of Highclere off the A34

£ ☕ S *(plant centre)*

A drive through the rolling parkland of Highclere, set within wooded hills and designed by Lancelot 'Capability' Brown, culminates in the grand early-Victorian splendour of the castle itself, designed in neo-Elizabethan style by Charles Barry. An older house existed here, which was entirely recased. The Gothic great hall, used as a sitting room, rises through the full height of the house, and the grander interiors include the library and dining room. Many fine family portraits, especially of the Herberts, Earls of Caernarvon, fill the walls.

The 5th Earl was probably the best known, as co-discoverer of the fabulous tomb of Tutankhamun in 1922. A few Egyptian artefacts, discovered in a hiding place in the house in 1987, are now the centre of a display in the basement.

The park and gardens of Highclere are among the finest in Hampshire, with 18th-century temples in the landscape, and a sequence of formal gardens.
Jul–Sept, Wed–Sun and BH weekends Sun–Mon, 2–6pm. Also Easter and May BH, Sun–Mon, Whit, Sat–Mon. Tel: (0635) 253210.

HINTON AMPNER HOUSE *

Map p.150, F3
8 miles E of Winchester on the A272

£ ☕

Situated in unspoiled Hampshire countryside, commanding panoramic views over the peaceful countryside, Hinton Ampner as it stands today is largely the work of Sir Ralph Dutton, who had it remodelled in the Georgian style in 1936. Shortly afterwards, having restored and refurnished it, he relinquished it to a school for the duration of the war. Then in 1960 a fire virtually wrecked the whole building. Sir Ralph had it rebuilt and replaced the much of the furniture. The house contains a fine collection of Regency furniture, pictures and porcelain.
***House**: April–Sept, Tues–Weds 1.30–5.30pm; also Sat–Sun in Aug. **Gardens**: April–Sept, Tues–Weds, Sat–Sun and BHs 1.30–5.30pm. Tel: (0962) 771305 or 771023.*

JANE AUSTEN'S HOUSE * *

Map p.151, D2

1 mile S of Alton off the A31

(£) (S) 🚶 ♿ *(ground floor)* ✕

Novelist Jane Austen spent much of her life in Hampshire, and the latter part of it at Chawton, shortly before moving to Winchester, where she died in 1817. Jane's brother Edward inherited Chawton estate and renovated the former alehouse for his mother and sisters.

After World War II Mr T. Edward Carpenter re-opened it as a museum and it remains as a shrine to one of our finest novelists. The rooms have been restored just as the Austens would have known them with much of the original furniture, including the work table where *Mansfield Park*, *Emma* and *Persuasion* were written. Perhaps most poignant of all is the donkey carriage in which Jane travelled around when she was seriously ill and too weak to walk. Within a few months of moving to Winchester she was dead; she is buried in Winchester Cathedral.

Apr–Oct, daily 11am–4.30pm;. Nov, Dec, Mar, Weds–Sun; Jan, Feb, Sat–Sun. Tel: (0420) 83262.

KING JOHN'S HOUSE, ROMSEY * *

Map p.143, B2

Off Church St, Romsey

(£) ✕

A chance discovery in 1927, of a medieval stone window in a row of slum cottages, revealed an intact 13th-century hall house complete with its original roof timbers – and graffiti on the plaster walls inscribed by the retinue of Edward I during a royal visit of 1306. A charitable trust now runs the building and the Tudor house next to it.

The connection with King John is fanciful, since the building was erected after his death. It was probably one of the buildings of the men's infirmary, which formed part of a hospital complex for Romsey Abbey. From the 16th century the house's social fortunes declined; a unique relic from the 17th century is the ground floor (part of which is exposed), made from cattle knuckle bones pressed into the clay.

Spring BH–Sept, Mon 2–4pm, Tues–Sat 10.30am–12.30pm and 2–4pm; Sats in Apr, May and Oct 2–4pm. Tel: (0794) 512200 or 512285.

MOTTISFONT ABBEY *

Map p.143, A1

3½ miles from Romsey off the A3057

(£) (S) ♿ (i)

The large house by the River Test, built in brick, stone and flint, was originally a 13th-century Augustinian priory church. There are few remaining signs of that, except at the rear where windows break through the lines of medieval arches.The front elevation has an 18th-century classical centrepiece in red brick, with brick Elizabethan corner towers, flanked by 18th-century stone wings.

Access to the house's interior is very restricted. Entrance is via the medieval cellarium in the semi-basement, and most of the house's living rooms are contained within what was originally the nave. Little medieval fragments abound. The drawing room is decorated with Rex Whistler's *trompe-l'œil* paintings of trophies and smoking urns on the wall plaster.

The house's setting is superlative, with shaded woodland walks, the fast-flowing river, acres of close-mown grass and the walled rose garden (see p.20).

*Apr–Sept. **House:** Sun–Weds 1–5pm. **Gardens:** Sat–Weds 12am–6pm, June 12am–8.30pm. Tel: (0794) 41220 or 40757.*

ROTHERFIELD PARK HOUSE *

Map p.151, E2

6 miles S of Alton on the A32

(£) ☕ 🚶 ♿ ✕

Rotherfield Park is the home of Sir James Scott, Bt., the Lord Lieutenant of Hampshire, and has been in his family for nearly 200 years. The house underwent a significant change in the 1880s when it was 'romanticized' by the addition of a number of turrets and towers. The result is an interesting example of Victorian Gothic architecture, set in a fine area of Hampshire parkland (for gardens see p.21). The interior is an unspoilt example of Victorian grandeur with typical trappings of that era, including a stuffed duck-billed platypus – and watch out for the three stuffed Indian tigers looking down over the banister.

*__House:__ All BHs, Sun–Mon; June–Aug, 1st week of month. **Grounds:** Apr–Sept, Thurs, Sun 2–5pm. Tel: (042058) 204.*

STANSTED PARK * *

Map p.139, A3

3 miles N of Havant, entry gates at Rowlands Castle

(£) ☕ (S) ♿ *(ground floor)* ✗

The 'Upstairs, Downstairs' version of life in a large country house is on view at Stansted Park. Upstairs is the elegance and style of the family seat of the Earl and Countess of Bessborough: the blue drawing room with its Continental furniture and pictures; the dining room where rare pieces of china and fine porcelain are displayed; tall hallways containing early 18th-century Brussels tapestries.

Downstairs are the beautifully restored old kitchen and staff quarters. Also on view is the prized 17th-century vaulted cellar. The grounds are a delight, featuring the Victorian walled gardens where Harry Dodson of the popular *Victorian Garden* television series was a journeyman gardener. Nearby is the chapel where John Keats was inspired to write some of his finest verse.

Easter Sun and May–Sept, Mon, Tues 2–5.30pm. Tel: (0705) 412265.

STRATFIELD SAYE HOUSE AND GARDEN * *

Map p.156, B2

9 miles N of Basingstoke on the A33

(£) ☕ (S) ♿

Stratfield Saye House was bought by the nation for the Duke of Wellington as a mark of gratitude for his victory at the Battle of Waterloo, and was opened to the public in 1974. A tall column topped by a statue of the Iron Duke at the entrance to the estate sets the scene. The house is packed with mementoes of the Duke's life and times; even the funeral carriage used at his burial is housed there, having been moved from St Paul's Cathedral where it was kept for many years. The house is also noted for many innovations of Victorian times such as steam baths, radiators and main drainage. In the grounds, many people will want to visit the grave of the Duke's trusty warhorse, Copenhagen, which carried him during the Battle of Waterloo. Copenhagen had ten years of retirement in the adjoining parkland and his remains were laid to rest there, marked with a special gravestone.

May–Sept, Sat–Thurs 11.30am–4pm. Tel: (0256) 882882.

THE VYNE * *

Map p.155, C4

3 miles N of Basingstoke on the A340

(£) ☕ (S) ♿ *(ground floor)* ✗

The Vyne at Sherborne St John is a magnificent Tudor house which was built for Lord Sandys, Lord Chamberlain to Henry VIII. Henry and later Queen Elizabeth I liked it so much that they both made several visits. Extensive alterations were made around 1654 by Chaloner Chute, who was speaker in the House of Commons, and architect John Webb built the earliest classical portico for a country house in England. It remains the most prominent feature to this day. Of particular note are the long gallery of linenfold panelling, and the chapel which contains exquisite Renaissance glass from around 1520. There is also a grand Palladian staircase.

The house, which was bequeathed to the National Trust in 1956, is set in 500 acres of woodland with gardens and lawns sloping down to the lake.

Apr–Oct, Tues–Thurs, Sat–Sun 1.30–5.30pm (house), 12.30–5.30pm (garden); BHs 11am–5.30pm. Closed Tues following BH Mon. Tel: (0256) 881337.

CASTLES & FORTS

CALSHOT CASTLE * *

Map p.137, C3

2 miles from Fawley off the B3053

When Henry VIII feared the threat of French invasion in the 1540s, he ordered the construction of a string of castles and forts along the coast from Cornwall to Kent. Calshot was one of the smaller castles, a stone keep with sheer walls punctuated by a few deep windows, and a moat. Although it was not used in warfare at the time, Calshot played a role in defence up to the 1950s. It guarded the entrance to Southampton Water, and saw most active duty from the 1890s. The Admiralty used Calshot as its seaplane base in World War I, and the RAF took it over for seaplane training after 1918. In World War II it resumed its offensive role, having witnessed the exciting air races for the Schneider trophy in the 1920s and 30s. The RAF finally left in 1953. English Heritage have restored various parts of the castle to their Tudor appearance, others to the late-Victorian barracks. Photographic displays recall the great days of the flying boats.

Apr–Sept, daily 10am–6pm. Tel: (0703) 892023.

FORT BROCKHURST * *

Map p.138, C2

In Gosport off the A32

(grounds)

Like many of the massive defences which were built in the 19th century to protect the naval dockyard at Portsmouth, Fort Brockhurst was used for defensive purposes as late as World War II. This fortification is particularly interesting in that it still retains its freshwater moat.

A central exhibition explains Prime Minister Lord Palmerston's plans to build a chain of fortresses as a defence against possible French invasion. In the event the attack never came, but the forts were put to use in the two World Wars.

Fort Brockhurst is today an outstanding example of Victorian defences with its huge parade ground, earthen gun ramps, keep and some of the original armaments. Several special events are staged here every year.

Apr–Sept, daily exc. Mon, 10am–6pm; Oct–Mar, 10am–4pm. Tel: (0705) 581059.

FORT NELSON * *

Map p.138, B2

2 miles E of Fareham off the M27 (junction 11)

Fort Nelson is one of the mighty defences built around Portsmouth in the 1860s to protect the naval dockyard from possible French attack, and is being developed by the National Royal Armouries Museum and Hampshire County Council to show the development of artillery through the ages. Exhibits range from a 20-ton bronze Dardanelles gun of 1464 to components of the Iraqi supergun which were impounded by British Customs officials in 1990.

The massive fortification includes a central tunnel, bored deep in the chalk under Portsdown Hill, and the shell-proof barrack block. The parade-ground is now used to display many of the large guns, and is also the arena for special events and firing days held during the year.

The Portsdown Artillery Volunteers, part of the Palmerston Forts Society based in Fort Nelson, regularly recreate gun drill of the 1880s, using authentic guns which represent the fort's original armament.

Easter–Nov, Sat–Sun and BHs 12–4.30pm (last tour). Tel: (0329) 233734.

HURST CASTLE * *

Map p.135, E4

5 miles from Lymington off the B3058

Dating from 1541, Hurst Castle was built as part of Henry VIII's chain of defences against France. It was designed on geometrical principles, a nine-sided single storey enclosing a higher 12-sided tower.

It sits at the very tip of a long spit, protruding half-way across the stretch of water between the mainland and the Isle of Wight, and it is reached either by the Keyhaven ferry or by walking along the shingle bank from Milford.

The castle entrance is in one of the great brick wings added in the 1860s, when war with France threatened again. The castle had already been extended twice in the 19th century because of the need to accommodate larger guns; the narrow gauge railway over the drawbridge was installed to carry heavy weapons and shells.

There have been a series of lighthouses on the spit since the 1780s (the present one was built in 1865), and at one time there was a small community living out here, complete with an inn. The army garrison only left in 1945. The property is now cared for by English Heritage.
Apr–Sept, daily 10am–6pm; Oct–Mar, Sat–Sun 10am–4pm. Tel: (0590) 642344.

PORTCHESTER CASTLE * * *
Map p.138, C3
3 miles E of Fareham off the A27

£ S ♿ *(ground floor)*

Portchester, sheltered in the natural harbour which still protects Britain's Navy, was recognized for its strategic importance centuries ago, and the massive castle which looks out from the water's edge is a permanent reminder of this.

It was the Romans who first established a fort here, and the 18ft walls which still stand are regarded by historians as among the finest remaining examples of Roman fortification in northern Europe. Within the vast outer walls are the later additions. The large keep was added in the late 12th century and the external walls are extremely well preserved. Also within the castle grounds is the parish church of Portchester, St Mary's, a fine example of Norman architecture. It formed part of an Augustinian priory founded in 1133 by Henry I.

The rise in the importance of Portsmouth led to Portchester's decline, and the castle is now in the care of English Heritage.
Apr–Sept, daily exc. Mon 10am–6pm; Oct–Mar, 10am–4pm. Tel: (0705) 378291.

SOUTHSEA CASTLE * *
Map p.138, E3
On Southsea seafront.

£ *(children under 13 free from April)* S

Southsea castle was one of a chain of massive fortifications built by King Henry VIII to defend his expanding fleet of warships based in Portsmouth harbour. It was completed in 1545 using stones from the abbey at Beaulieu, which had just been dissolved. It is said that Henry was watching from the castle when his flagship, the *Mary Rose*, set out to do battle with the French and suddenly turned turtle, taking 700 crewmen to a watery grave.

The castle retains many Tudor features but most of what is seen today dates from the 19th century. There is a wide range of artillery spanning the years, along with other militaria which have played a role in the history of the area. From the battlements there are spectacular views across Spithead to the Isle of Wight.
Daily 10.30am–5.30pm. Tel: (0705) 827261.

SPITBANK FORT *
Map p.138, E3
Off Portsmouth.

£ ☕ 🚶

Spitbank Fort, rising from the sea a mile off Portsmouth, is a monumental example of Victorian engineering and architecture. It was bought from the Government in 1980 and parts have been converted to living accommodation available for rental.

Most, however, has been restored to its original use. You can see how the 156 men who manned the fort lived, using coal ranges, oil lamps and hammocks. Replicas of the huge 38 ton guns and 800lb shells are on view and you can explore the maze of passages and rooms which make up the castle. One passageway, 400ft long, can be investigated by the courageous with just the light of a candle.

Boat trips from Gosport Pontoon and Clarence Pier at Southsea run every 75 minutes, weather permitting, and take about 15 minutes. For the ferry trip and a guided tour you should allow at least two hours.
Easter–Sept, daily exc. Mon 10am–5pm. Tel: (0329) 664286 or (0831) 608383.

GARDENS

BOHUNT MANOR * *

Map p.152, E1

At Liphook on the A3

£ ♿ *(ground floor)* ✗

The ducks which come quacking from the lake at the first hint of food are a popular feature of the gardens at Bohunt Manor. But beware! One of them, large and black and white, can be a real tyrant. He is one of many ducks which have ended up at Bohunt for a variety of reasons and probably his bad temper had something to do with the decision to find him a new home.

The lake is the main feature of this garden but that does not mean the rest should be ignored. The expanse of neatly trimmed lawn which sweeps down to the water is guarded by two copper beech trees. Around the corner and over a wooden footbridge, mature beech, oaks and limes provide a shady habitat for daffodils and bluebells. Here, too, are azaleas – and watch out for the handkerchief tree, and the judas tree which, despite an unfortunate accident with a tractor, shows signs of a remarkable recovery. The front of the house is veiled by a magnificent *Fermontia Californicum* which has a mass of yellow flowers.

All year, daily 9am–6pm. Tel: (0428) 722208.

BRAMDEAN HOUSE * *

Map p.150, F4

8 miles E of Winchester on the A272

£ ✗

The gardens at Bramdean rank as the pin-ups of the horticultural world, having featured in books, magazines and calendars. The lawns were once used in an advertisement for Fisons.

There is plenty of variety here, but of particular interest are the double herbaceous borders which have been laid out as mirror images with a central pathway leading to a pool and a fountain. Other features in the five-acre garden include the borders which have been planted to attract different species of butterflies.

In the walled garden, part of which has been set aside as a nursery, many varieties of apple trees have been trained cordon style against the wall. Older apple trees were planted by a young gardener called Baker who, as a teenager, joined the Coldstream Guards in World War I and was killed in action in France. The trees are regarded as an informal and sentimental memorial to him.

Open on NGS days and by appointment.
Tel: (0962) 771214.

EXBURY GARDENS * * *

Map p.137, D1

6 miles E of Brockenhurst off the B3054

£ ☕ S ♿ *(wheelchair loan)*

Exbury boasts one of the finest and most famous rhododendron gardens in the world. The sheltered location on the east bank of the Beaulieu River, and the acid forest and heath soil, have proved ideal conditions, and Exbury is justifiably well-visited in May and June when the many vibrant colours and scents of the rhododendrons and azaleas are at their best. In autumn the magnificent collection of specimen trees makes the gardens equally breathtaking.

The main gardens cover almost 250 acres, with water features and river viewpoints, and there are walks through every part, some on tarmac paths, others across grass or gravel. Perhaps the best aspect of Exbury is that visitors can each make their own itinerary, and it is very easy to get away from other visitors. (The great house, a truncated triangle in plan, is private. There are glimpses of its wistaria-hung portico.)

The gardens were the life's work of Lionel de Rothschild, a member of the banking family, who began to make them in 1919 after he bought the estate at Exbury from the Mitford family. He made a million new plantings, and spared no expense. Exbury Gardens incorporate not only the Rothschild collections of rhododendrons and azaleas, but also of magnolias, maples and camellias.

Mar–Oct, daily 10am–5.30pm. Tel: (0703) 891203.

FURZEY GARDENS, MINSTEAD * *

Map p.142, E3

At Minstead off the A31

£ ☕ S ♿

Deep among the wooded lanes of Minstead lies Furzey Gardens. Work began in 1922, and since then eight acres of rough gorse grazing have been transformed into an informal garden of trees, shrubs, water, and above all spring and early summer blossom. As with many New Forest gardens, Furzey's great speciality is in acid-loving azaleas, rhododendrons and heathers, and the colours can be quite exhilarating, especially when the bluebells still carpet the wooded areas. The trees provide good autumn colour and whatever the season there are plants to be seen and views into the wooded valleys to be enjoyed.

The thatched house covered with climbing plants on the rise at the centre of the gardens is a private religious retreat. The house is the same age as the garden, but other houses open to view are older, notably the little Tudor, black weatherboarded and thatched cottage, and the barn used as a base by visiting groups of schoolchildren. Attractions include a gallery selling local art and craft work.

All year, daily 10am–5pm. Tel: (0703) 812464.

GREATHAM MILL * *

Map p.151, F4

7 miles SE of Alton off B3006 just before A325

£ *(adults)* 🐕

The way into this fascinating unspoilt garden is across a wooden footbridge over the chuckling mill stream. It is a perfect introduction for what is to come.

Everything is wonderfully informal in true cottage garden style. In a shady corner a honeysuckle makes a splendidly compatible partner for a big old apple tree. Wild flowers and grasses are left to do their own thing beside the stream, providing a natural home for small mammals and insects. A lawn, edged with a stone wall on one side and a slender yew hedge on the other, makes a lovely suntrap. But amid all this natural informality, do not be fooled into thinking that some of the plants and shrubs making up the overall picture are commonplace. A close look at some of the name tags will surprise you.

The front of the 17th-century millhouse is clothed with a magnificent wistaria which looks as though it could be as old as the building itself. It is nearly sixty years since the mill was last used for grinding corn.

Mid Apr–Sept, Sun and BHs 2–6pm. Other days by appointment. Tel: (04207) 219.

HOUGHTON LODGE * *

Map p.148, E3

1 mile SW of Stockbridge off the A30

£ S 🚶 ♿ *(in Hydroponicum)* ℹ

The beautiful waterside gardens of the Lodge are open to the public and so provide an opportunity to gain the banks of the River Test. The gateway from the road is through what appears to be a ruin, but this is artificial for the Lodge was built, shortly before 1800, in the then popular 'Gothick' style. The architect is unknown but his work resembles that of Nash who designed London's Regent Street at about that time. The main layout of the grounds is traditional, with mature trees, ingenious topiary work, a sunken garden, herbaceous borders and lawns sweeping down to the river. But in the walled garden is the Hampshire Hydroponicum 'a garden of the future in a garden of the past'. It is based on hydroponics, the technique of growing plants in nutrient-rich solutions without soil. The technique is in increasing use throughout the world, particularly where local conditions are unfavourable to traditional horticultural methods, and the Hydroponicum is an important scientific development as well as a tourist attraction.

Mar–Sept, daily 10am–4.30pm.
Tel: (0264) 810177.

JENKYN PLACE, BENTLEY * *

Map p.151, B4

5 miles NE of Alton on the A31

£ ♿ 🐕

Fifty years ago, during the dark days of war when Britain was finding it hard to feed itself, most of this seven acre garden was used for growing vegetables, and cows grazed on what is now the terrace. After the war, the gardens gradually evolved without any real master plan and are now made up of 16 different sections, each with its own identity. The rose garden was formerly one of two tennis courts and now includes a geometrical pool. The other tennis court became the formal pavilion garden. The sundial garden is filled with large tubs in a paved area. The origin of the Dutch garden has become shrouded in the mists of time. The lion garden takes its name from the statue of a sleeping lion, a copy of the original on the tomb of Pope Clement XIII in Rome.

On a poignant note, there is a garden seat which serves as a memorial to Peter Passey, a former head gardener who was largely responsible for making the garden what it is today.
Apr–Sept, Thurs–Sun and BH Mons 2–6pm. Tel: (0420) 23118.

LITTLE BARN GARDEN & BARNHAWK NURSERY *

Map p.141, C4
1 mile W of Woodgreen off the A338

£ 🚶 ♿

Little Barn is a collector's garden, displaying a year-round variety of plants and trees in its 2½ acres. The mature, informal gardens are noted for their variety of colour and texture: azaleas and rhododendrons, camellias and magnolias, and many rare shrubs, in rock, scree, woodland and boggy garden areas. The nursery specializes in the types of plant and shrub displayed in the main garden.
Apr–Oct, Fri–Sat 9am–6pm. Tel: (0725) 22213.

LYMORE VALLEY HERBS *

Map p.136, F1
3 miles W of Lymington off the A337

£ ☕ S ♿ 🐕

On a turning from the A337 west of Lymington, Lymore Valley Herbs is a new venture in a courtyard of old farm buildings refurbished as small business units. A walled courtyard garden (reached through the shop) of herbaceous borders and gravelled walks displays many plants, especially herbs. The centrepiece is a small Tudor knot garden, and rose pillars and water features set off the display. Many different varieties of herbs are for sale.
Mar–Dec, daily 9am–5pm. Tel: (0590) 642008.

MACPENNY NURSERIES, BRANSGORE **

Map p.135, C1
4 miles N of New Milton off the A35

☕ *(near by)* S 🚶 *(by appointment)* ♿ i

A 12-acre garden near Thorney Hill, by Bransgore, Macpenny's was once a gravel pit. This relic of one of the area's main industries has been transformed into a densely planted woodland garden which specializes in rare and choice plants. It has herbaceous plants as well as camellias, rhododendrons, azaleas, and heathers, all of which thrive in the region's soils. Fine stately trees and hilly paths are the keynotes.
All year, daily. Mon–Sat 9am–5pm; Sun 2–5pm. Tel: (0425) 72348.

MOTTISFONT ROSE GARDEN **

Map p.143, A1
3½ miles from Romsey off the A3057

£ ♿ 🐕

Since his childhood Graham Stuart Thomas, the doyen of English rose gardeners, had collected and nurtured old varieties of roses. Their colours and scent are incomparable, and in 1972 his collection became the nucleus of a new rose garden planted by the National Trust within the old walled garden at Mottisfont Abbey (for house, see p.14). It has since been recognized as the national collection of ancestral species and 19th-century rose cultivars. All are labelled: Moussou du Japon, Comte de Charbord, Climbing Lady Hillingdon… One of the few new roses is appropriately named Graham Thomas.

Many old roses have a relatively short blooming period, so the gardens are at their very best in midsummer; nevertheless, colour is maintained through the whole season. Some 300 varieties of rose are grown in the garden, and it has already been almost doubled in size; the original area has borders edged by box hedges, the newer part is more open with paving stones set as paths within the flower beds. Both areas have seats and arbours.

Apr–Sept, Sun–Thurs 2–6pm; also evening openings in June (phone for times). Tel: (0794) 41220 or 40757.

PETERSFIELD PHYSIC GARDEN *

Map p.146, B2

Centre of Petersfield, just off The Square.

♿ 🍽

This walled garden is a delightful, intriguing and unexpected gem right in the middle of the busy town of Petersfield. Physic gardens owe their name to the species of plants grown in them, many of which were considered to possess medicinal properties. The increasing popularity of natural medicine shows that the old botanist doctors were nearer the truth than they are often given credit for.

In 1988 Major John Bowen gave the garden to the Hampshire Gardens Trust for the education and enjoyment of the public. Part is laid out in the geometric style typical of 17th-century physic gardens, but there are also areas with trees, roses and herbaceous plants and an informal orchard. In the centre of the garden is a sundial which commemorates Major Bowen.

Also remembered in the gardens is the botanist John Goodyer who lived and worked in the Petersfield area in the 17th century. He grew and recorded many plants in detail and used his skills with some degree of success on his family, friends and neighbours.

Daily, 9am–5pm. Tel: (0730) 268829.

ROMSEY MEMORIAL GARDENS *

Map p.143, B2

At Romsey, W of the A3057

♿

Filling most of the area between two of the channels of the River Test (originally cut as mill streams) on the western edge of Romsey, the Memorial Gardens were established in remembrance of those who had fallen in World War I. The stone memorial and a gun brought back by Earl Mountbatten from the Burma campaign evoke memories of wartime, but the lawns and standing clumps of trees have a serene air. The countryside is not far away, and footpaths and small bridges lead west of the park to the River Test itself. The bridge across the river stands over sluice gates, up which the salmon had traditionally leapt on returning to their breeding grounds.

ROTHERFIELD PARK *

Map p.151, E2

6 miles S of Alton on the A32

£ ♿

The gardens and grounds at Rotherfield Park at East Tisted are a challenge, to say the least, for the staff who maintain them. They are on top of a hill, exposed to the wind and rain – and Sir James Scott, the owner, jokes about there not being much between Rotherfield and Siberia, apart from perhaps Midhurst!

Although the garden is at the top of a hill, there is no problem getting around, even for people in wheelchairs. There is a good mixture of elderly trees, now interspersed with much younger ones which have taken the place of those damaged in recent hurricanes. The rose garden in particular is a peaceful corner. Head gardener Ron Nettle is especially proud of his trained fruit trees and claims to have one of the finest collections in the country. The vegetable and flower garden are separated by a magnificent pair of wrought-iron gates.

From the front of the house (see p.14) there is a panoramic view across the valley to Plash Wood with the village and its picturesque cottages set out below.

Apr–Sept, Sun, Thurs 2–5pm.

ROWANS WOOD GARDEN *

Map p.143, B3

West of Ampfield, just S of the A31

£ ☕ 🍽

The high winds of recent years have enabled the owners of these gardens to replace losses among the fine trees with new planting. This has opened up more handsome views down towards the New Forest. Rowans Wood covers two acres, and is particularly well endowed with rhododendrons, azaleas, camellias and spring flowering bulbs. Hostas are a speciality: over 50 varieties are grown.

Late Apr–May, Weds 2–5pm.

SIR HAROLD HILLIER GARDENS & ARBORETUM * * *

Map p.143, B3

3 miles NE of Romsey off the A31

£ ☕ *(Jermyn House)* S *(plant centre)* ♿ ✗

One of the most complete collections of hardy trees and shrubs in the British Isles is to be found in the Hillier Gardens. The collection of plants from all the world's temperate zones was begun by the late Sir Harold Hillier, third-generation plant nurseryman, in 1953. He gave the collection to Hampshire County Council in 1977, who have administered its 160 acres since.

The undulating ground and surrounding older woodlands give the gardens a variety of vistas and different aspects; every tree is labelled, and bulbs and smaller plants are mixed with the trees and shrubs on which the firm of Hilliers have long built their reputation. The garden is designed to have an impact and colour in every season: winter witch hazels, spring blossom and rhododendrons, summer shrubs and herbaceous perennials, and autumn foliage. As befits a nursery, there is considerable information available in the form of factsheets, guided tours and workshops, and plants are for sale from the Hillier nurseries.

Mar–Nov, daily 10.30am–5pm.
Tel: (0794) 68787.

SPINNERS, BOLDRE * *

Map p.136, E2

At Boldre off the A337

£ S *(plant centre)* ♿ ✗

The wooded slopes down to the Lymington River at Spinners, near Vicars Hill, contains a superb variety of fine trees and shrubs and a wide range of herbaceous plants. Magnolias, maples, azaleas, rhododendrons and hydrangeas are among the specialities here, and many of its rare hardy plants are available for sale. The gardens are arranged as a circular walk, which winds through the trees and borders and down the hillside, with new views always opening around the carefully contrived corners.

Apr–Sept, daily exc. Mon 10am–6pm.
Tel: (0590) 673347.

The rose garden at Mottisfont Abbey.

COUNTRY PARKS & NATURE RESERVES

ALICE HOLT FOREST * *

Map p.152, B1

6 miles NE of Alton off the A31

S ♿ i

Alice Holt Forest was once the haunt of highwaymen who preyed on travellers, until an act of Parliament declared that vegetation had to be cleared for 200ft on each side of the track, preventing the marauders from lying in wait unseen.

Today you won't come across any highwaymen, and any clearing that takes place is part of a carefully managed conservation scheme to encourage plant and animal life. Deer are often seen but badgers and foxes are more secretive, coming out mostly in the evening and at night. Birds are plentiful and include warblers and chiff-chaffs. There are up to 28 different species of butterflies, including the purple emperor and white admiral. The Forestry Commission visitor centre provides guides to clearly marked trails. *Open all year. Tel: (0420) 23666.*

BERE FOREST

Map p.145, E2–E4

5 miles NE of Fareham on the A32

The Forest of Bere was once part of a vast area of woodland stretching over much of southern Hampshire from Romsey to the Portsmouth area. It was popular with royalty, who hunted the deer and wild boar, and later its timber was used to build some of the great British warships.

Today only small pockets of the forest remain. A popular spot is in the Meon Valley, just north of Wickham. Woodland trails and bridleways are clearly marked, and although wildlife abounds, the best time to see it is during the week when there are fewer visitors. Bluebell time in the spring is a particularly good time for a visit. *Open all year, free car park, toilet facilities.*

FARLEY MOUNT COUNTRY PARK * *

Map p.150, F2

4 miles W of Winchester off the A3090

♿ *(limited)*

High up on Farley Mount is a monument, visible from a long distance, which invariably attracts visitors for it is easy of access with a footpath leading up to it. It commemorates a horse which, while out foxhunting with its master in 1734, jumped into a chalk pit 25ft deep. Horse and rider not only survived, but later went on to win a race.

The Country Park comprises over 1000 acres of unspoilt countryside and consists of three quite distinct habitats: Crabwood, an ancient woodland of oak and hazel: Pit Down, a chalk down rich in flowers and butterflies; and the relatively modern Westwood, a Forestry Commission Plantation. The Park is ideal for a casual ramble but it also has an educational purpose. There is a fully equipped school-room available for pre-booked groups. *Tel: (0962) 846034.*

HAREWOOD FOREST *

Map p.149, B1

3 miles E of Andover off the A303

A good point to start exploring this ancient remnant of England is that marked as 'Old Pound' on the A303. The Forest is suitable only for walking, but it is crisscrossed by good footpaths, some of them concreted over – a reminder that the Forest was used as a bomb store, hidden from aerial surveillance by the trees, during World War II. Not far from the point of departure one of these concrete tracks leads to the site of an ancient tragedy, marked by a monument known as Deadman's Plack, erected in 1775. According to the story,the Saxon King Edgar (959–79) charged a certain earl Ethelwold to report on the fitness to be queen of a maiden called Elfrida. Ethelwold fell for the maiden and, determined to have her for himself, reported back unfavourably. When Edgar discovered the truth he killed the earl at this spot.

HOLLY HILL WOODLAND PARK

Map p.144, F2

Just SW of Sarisbury

More than 70 acres of the grounds of a former mansion provide an unexpected and welcome rural recreation area in a district which is rapidly being developed with housing. Holly Hill Woodland Park, not easy for strangers to find, is a splendid wilderness in a valley of mature woodland, leading down to the banks of the River Hamble. The site includes five acres of lakes on different levels. While the pathways are well maintained, a minimum of management ensures that the natural atmosphere is preserved Unless you have a good sense of direction, do not be surprised if you find yourself temporarily lost.

Open all year, free car park, toilet facilities.

ITCHEN VALLEY COUNTRY PARK *

Map p.144, C4

4 miles NE of Southampton off the A27

Eastleigh council has recently bought 440 acres of mostly unspoilt fields and woodland to preserve breathing space between Eastleigh and Southampton. It provides opportunities for walking, horse riding and picnicking, with a rural adventure playground for children.

The park is being managed without the use of pesticides or artificial fertilizers. Consequently a diverse range of plant- and wildlife is thriving, making the area of great interest to naturalists. Events are held throughout the year, including a fascinating look at folklore and other rural traditions, and guided walks are a regular feature. There is a visitor centre with educational, refreshment and toilet facilities. Dogs are welcome provided they are kept on a lead.

Open all year, ample car parking.
Tel: (0703) 466091.

LAKESIDE

Map p.144, C1

Southampton Road, Eastleigh

Lakeside is an attractive and relaxing location incorporating three lakes and providing facilities for a wide range of leisure activities. There is sailing, windsurfing and canoeing for those who do not mind taking an accidental dip. Those who prefer to keep their feet dry might enjoy model boating, or fishing. On shore there are picnic areas and open spaces for informal ball games.

Lakeside, like Itchen Valley, has been established in the area between Eastleigh and Southampton to try to preserve a green belt. Noise from the nearby motorway, railway and airport is a constant reminder that this is but a small sanctuary in a built-up area.

Open all year, car parking.

LEPE & CALSHOT FORESHORE COUNTRY PARK * *

Map p.137, D2

Between Lepe and Calshot

Lepe Country Park occupies the narrow stretch of land between the Solent and the New Forest to the west of Southampton Water. The shingle beaches and wild natural habitats continue along the coast to Calshot, where the shingle forms a long spit at the entrance to Southampton Water.

The Country Park is managed by Hampshire County Council, and provides a variety of environments. Swimming is available off the shingle and sand beach, although the closeness of the passing ships suggests that the channel is soon deep. Wooden groynes help to trap the ever-shifting beach and prevent erosion, and many parts of the beach are designated dog-free. Close to the entrance of the main car park, where the Dark Water river flows into the sea, reed beds and marsh vegetation grow.

Further round the headland, the closest point to the Isle of Wight, the brackish ponds on the inland side attract a huge variety of wildfowl. The great concrete platforms were the site of the construction of the floating Mulberry Harbour which was towed across to Normandy for the D-Day landings in 1944.

The foreshore at Calshot has similarly been designated a country park. The long, wide shingle beach there offers possibilities for swimming and bird- or ship-watching. *Open all year. Pay and display parking. Tel: (0703) 899108.*

MARTIN DOWN * *

Map p.140, C3

3½ miles N of Cranborne off the A354

Martin Down is preserved as a National Nature Reserve. Its importance lies in its variety of downland natural habitats as well as its wealth of prehistoric monuments. The Bronze Age earthwork of Grim's Ditch and Bokerley Ditch, with a pair of banks each 12 yards wide, enclosing some 16 square miles, now forms part of the Hampshire border. A smaller earthwork enclosure and a row of tumuli (earth burial mounds) confirm the site's prehistoric importance.

The landscape of Martin Down sweeps down from its north-west corner, at over 400ft one of Hampshire's highest points. It varies from herb-rich turf, still extensively grazed by sheep, to long grass and scrub and, at the southern end of the reserve behind Martin village, heath on the chalk. The Down is home to many varieties of butterfly and bird, and there is public access across the reserve except where the demands of agriculture or precious natural habitats demand otherwise. Car parks are available beside the A354, at the Down's highest point, and at the further end of Sillen Lane east of Martin village.

OLD WINCHESTER HILL *

Map p. 145, B2

2 miles W of Corhampton off the A32

This chalk downland nature reserve is crowned by the clearly defined ramparts of an Iron Age fort, dating back to the last 5000 years BC. It is a fine example of a chalk habitat, with a mix of open grassland, scrub and woodlands – principally juniper, yew and beech. It boasts rich and varied plant and animal life, and there are several species of butterflies and birds to be seen, including skylark, goldcrest and kestrel. Parking on the road is limited and, as there is no admission charge, the reserve can become fairly busy on fine weekends, when many people come to enjoy the several walks and fine coast and country views.

QUEEN ELIZABETH COUNTRY PARK * *

Map p.146, C2

3 miles S of Petersfield on the A3

☕ ♿ ♿ ⓘ

The Queen Elizabeth Country Park incorporates a fascinating mixture of deep forest and high open downland and also stages recreational events ranging from grass skiing to paragliding.

The hub of the park is the Centre building with shops, a café, a small theatre and toilet facilities. From there you can enjoy long woodland walks or a hike to the top of Butser Hill, with its magnificent all-round views with the coastline to the south and the heathlands of north Hampshire and Surrey to the north. For the less active there are special driveways to remote parts of the park. Throughout the year there is a full programme of activities and exhibitions. *Open all year. Centre facilities are limited during the winter. Parking (small fee). Tel: (0705) 595040.*

ROYAL VICTORIA COUNTRY PARK *

Map p.144, F1

4 miles E of Southampton off the M27 (junction 8)

£ ☕ ♿ *(limited)* ⓘ

The Royal Victoria Country Park is on the site of a large Victorian military hospital which was demolished in the 1960s. Only the Royal Chapel remains as a landmark on the edge of Southampton Water; it now houses a museum tracing the history of the hospital from the Crimean War. From the viewing gallery at the top there are spectacular coastal views.

Although there are plenty of natural and scenic attractions, this is very much a park for people, and several special events are held here, including steam and caravan rallies. The park centre houses refreshment facilities and there is a picnic and barbecue area. A narrow gauge steam railway has been established on part of a former branch line. *Easter–Oct. Tel: (0703) 455157.*

SIR GEORGE STAUNTON COUNTRY PARK * *

Map p.139, A2

1 mile N of Havant on the B2149

(ornamental farm)

As a boy in 1792, George Staunton went to China as page to Lord McCartney, who headed the first British mission there. He later became head of the British East India Company, and bought the estate in 1820 to establish his collection of rare Chinese species. The park comprises nearly 1000 acres containing widely differing attractions. Children in particular will enjoy being able to pat and stroke some of the smaller farm animals. For the country lover there are heritage trails and guided walks, and serious horticulturalists will be fascinated by Sir George's collection.

Easter–October, daily 10am–5pm; winter, farm only, weekends 10am–4pm. Tel: (0705) 453405.

UPPER HAMBLE COUNTRY PARK *

Map p.144, E2

4 miles E of Southampton off the M27 (junction 8)

This park covers 400 acres set among mature woodlands on the banks of the River Hamble. It is a must for nature lovers and botanists as the various types of habitat support a wide range of plant and animal life in a fairly compact area. The river here is tidal as far inland as the mill at Botley, and supports fresh and saltwater creatures. Kingfishers and herons are river residents.

Nature trails of varying lengths take in the wooded valley slopes, the shoreline and open meadowland. Some of them can be fairly tough going. There is an activities centre, a permanent scout campsite and areas set aside for picnics and ball games. Admission to Manor Farm (see p.32) is extra.

Open all year, parking charge in season. Toilet facilities. Tel: (0489) 787055.

WAGGONER'S WELLS * *

Map p.152, D4

2 miles E of Grayshott off the B3002

Waggoner's Wells are a series of three man-made ponds set among beech woodlands. They were originally created by building dams across the Downwater Stream to provide power and water for the 17th-century ironworks which were established here. Nature has now obliterated most evidence of industrial activity, though industrial archaeologists will find the area interesting.

The lakes were acquired in 1919 as a memorial to Sir Robert Hunter, one of the founders of the National Trust. They adjoin Ludshott Common and the wooded slopes to the north. The middle lake is stocked with trout for fly fishing, while the two either side are for coarse fishing with tench, roach and perch. Not surprisingly, kingfishers are among the bird life which visitors might expect to see. There are car parks and picnic areas and details are available at Grayshott Post Office.

Open all year.

WATERSHIP DOWN * *

Map p.154, C4

3 miles SE of Burghclere off the A34

This great chalk hanger in the North Hampshire Downs was made famous by the novel of the same name by Richard Adams about a group of rabbits, p[ublished in 1972 to great acclaim. The too-good-to-be-true placename is quite real, and the down's bulk has become a nature reserve. The steep slopes – rising almost sheer for 300 feet on the north face – are still home to considerable rabbit colonies, as well as a great variety of bird and plant life. There are isolated farms and cottages on the shallower slope, at the bottom of which runs the ancient Portway track. One steep, minor road rises up the scarp from the villages of Sydmonton and Ecchinswell; parking places are available at its top, and at the easternmost end of the Down, by the lookout point on the B3051.

WELLINGTON COUNTRY PARK * *

Map p.156, B2

8 miles N of Basingstoke on the A33

Wellington Country Park, associated with Stratfield Saye House (see p.15) but separate from it, consists of 300 acres of countryside and parkland, catering for a wide range of recreational interests. There is boating, windsurfing and fishing on the lake, pony trekking, an adventure playground, crazy golf and a miniature steam railway. Clearly marked nature trails have been established and the deer park is always fascinating. The National Dairy Museum provides an interesting insight into how we used to get our daily pintas before the industry was automated, and there is a children's farmyard with small breeds.

Camping and caravan sites are available in peaceful woodland glades and there are shopping and toilet facilities. For day visitors there is plenty of car parking space and picnic areas.
Mar–Oct, daily 10am–5.30pm; winter, weekends. Tel. (0734) 326444.

THE WILDGROUNDS, GOSPORT
Map p.138, D2
In Gosport, off Rodney Close

Wildgrounds, as its name suggests, is a fascinating 67-acre nature reserve oasis in an otherwise crowded corner of urban Hampshire. It was acquired by the local council in 1966 and now supports a wide range of animal, bird and plant life.

If you are lucky you might catch a glimpse of deer, foxes or badgers, and birds include woodpeckers and the tiny goldcrest. There are two trails through the reserve and special areas have been developed to attract butterflies and amphibious creatures. This is a serious wildlife sanctuary so do not expect any commercial facilities.

Permits for up to four people, valid for the month of issue, are available at the Town Hall, High St, Gosport. Children should be accompanied by adults and dogs are not allowed.

YATELEY COMMON * *
Map p.157, C2
12 miles NE of Basingstoke on the A30

Yateley Common sits close to some extensive urban development, but it is skilfully managed by Hampshire County Council to meet the recreational needs of people while maintaining a natural habitat for wildlife.

Wyndham's Pool nature trail is a well laid-out path and notes are available pointing out interesting features found en route. Wyndham's Pool itself has a wide range of coarse fish, notably tench and carp, and also supports several species of waterfowl. Other birds include linnets, goldfinches, yellowhammers and stonechats, while birds of prey hover above waiting for an opportune meal. Butterflies include the spectacular red admiral, the yellow brimstone and the silver-studded blue. The emperor dragonfly is to be found near the poolside.

There are car parks and picnic areas and rangers are based on site.
Open all year.

FARMS & ZOOS

BIRDWORLD AND UNDERWATER WORLD * *

Map p.152, B1

3 miles SW of Farnham on the A325

A colourful mixture of species from all corners of the earth have been brought together at Birdworld, providing a fascinating day out. Perhaps the most interesting time to visit is the peak of the breeding season in May and June, when keepers are busy looking after new arrivals.

Birdworld is involved in a big breeding and research programme, making sure that rare and threatened species continue to survive. These include South American seriamas and Humboldt penguins which are sent to other establishments around the world. The most spectacular are the large macaws which fly freely around the site, making their homes in wooden beer barrels erected on tall posts.

Underwater World is a large indoor aquarium with a range of tropical freshwater and marine fish which are just as colourful as the birds outside. It is an interesting diversion if the weather is wet.

April–Sept, daily 9.30am–6pm; Mar and Oct, till 5pm; Nov–Feb, till 3.30pm. Tel: (0420) 22140.

BUTSER ARCHAEOLOGICAL FARM *

Map p.146, C2

4 miles S of Petersfield off the A3

Pre-booked parties:

Butser Archaeological Farm, established on an isolated site on the western edge of the South Downs, claims to be unique. It is a fascinating attempt to recreate an Iron Age settlement using only the materials and tools that ancient people would have had at their disposal. The project is also attempting to revive some of the ancient breeds of sheep, goats, cattle and poultry.

Life on the settlement is undoubtedly tough, especially when the weather is poor. The huge, thatched roundhouse which is being built illustrates just how much modern construction methods are taken for granted. Special grain storage pits are being dug, and a Romano-British style kiln is being established where simple clay pots will be fired. Fortunately essential modern facilities are available, too.

Easter to November, Sun–Fri 10am–5pm, Sat 2–5pm; phone in winter for availability. Tel: (0705) 598838.

CHOLDERTON RARE BREEDS FARM * *

Map p.147, B3

4 miles S of South Tidworth off the A338

As farming methods change, many species of specially bred farm animals face extinction as they no longer have an economic role to play. Cholderton Farm, established in 1987, provides a haven for a wide variety of such species, including a noble Shire Horse, Exmoor Ponies, and various goats, rabbits and sheep. The Farm covers some 50 acres on the Hampshire–Wiltshire borders with superb views. Apart from the animals themselves, there are a number of planned attractions, including a rose garden, a water garden, picnic areas and an excellent restaurant. The Farm is particularly suitable for children, who are encouraged to wander among the animals and pet and feed them.

April–Oct, daily 10am–6pm. Tel: (098064) 438.

DEER SANCTUARY, BOLDERWOOD * *

Map p.143, F1

N of A35

Specially-constructed platforms within the 19th-century arboretum and ornamental tree plantation at Bolderwood offer perhaps the most intimate views of the deer which roam the New Forest. A former farm has been turned into a sanctuary, within which only keepers and deer may enter, with public viewing over the sanctuary fences. Ever since the New Forest was established by William the Conqueror as a royal hunting forest, the deer have had special status. Attempts to eradicate them after 1851 succeeded in reducing numbers to a fraction of their former size; and although deer populations recovered, today there are perhaps 1500 deer, of five species, in the forest. The most common variety is the fallow deer. Red deer and roe deer are next most populous, with the small, exotic sika and muntjac deer relative rarities. Deer numbers are controlled to protect trees and crops.

FINKLEY DOWN FARM PARK * *

Map p.149, A1

Just N of Andover

A very popular place in spite of high admission charges, and particularly intended to interest children, the Farm Park is right on the northern edge of Andover, near Picket Post. Paddocks and grassed areas with pens, barns and stables enclose the grey Victorian farmhouse (not open to view), and within them a great variety of farm animals and domestic pets are on show. These range from horses and ponies to breeds of pigs and varieties of poultry both rare and common. Some barns contain tableaux of traditional farm life or old farm carts. Emphasis is placed on the educational side, with poster displays and information points, as well as a lecture room for school parties.

April–Sept, daily 10.30am–6pm.
Tel: (0264) 352195

THE HAWK CONSERVANCY * *

Map p.148, A2

3 miles W of Andover off the A303

A quarter of a century ago, the site of the Conservancy was open farmland. All the trees and shrubs have been planted since the mid 1960s and have developed into a woodland garden, worth a visit in its own right apart from its spectacular inhabitants.

The Conservancy's collection of owls is the most comprehensive in Britain, ranging from the relatively large European Eagle Owl to the tiny Scops Owl. Some, like the Spectacled Owl from the rain forests, are becoming increasingly rare as their natural habitats diminish so the Conservancy discharges a vital scientific role in preserving the species.

Prime attraction, of course, are the birds of prey – hawks, eagles and falcons – all of which have been trained. You can even have your photo taken with one of these hunters settled on your wrist. Weather permitting, flying demonstrations are given every day at noon, 2pm, 3pm and 4pm. The birds will not fly on wet days.

Mar–Oct, daily; summer 10.30am–5pm, spring and autumn till 4pm. Free parking.
Tel: (0264) 772252.

HOLIDAYS HILL REPTILIARY *

Map p.143, F1

Near Lyndhurst, beside the A35

An inconspicuous track off the A35, with a Forestry Commission sign beside it, leads through the woods of what was one of the very earliest 17th-century tree inclosures to the Commission's reptiliary. It is designed to show visitors the range of English reptiles found in and around the New Forest. In a series of rounded concrete pens, with walls about a yard high, the reptiliary provides habitats for the adder, grass snake, slow worm, sand and common lizard, smooth snake, and various frogs and newts. Visitors have to be very keen-eyed to see all of the reptiles, which often hide or blend in with their surroundings.

There is a series of bicycle and walking routes through the inclosures from the reptiliary, with one circular route taking in the Knightwood Oak (see LYNDHURST).

Apr–Sept, daily 8am–8pm.

LONGDOWN DAIRY FARM * *

Map p.143, F2

Near Ashurst off the A35

Longdown is a thriving example of farming combined with tourism. It is a working dairy farm which also caters for a wide range of visitors, especially children. Dairy farming remains the central activity on the Pass family farm, and visitors are welcome to watch

the afternoon milking in the computerized parlour. There are many different animals – cows, goats, pigs and poultry. Some breeds are rare or ancient, such as the 'Iron Age' pigs, pygmy goats, Norfolk Bronze turkeys and Embden geese. Many gentler animals are kept for children to pet and stroke. Educational visits are a speciality.
Easter–Oct, daily 11am–5pm. Free parking.
Tel: (0703) 293326 or 293313.

MARWELL ZOO * *

Map p.144, B2

6 miles S of Winchester off the B2177

£ ☕ S ♿ 🚻 🐕 *(kennels)*

Although Marwell Zoo has rides, gift shops and an adventure playground, it also has a serious purpose. The zoo is dedicated to the conservation of endangered species and a successful breeding programme has already ensured that many animals are now surviving in their natural habitats all over the world.

At Marwell, founded in the 1970s and set in 100 acres of Hampshire parkland, most of the animals roam in large, open enclosures. While visitors are essential to the zoo's future, the emphasis is on the well-being of the animals. They can be seen at their best from special walkways, or from the narrow gauge railway which threads a scenic route through the enclosures. There is also an education centre – housed in a magnificent listed Tudor mansion – for learning more about the various species, and during some school holidays and weekends there are family animal handling sessions. Two novel attractions, introduced in 1992, are the 'World of Lemurs', showing these eerie little creatures in their own community, and an 'encounter village' where visitors can make friends with domesticated species.
All year, daily 10am–6pm (4pm in winter).

NEW FOREST BUTTERFLY FARM * *

Map p.143, F2

1 mile S of Ashurst off the A35

£ ☕ S 🚶 *(for groups)* ♿ 🐕 i

In a variety of indoor habitats under large glazed roofs, visitors to the Butterfly Farm can see many different and exotic types of butterfly in their usual surroundings. A cottage garden setting offers the chance to see many fast-disappearing British moths and butterflies, including red admirals, tortoiseshells and fritillaries, as well as colonies of bees and wasps. More exotic is the steamy tropical garden, where many of the world's most beautiful creatures are housed among the banana and lemon trees and trailing passion flowers. Some of the world's ugliest or most tantalizing creatures are to be found in the insectarium; children especially enjoy looking at the tarantulas, scorpions, stick insects and beetles. The farm's outdoor attractions include dragonfly ponds, and wagon rides drawn by heavy horses through the woods.
Easter–Oct, daily 10am–5pm. Tel: (0703) 292166.

NEW FOREST OWL SANCTUARY * *

Map p.134, A4

1 mile S of Ringwood off the B3347

£ ☕ S ♿ 🚻 🐕 i

Saving the barn-owl from possible extinction was the motive force behind the establishment in 1975 of the Owl Sanctuary, just to the east of Ringwood. Now, owls from all over the world are kept here in reconstructed habitats within enclosures festooned with plaques bearing the names of their sponsors. The great horned owl for one, 'fiercest and most savage of all predatory birds', blinks at visitors from behind its wire and the signs warning visitors to keep their fingers away. Tiny Little owls and snowy-white Arctic owls are kept in the reconditioned hangar which also forms the visitor entrance and information area. The sanctuary receives many visitors, and the frequent displays of owls, and other birds of prey, flying in the lecture room and in the open air are deservedly popular.
All year, daily, 10am–5pm. Tel: (0425) 476487.

PAULTONS PARK * *

Map p.143, D1

At Ower, 4 miles S of Romsey off the A36

£ ☕ S ♿ *(wheelchair loan)* 🚻 🐕

The 140 acres of parkland in the amusement park were originally the gardens of a country house, which has since been demolished. The superb cedar trees survive, one of the proudest features of the garden which is the setting for aviaries and ponds containing exotic birds and 100 species of wildfowl. A huge lake, covering ten acres, lies at the garden's heart. A 19th-century waterwheel and the grand bridge over the lake are among its many features.

Paultons Park is one of the premier tourist attractions in Hampshire. It is situated close to the M27, so access is easy, and the park has many features aimed at children, from games in Kids' Kingdom and the Magic Forest, to mazes, pets' corners, flying saucers, and board walks in the land of the dinosaurs. A Village Life Museum illustrates forest ways at the turn of the century, and the Romany Museum has a unique collection of gypsy vehicles and craft work. Transport around the park is on the Rio Grande train.

End of Mar–Nov, daily 10am–6.30pm. Tel: (0703) 814455.

SEALIFE CENTRE * *

Map p.138, D3

Clarence Esplanade, Southsea

(talks)

Some of the fascinating mysteries of life under the sea are revealed at the Sealife Centre, where visitors enjoy a close quarters look at this otherwise hidden world. the centre also has a scientific purpose; research staff conduct studies into marine creatures and their environments. There is also an extensive breeding programme, and a constant stream of casualties, which are brought to the centre by members of the public to be treated and nursed back to health before being released back into the wild.

Sealife is divided into several theme areas, ranging from the shoreline to local harbours, British sharks and an intriguing look at some of the unusual perils to be encountered in the depths. Favourite with the children is a touch pool, where they can actually handle fish in the water.

The centre has a shop and restaurant facilities, a picnic area and a children's play area which includes a reconstructed rock pool.

All year, daily 10am–6pm (9pm in summer holidays). Tel: (0705) 734461.

TITCHFIELD HAVEN

Map p.137, B4

Head for Titchfield off the A27

When the Earl of Southampton had a dam built across the mouth of the River Meon in 1611 he might not have done the town of Titchfield much good in terms of trade: what was becoming a thriving port was cut off from the sea, and the canal which was built was nowhere near big enough to be of much good. What he did, however, was to create a new environment which was very much to the liking to a variety of animals, birds and plants. Today Titchfield Haven is a major nature reserve regarded as an internationally important breeding and visiting ground.

Such is the importance of the site that admission is outside the breeding season, from August to the end of March, is only by prior arrangement, and visitors must be accompanied. The site is best suited to the serious naturalist who will be content to watch the natural world from a hide.

Contact Naturalist Warden, Haven Cottage, Hill Head, Fareham. Tel: (0329) 662145.

UPPER HAMBLE FARM MUSEUM

Map p.144, E2

4 miles E of Southampton off the M27 (junction 8)

Manor Farm, set in a corner of the Upper Hamble Country Park (see p.00), is a fascinating insight into traditional farming methods. This is no museum, however, but a working farm. The barns, sheds and shelters contain implements that would have been used from the turn of the century to the 1950s. Many of the crops are cultivated with horse-drawn machinery or using veteran tractors and the woodland, too, is worked in traditional coppice style. Farm implements are made and repaired in the smithy and the wheelwright's shop.

The fine old farmhouse shows the simple way of life of the farm bailiff and his family in the early 1900s, with the authentic furniture and equipment of the milkhouse, scullery, parlour and bedrooms. In the garden there is an authentic three-seat privy.

Easter–Oct, daily; Nov–Easter, Sun only 10am–dusk. Tel: (0489) 787055.

ARCHAEOLOGICAL SITES

BASING HOUSE **

Map p.156, E1

1 mile E of Basingstoke off the A30

The site of Basing House has been important in archaeological terms since Iron Age times and the Romans and Saxons also had settlements there, making use of the resources of the River Loddon.

But it is the siege of Basing House during the Civil War and its subsequent destruction which have made it famous. The house was built by Sir William Paulet, the First Marquess of Winchester, and it was probably the most sumptuous palace in the kingdom at that time. That was until the Civil War when John, the Royalist 5th Marquess of Winchester, held out against Parliamentary troops.

The siege started in May 1645 and lasted until November when Oliver Cromwell himself led a dramatic final storming with a formidable force of 7000 troops. John was captured and sent to the Tower. The house was left in ruins and villagers raided the stones to build their own cottages. The site was subsequently cleared and landscaped to form gardens for another large house built by the Duke of Bolton but that, too, met a dramatic end when it was destroyed by fire in 1740.

The site was bought by Hampshire County Council in 1970 and excavation work continues from time to time. It includes the great earthwork ditch which was orginally built in the 11th century, but the most recognizable building is the old dovecote, where up to 500 birds were kept for eggs and meat. The entrance to the ruins is over an old canal bridge built in the 1790s but which now blends in with the surroundings.

Battles from the Civil War are occasionally re-enacted and there is also a programme of theme events during summer months.

Apr–Sept, Weds–Sun and BHs 2–6pm.
Tel: (0256) 467294.

BEACON HILL **

Map p.154, C3

2 miles S of Burghclere off the A34

Sitting on the highest part of the North Hampshire Downs, at some 870ft, Beacon Hill is crowned by an important Iron Age hillfort. It is one of a cluster of fortifications from the Bronze and Iron Ages in this part of the county, and its banks are especially well-preserved. They are some 7ft high, and together with the 10ft deep ditch encircle an area of 12 acres. The original entrance is on the south side, with additional defensive banks, and the enclosed area contains many grassy mounds which were the position of the original huts, each some 7 or 8 yds across.

Access is from the nearby car park off the main A34, and the path is very steep. The fine and extensive views are the best reward for the climb. Within the enclosure of the fort is the grave of the 5th Earl of Caernarvon, co-discoverer of Tutankhamun's tomb, who died in 1923 shortly after the discovery. His home, Highclere Castle (see p.13) and its surrounding parkland are clearly visible from the top of Beacon Hill.

BISHOP'S WALTHAM PALACE **

Map p.144, C3

6 miles E of Eastleigh on the B2177

The ruins of Bishop's Waltham Palace represent a 500-year period in British history, beginning with one of the wealthiest and most influential men in the country and ending amid the turmoil of the Civil War.

The palace was built in the 12th century by the Bishop of Winchester, Henry de Blois, and over the next 200 years it became increasingly important and was a favourite with royalty. Henry III stayed there on several occasions.

In the 14th century another Bishop of Winchester, William Wykeham, who was one of Edward III's most important advisers, had

the palace extensively renovated but retained most of the outer walls. He engaged the best stonemasons and carpenters normally employed building the great cathedrals.

After Wykeham's death the palace was inherited by Bishop Henry Beaufort who continued the rebuilding work and added a new storey to the west tower for his private accommodation. Queen Mary stayed there while waiting for her betrothed, King Philip of Spain.

The end came after the Battle of Cheriton in 1644 when the Royalist garrison was forced to surrender. Contemporary reports say the palace was 'in ashes'.

Easter–Sept, daily 10am–6pm; Oct–Easter, Tues–Sun 10am–4pm. Tel: (0489) 892460.

BURY HILL *

Map p.148, B3

1 mile S of Andover off the A343

There is a permanent debate as to whether archaeological sites should be stripped down for total inspection, as archaeologists want, or whether they should be left undisturbed in a 'romantic' condition. Bury Hill Fort belongs emphatically to the second class. It is maintained by Hampshire County Council but only the outer ramparts form part of a public footpath, the large, flat internal section being part of a private farm. The entrance to the fort is on the right hand of the road leading west from Upper Clatford.

The footpath that runs round this centre is well trodden, so there is no difficulty of access but the gnarled roots underfoot, and the trees and bushes arching overhead give it an eerie atmosphere. The fort is very simple in shape. Some time about 300 BC a ditch some 11ft deep and 5ft wide was excavated, the earth being thrown up to form an embankment about 6ft high. The dense vegetation has obscured much of the detail but it is still possible to work out the plan, including the two causewayed entrances, one of which is the modern entrance. There was a second phase of building about 1 BC and the fort was probably occupied until about the end of the 1st century AD.

DANEBURY HILL FORT **

Map p.148, D3

2 miles NW of Stockbridge off the A30

The most evocative approach to this spectacular hill-fort is up the rough track from Longstock. For the more hurried or the sedentary, the easiest approach is from the byroad which runs past Danebury, whence a drive leads up to the site. Unlike Bury Hill (see above) this is an active, not to say very busy, site with interpretation boards and units for the layman explaining every aspect of Iron Age life. The hill-fort consists of massive defensive earthworks enclosing a 13-acre site. Commenced about 500 BC, it was in continued use for over 400 years, being abandoned shortly before the Roman conquest of Britain. Archaeologists have been exploring the site for over 20 years, producing a wealth of Iron Age artefacts which are now in Andover Museum. At least two hours should be devoted to exploring the site.

Open at all times. Tel: (0962) 846034.

FLOWERDOWN BARROWS, LITTLETON

Map p.149, E3

2 miles NW of central Winchester off the A272

This burial site stands on the edge of the common at the southern end of Littleton, behind the bus shelter. The larger of the two tumuli is a disc barrow which is still unexcavated but is normally expected to cover a female burial. The central mound is 98ft across and surrounded by a ditch 20ft wide and an outer bank also 20ft wide. The mounds are probably representative of the early bronze age (2100–1500 BC) 'Wessex culture'.

LADLE HILL **

Map p.154, C3

Just SE of Old Burghclere

Part of the great chalk scarp which includes Watership Down, Ladle Hill's special importance is that it has an Iron Age hillfort on top which was left unfinished. To the casual visitor this gives

The Mizmaze, Breamore Down.

it a rather ragged appearance, but it has been invaluable in helping archaeologists unravel the sequence of building operations for these 3000-year-old forts.

Portions of the very first marking-out ditch are still visible, but this has been largely obliterated by the digging of the principal defensive ditch, the topsoil from which was dumped in the central enclosure. Only some parts of the rampart, made from the chalk rubble beneath the topsoil in the ditch, were ever constructed, and the topsoil was never put back onto the defensive bank before the fort was abandoned.

The hilltop also boasts a number of earlier, Bronze Age burial mounds of various forms – round, saucer, bell and disc barrows. These have their counterpart in the so-called Seven Barrows on nearby Lower Woodcott Down. In the Bronze Age, this downland region was a centre for settled agriculture; cattle were penned during winter in embanked enclosures, some of which can still be made out on Ladle Hill, and their dung was spread on the small embanked fields like those below Ladle Hill on Great Litchfield Down, close to the A34. All these features are accessible on the network of paths and tracks which cross the countryside.

THE MIZMAZE, BREAMORE DOWN * *

Map p.141, B2

2½ miles from Fordingbridge off the A338

Encircled by yew trees on the down above Breamore, the Mizmaze is one of Hampshire's great curiosities. It is a turf maze, a continuous turf path which loops its way within a circle 80ft across, finally reaching the central mound. This ancient maze, like those at Wing, in Leicestershire, and Hilton, Cambridgeshire, is not of the Hampton Court variety, with blind turnings and dead-ends, but a circuitous labyrinth, like the Minotaur's in ancient Crete. In the Middle Ages these mazes had a religious significance, for penitential rituals; but Breamore Down is a secluded place with a number of ancient burial mounds, on one of which the maze itself is placed. So nobody knows quite how ancient this site is. The antiquarian interests of Sir Edward Hulse saved the Mizmaze from almost total decay in 1783, and it has been maintained by the Breamore estate since.

A network of public footpaths connects the Mizmaze with the nearby villages. The most straightforward route is up the track which runs alongside Breamore House, and rises onto the down. A signboard points into the mysterious wood in which the maze lies.

ODIHAM CASTLE *

Map p.156, E3

7 miles E of Basingstoke off the B3349

As archaeological ruins go, Odiham Castle, or King John's castle as it is known locally, is rather disappointing. The crumbling stonework of the keep is in a dangerous condition and visitors are warned to keep clear for fear of falling masonry. That said, it is in such an idyllic location, beside the restored Basingstoke Canal, that it is worth a visit, even though cars have to be parked up to half a mile away.

The castle was built at the beginning of the 13th century. It is said that King John stayed here when he was on his way to put his seal to the Magna Carta at Runnymede. The site is now preserved by Hampshire County Council with constant free access.

ROCKBOURNE ROMAN VILLA * *

Map p.141, C2

2 miles from Fordingbridge off the B3078

£ S ♿

In 1942 a farmer out ferreting discovered what turned out to be one of the most interesting Roman villa complexes in the south. Initial excavations revealed a mosaic floor, and systematic investigation of the site between 1956 and 1982 uncovered the sequence of buildings which occupied the site between the 1st and 5th centuries AD. Some of the mosaic floors, with geometric patterning, and the underfloor heating systems of the bath house, are uncovered during the opening season, while the outlines of the rooms and buildings which have been covered over again are marked out in the grass.

The site was bought after its discovery by the local antiquarian A. T. Morley Hewitt, who then organized its excavation, and since 1979 the villa has been owned by Hampshire County Council. Entrance to the site is via the museum, dedicated to Hewitt, which displays many artefacts found on the site. Rockbourne villa was part of a thriving local economy, and the routes of many Roman roads survive in the region as testimony to that.

Apr–Sept, daily 2pm–6pm; July–Aug, daily 10.30am–6pm. Tel: (07253) 541.

SILCHESTER ROMAN TOWN * * *

Map p.155, B4

7 miles N of Basingstoke off the A340

The great Roman town of Calleva Atrebatum at Silchester, or what remains of it, is for the most part buried beneath the fields in this quiet corner of North Hampshire. But some dramatic reminders remain, including the vast town wall and the site of the huge amphitheatre where as many as 4000 people would have watched gladiators engaged in bloodthirsty pursuits.

Many of the Roman artefacts unearthed over the years can be seen in the Calleva museum at Silchester, which was opened in 1951 as part of the Festival of Britain celebrations, but most of the important and valuable items are on display at another museum in Reading, a few miles away. Excavations still continue during the summer months, although most archaeological investigations have long since been completed and the results properly recorded.

To the untrained eye the remains of the wall, about one-and-a-half miles round, are the most striking relics. The wall had four main gates but only the one to the south is still visible. It is possible to walk the full length around the walls, using public paths, but access is not allowed to the fields within the ramparts. If time is against you it is possible to drive to the best preserved section between the south gate and the village church.

Calleva Museum: *Daily, daylight hours. Free.*
Reading Museum: *Mon–Sat. Free.*

TITCHFIELD ABBEY *

Map p.137, B4

2 miles W of Fareham on the A27

Titchfield Abbey was founded in 1232 by Peter de Roches, a Bishop of Winchester, and was occupied for 300 years by Premonstratensian White Canons. It had one of the finest monastic libraries of the times with more than 200 volumes. There were great national occasions here, too. The abbey was the scene of the marriage of Henry VI and Margaret of Anjou in 1445. Artificial ponds were created nearby where fish were kept as a source of food, and they can be seen from a public footpath to the west of the abbey.

After the Dissolution of the Monastaries Henry VIII gave the abbey to Thomas Wriothesley, Earl of Southampton, as a reward for his help in what was termed 'the King's great business'. He had it converted into a mansion which was called Place House. Subsequently the 3rd Earl of Southampton was a patron of William Shakespeare and it is widely accepted that the Bard must have written some of his works at Titchfield and that some of his plays may even have had their premières there.

LONG-DISTANCE FOOTPATHS

THE CLARENDON WAY * *

Between Winchester (map p.149, F3) and Salisbury, Wilts (map p.147, F1)

This 24 mile long-distance footpath connects two of England's most exquisite little cities, Salisbury and Winchester. Like its sister footpath, the Test Way (see below), it can be walked in one go or in different stretches. It takes its name from Clarendon Park, on the eastern side of Salisbury. This was the site of Clarendon Palace, a royal hunting lodge of the Norman kings which became a great mansion of the Plantagenets, but nothing now remains of this except for a low wall near the Way. The Way crosses the River Test at Broughton, goes through Farley Mount Country Park (see p.24) and ends in Winchester at the ruins of the Roman wall which once surrounded the city. As with the Test Way, Hampshire County Council has provided a simplified plan for walkers.

THE HANGERS WAY * *

Between Petersfield (map p.146, B2) and Alton (map p.151, C2)

Hangers is the name given to the steep, wooded hillsides which run in a ridge across north Hampshire from Petersfield to Alton. Ever since the days of the great naturalist, Gilbert White, they have held a special fascination for country lovers, and this 17-mile trek takes in some of the best rural scenery to be found anywhere.

It starts at Petersfield, itself a fine example of a rural town – but most hikers will want to head straight for the open country. That begins at Steep, which has connections with the poet Edward Thomas. After passing Ashford Chase the trail heads up onto Shoulder of Mutton Hill where there is a memorial to Thomas.

Hawkley is the first village on the route and the Hawkley Inn has a fine range of real ales to quench any thirst. From there it is on through Gilbert White country to his home at Selborne, where you can find out more about him at The Wakes museum or search for his simple grave in the churchyard. This is about half way, and is a good breaking off or starting point for those who would rather not make the trip in one go.

North of Selborne the path passes damp hollows which were once the medieval fish ponds of Selborne Priory. Binswood is described as an ecological jewel, managed by the Woodland Trust as an example of past land use. From East Worldham to Alton the path leads past redundant hop fields and on to King's Pond at Alton, which was formed in the 18th century for the paper making industry.

There is an infrequent bus service between Alton and Petersfield and it is best to check for times. Both towns are served by rail, but there is no direct link between them.

THE SOLENT WAY * *

Between Milford on Sea (map p.135, E3) and Emsworth (map p.139, B2)

Hampshire's coastal variety is well illustrated along the 60-mile length of the Solent Way. The first stretch of the walk from Milford follows the shingle spit to Hurst Castle and then takes the ferry back to Keyhaven. Continuing through the marshes, rich with bird life, and crossing the river at Lymington, the route turns inland, with occasional glimpses of the Solent waters, across Beaulieu Heath to Hythe. Here another ferry takes the walker to Southampton, and the way continues over the soaring Itchen bridge to Woolston and Hamble, yachting capital of the Solent. A small ferry across the Hamble River continues the route through the nature reserves and unspoilt coastline beyond Warsash.

After this peaceful interlude, the Solent Way reaches built-up areas again at Gosport, and takes the ferry past the naval dockyards over to Portsmouth. Next stop is the seaside town of Southsea. Beyond that and Portsea Island, Langstone Harbour is an unspoilt wilderness, with a snaking shoreline of 16 miles. Around the Farlington Marshes at the top of the harbour, the path continues to Langstone and Warblington, reaching its end on the West Sussex boundary.

THE TEST WAY * *

Between Totton (map p.143, D2) and Inkpen, Berks. (map p.153, A4)

The Test Way extends for 46 miles, following the valley of the River Test from Totton at the tidal head of Southampton Water in a north-westerly direction to Inkpen. It offers a variety of beautiful scenery – river, hills, woods, handsome villages, chalk land and clay. Dedicated walkers can cover the entire length in four days but it is perfectly possible to pick up various lengths for a day's easy strolling.

Beginning at Redbridge, at the end of the M271, and crossing the reedy marshes, the path follows the east bank of the river to Nursling, passing under the M27. At Lee it crosses the Test, follows the flood plain to Moorcourt, and from there continues north to Romsey. The path gives an excellent view of the stately porticoed front of Broadlands (see p.12). After a short distance on the A31, the path skirts Romsey, leaving the river again to follow the lanes through Awbridge.

At Mottisfont the pathway again follows the village lanes, skirting the grounds of Mottisfont Abbey (see p.14), to leave the roadways behind. Further north, the pathway recrosses the Test, then joins the track of the disused Andover to Romsey railway line. At King's Somborne, the Test Way crosses the Clarendon Way (see above).

Beyond Marsh Court, Stockbridge, and Leckford, the footpath finally parts company with the old railway, to make its way through the woods and hills above Wherwell to Longparish. Here it climbs into the hills until rejoining the river at St Mary Bourne. The Test here is a tiny river, and it is the course of one of the tributaries, the Bourne Rivulet, that the Test Way follows on its last stage, through Ibthorpe and finally onto the Wiltshire chalk escarpment.

Hampshire County Council has published an excellent simplified plan of the route, obtainable from most Tourist Information Centres in the county.

THE WAYFARERS WALK * *

Between Emsworth (map p.139, B2) and Inkpen, Berks. (map 153, A4)

The Wayfarers Walk is a 70-mile marathon from the coast at Emsworth through the middle of Hampshire to the highest point in the county 800ft above sea level on the border with Berkshire. There are many good stopping and starting points on the route with road, rail and bus links.

The beginning of the route passes through the urban areas around Havant and the built-up district north of Portsmouth before reaching the countryside. At Denmead, once deep in the Forest of Bere, the path takes on a rural character, heading on towards Hambledon and then Soberton and Droxford in the beautiful Meon Valley.

From Droxford the path climbs high over the down through typical Hampshire sheep country and then drops down to Cheriton, scene of a bloody Civil War battle, and Tichborne, near the source of the River Itchen.

Alresford, about half way, is the largest town on the route and has a regular bus service to Alton in the north and Winchester to the south. From there the trail leads up the Candover Valley, crossing an ancient track used by cattle drovers from Wales heading to the markets in London. Keeping a safe and respectable distance from overgrown Basingstoke, the route passes Dummer, childhood home of the Duchess of York, and on by Deane and Oakley.

The final leg is a steep climb back into the downland with its spectacular views over much of southern England. On a fine day it is said you can see five counties from Inkpen Beacon. This is also the end of the Test Way, which starts on the outskirts of Southampton. It is an isolated spot, so do not expect any public transport to come along.

BEACHES

BARTON ON SEA BEACH

Map p.135, D2

Near New Milton off the A337

The mile-long beach, a mixture of shingle and sand, lies at the foot of sand, clay and gravel cliffs. These were famous in the 18th and early 19th centuries as a source of fossils (one particular type of fossil is named after Barton), and as a smugglers' haven. Terraced pathways lead down from the clifftop village and car park to the unfussy beach, where breakwaters made of giant stones testify to the instability of the cliffs. From Barton, there are sweeping views of Christchurch Bay down to Hengistbury Head, and across to the Needles on the Isle of Wight. There is a pay and display car park.

HAYLING BAY

Map p.139, D1

S coast of Hayling Island via the A3023

There is something to suit most tastes and age groups at Hayling Bay, the beach on the south of Hayling Island. For those who like funfairs, kiss-me-quick hats and hot-dogs while they are getting a sun tan, you have all you can hope for. Others who prefer peace and solitude should move either to the east or the west. The further you go the quieter it tends to be. The beach itself seems clean and well maintained. It faces south and gets the best of the afternoon sun but the shingle can be tough on soft feet. There is good and ample car parking though at peak times in the summer it might be as well to arrive early.

LEE-ON-THE-SOLENT

Map p.138, D1

4 miles W of Gosport on the B333

This is a favourite spot to watch the comings and goings of ships as they head towards Southampton, but Lee-on-the-Solent has never quite made it as a serious resort. Many of the pre-war facilities, such as the pier and the amusement complex with its tall viewing tower and cinema, fell into disrepair and were demolished during the 1960s. They have not been replaced. The beach is used mainly by local sun worshippers and dinghy sailors who are accustomed to the sight of the Esso oil refinery and the power station chimney in the distance to the west. While the beach appears clean, many regard it as being a bit too close for comfort to industry and docks.

MILFORD ON SEA BEACH

Map p.135, E4

2 miles E of New Milton off the B3058

A very long beach, with pebble and shingles stretching for miles to join with the cliffs and beach at Barton, and extending to the spit at Hurst Castle. Milford beach has few facilities, with one shop beside the car park – and certainly no amusement arcades. The high water mark is only thirty yards from the car park, so the beach is easily reached. The warnings of sharp underwater obstructions, however, suggest that it is not an ideal swimming beach.

The glory of Milford beach is the outlook, across the Solent to the Needles and the Isle of Wight, and the down the coastline to Dorset. There is a pay and display car park.

PARK SHORE BEACH

Map p.136, E3–E4

3 miles S of Beaulieu off the B3054

A number of narrow lanes run to the Solent coast from St Leonard's Grange and the East Boldre district, via Sowley. The public parts of the shingle shoreline offer secluded opportunities for watching birds, ships, and the world go by. Ironstone, the raw material for the former ironworks at Sowley Pond, is still washed up here. Swimming is for the intrepid.

SOUTHSEA

Map p.138, E3

Just S of Portsmouth

Loud and garish best sums up Southsea. The large funfair and amusement park at Clarence pier is extremely popular with the young, and South Parade Pier is proud to call itself one of the liveliest entertainment spots in the South. The hovercraft plying to and from the Isle of Wight can be an annoyance, but with four miles of beach it is not too difficult to find a quieter spot. The beach, like many along this stretch of coast, is mostly rather uncomfortable shingle, but it is well maintained. And if the sun and sea all get a bit too much there is always the large grass expanse of Southsea Common to back it up.

STOKES BAY

Map p.138, D2

Just S of Gosport

This is a comparative newcomer to the list of popular beaches, its reputation boosted in recent years by a number of EC Blue Flag awards for cleanliness. It is easy to forget that the large Naval Dockyard and the cross-Channel ferry terminal are just around the corner in Portsmouth Harbour. Stokes Bay tends to be used mainly by local people living in the urban areas of Gosport, and it is likely to be as busy on a warm summer evening after work as during the daytime. The beach is of shingle but it curves to the south-west so it is an ideal sun trap in the afternoons and evenings. Parking is no problem while the beach remains mainly for local use.

ABBOTTS ANN

Map p.148, B3
3 miles SW of Andover off the A343

The first known settlement on the site of Abbotts Ann was established in 50 BC by the Celtic Belgae leader Commius, who had accompanied Julius Caesar on the latter's two invasions. In 901, King Edward the elder granted the manor and others to Hyde Abbey in Winchester and the village became known as Abbott's Anna ('Abbott's brook'). From 15 houses in 1915 the village has expanded to over five times as many now. Of note is the thatch owl on top of the Old Bakery.

The **Church of St Mary the Virgin,** a 250-year-old church overlooking the water-meadows of the brook, was built by Thomas Pitt, known as 'Diamond Pitt', who made a fortune selling a large diamond to the King of France and was the forebear of two prime ministers. It is a medium-sized flint building with some 19th-century windows. Its real claim to fame is the perpetuation of the medieval tradition of awarding virgin's crowns. These were hung from the ceiling of the church on the funeral of an unmarried person of good character ('chaste in all senses') who was born, baptized and buried in the parish. There are currently 39 crowns hanging, the earliest being dated 1740 to John Morrant. The crowns are made of hazelwood ornamented with paper rosettes with five paper gloves representing a challenge to anyone disputing the worthiness of the virgin. The most recent crown is dated 1977.

ALDERSHOT

Map p.157, E3 * * *
15 miles E of Basingstoke off the M3

Aldershot is the home of the British Army. That was the purpose for which it was built, and although it has since been developed for the growing civilian population, the military influence is everywhere.

Aldershot was virtually deserted heathland until the middle of the last century, when the War Department made its first purchase of land on a site which is today occupied by the Princes Gardens. The growth of the army camp coincided with the development of the railway and the building of better roads.

The new barracks were built of timber, much of it shipped along the Basingstoke Canal which runs through the town. Brick-built barracks were to replace the wooden huts, and new roads were laid out to form the foundations of the Aldershot as we know it today. Queen Victoria was a regular visitor, staying at the Royal Pavilion and reviewing her troops in Long Valley.

Aldershot has changed its character several times over the years and in recent times many of the old barracks, known to generations of soldiers, have been replaced.

The **Aldershot Military Museum and Visitors' Centre** in Queen's Avenue tells the story of Aldershot from 1854 until the present day and includes a typical barrack room scene reproduced in an original Victorian building. There are nine other regimental museums and a military heritage trail is a popular feature. Details can be obtained from the Visitors' Centre which is open daily. The **Airborne Forces Museum** covers fifty years of military aviation, with displays including original briefing materials, weapons and equipment.

The **Royal Garrison Church of All Saints,** known locally as the Red Church because of its brick construction, is another imposing building. It was built in 1863 to serve the growing number of soldiers and now includes more than eighty memorials to outstanding servicemen.

The **Garrison Church of St Michael and St George** was built in 1892 as an Anglican church but became Roman Catholic in 1973. There is a stained glass memorial window dedicated to men of the Army Service Corps who died in the South African War. **St Joseph's** Roman Catholic Church was built in 1912.

The Wellington Monument, Aldershot.

The **Union Building,** dating from pre-Army times, was the old workhouse and was being used as a school for pauper children when it was taken over by the military in 1854. It has had many additions and alterations in the intervening years but it still retains its distinctive character.

Until the 19th century Aldershot had fewer than one thousand inhabitants. The manor belonged to the Tichborne family (see TICHBORNE) and the **Manor House,** rebuilt of brick in 1670, is one of the town's oldest buildings. It has been converted in recent years into offices but is still well cared for.

The **Prince Consort's Library,** overlooking Farnborough Rd, was a gift from Prince Albert to 'the Officers of the Army and Militia'. It cost £4000 when it was built in 1860. It now contains many valuable military records and reference books.

M The **Wellington Monument** is the most striking of Aldershot's memorials to its soldiers. It shows the Iron Duke on his favourite horse, Copenhagen, and the statue was originally on top of the Triumphal Arch at Hyde Park Corner in London.

M The **Heroes' Shrine** in Manor Park is a granite memorial to men who died in World War I. A walled sunken garden represents Britain's tribute not only to the men of Aldershot but also to all the towns and cities which were bombed in World War II. Stones used in its construction include those from Coventry Cathedral and Portsmouth Dockyard.

Union Street, known to thousands of servicemen and their families, is now an attractive pedestrianized precinct and the **Wellington Centre** is a purpose-built covered shopping mall opened in 1979.

Princes Hall, built in 1972 as part of a complex which includes a health centre, court and police station, is also a venue for live entertainment and there is a multi-screen cinema in the town centre.

Brickfields Country Park is a popular area on the outskirts of the town which includes a picnic area. Sporting facilities include a swimming pool complex, an ice rink, a nine-hole golf course and an outdoor ski slope.

Aldershot Military Museum: *Mar–Oct, daily 10am–5pm; Nov–Feb, daily 10am–4.30pm. Admission charge. Tel: (0252) 314598.*
Airborne Forces Museum: *All year, Tues–Sun 10am–4.30pm. Admission charge. Tel: (0252) 349619.*

ALTON

Map p.151, C2 * *
11 miles SW of Aldershot off the A31

Alton is a traditional centre for the brewing industry, once renowned for its fine ales and stouts. It maintains strong connections with brewing to this day, but this is no longer the sole industry on which the town relies for its prosperity.

It was the quality of the spring water which encouraged the Crowley family to establish a brewery at Alton, and hops, another vital ingredient, thrived nearby. As late as the 1960s there were few families who didn't have someone employed by Watney, Courage or Harp, and on some days the heady smell of spent hops permeated the town. Today Bass, which took over the Harp Lager brewery opened by Lord Louis Mountbatten in the early 1960s, is the custodian of the brewing tradition. Tours of the Manor Park Brewery can be arranged for groups and individuals but bookings are needed. They can be made at the Tourist Information Centre in Cross and Pillory Lane.

Being at the centre of an agricultural area, Alton was well known for its weekly cattle market – but that, too, has gone, following changes in farming practices. The old Market Square is now an attractive paved pedestrian area and a shopping precinct occupies the site of the former cattle pens.

The annual agricultural is still an important event in the town's calendar, though, and there's still some semblance of the weekly market when traders set up stalls in the Market Square selling anything from fruit and vegetables to clothes and pot plants.

The River Wey, which subsequently helps to swell the waters of the Thames, rises in a meadow about a mile on the Basingstoke side and flows for the most part unseen through a culvert under the town centre. But there has been concern in recent years about the lack of water in the river, particularly during the summer months, following several particularly dry winters.

St Lawrence's Church★ was the scene of a bloody encounter during the Civil War when Colonel John Bolle and his troops were killed trying to defend the town from Cromwell's Roundheads, led by General Waller. They made a desperate last stand inside the church but were eventually massacred. Bullet holes and pike marks can still be seen in the heavy oak south door. The loss of the town was a major blow to the Royalists.

The **Friends Meeting House** was built in Church St in 1672 by the Society of Friends, later known as the Quakers, who held some of their first meetings in Alton. The date, set in bricks in the boundary wall, can just be made out.

The **Curtis Museum★** was founded by William Curtis, a noted Quaker and botanist who died in 1799. Situated in High St, it contains a wealth of local interest including collections of Victorian Dolls, toys, books and puzzles, and sections on natural history and geology.

Fanny Adams was the name of an eight-year-old girl who met a gruesome death at the hands of a solicitor's clerk called Frederick Baker in 1867. After luring her from her home, he murdered her and cut her body into many pieces. At about the same time tinned meat was being issued to the Royal Navy for the first time and sailors with a macabre sense of humour called it Sweet Fanny Adams. Baker was later hanged at Winchester prison.

The **Watercress Line★★** terminates at Alton at the end of a ten-mile trip through the Hampshire countryside from New Alresford. The line was once part of a secondary route which linked London with Southampton and was, in fact, slightly shorter than the main line. However, because of the steep gradients and sharp curves in Hampshire, the line was never renowned for its speed. British Rail closed the track in the 1970s but it has now been re-opened by enthusiasts using an impressive range of steam locomotives. Trains on the Watercress Line share the same station as British Rail, making convenient connections.

Eggar's Grammar School, founded in 1642 thanks to the generosity and foresight of local landowner John Eggar, had a reputation for learning excellence and many of its pupils went on the achieve fame and fortune. During the 1970s a move to make the school comprehensive caused widespread public protest, but change was inevitable and Eggar's Grammar School has now become Alton College.

The **Sports Centre,** at the Chawton end of town, has swimming pools, fitness suites, squash courts and floodlit outdoor areas. At the other end of town, **Anstey Park** is a large open space with football and rugby pitches.

***Manor Park Brewery**: Tel: (0420) 541177.*
***Watercress Line:** Easter–Oct, Sat and BHs; mid June–mid July also Mon–Fri; mid July–Aug, daily; Jan–Easter, Sun only. Trips approximately ½-hourly. Tel: (0962) 733810.*
***Curtis Museum:** All year, Tues–Sat 10am–5pm. Tel: (0420) 82802.*

AMPFIELD

Map p.143, B3
6 miles SW of Winchester on the A31

St Mark's Church★ is Ampfield in miniature. Sitting beside the main A31, its churchyard is a wooded dell, filled with rhododendron and azalea blossom in late spring, and it is built in blue brick, made from local clays which have sustained a pottery and brick industry since Roman times at least. The great and the good of the High Church turned out in 1841 for the church's consecration, since it was inspired by Revd John Keble from nearby Hursley, and designed by William Yonge of Otterbourne, father of Charlotte.

The Hillier Centre arboretum on Jermyns Lane (see p.22) is the crowning glory of the wooded gardens which abound in the parish. Hillier's Nurseries have their head office in the brick-built, substantial, mid-Georgian Ampfield House a short distance towards Romsey from the church.

Braishfield, a mile north-west, is a more secluded, more agricultural village. Its red brick church of 1855 is by the celebrated William Butterfield.

AMPORT

Map p.148, B2 *

4 miles W of Andover off the A303

Amport stretches for the better part of a mile across the upper reaches of Pillhill Brook. The centrepoint of the village is a gentle curve of thatched houses overlooking the green and water-meadows. The manor was granted by William the Conqueror to Hugh de Port, giving the derivation of the name Anna de Port ('Port's brook') which contracted to Amport. It was long the home of the Marquesses of Winchester.

Amport House is on the south side of the brook at the west of the village. The current building dates to 1857 and has gardens laid out by Sir Edwin Lutyens. It is now the Royal Air Force Chaplains School.

St Mary's Church* is an imposing cruciform building with a 14th-century tower and some windows of the same period, but it was greatly altered in the 19th century. It contains a number of memorials to admirals and generals and there is a 400-year-old portable alabaster altar hanging in the central tower.

ANDOVER

Map p.148, A4 * *

16 miles W of Basingstoke on the B3400

Andover is a classic modern market town with ancient roots. Its name refers to its position on the Anton River ('Anton water') and it has been a centre of settlement and trade routes since neolithic times. From Roman times it sat on the hill above the strategic London to Exeter road. One of the first mentions of the town and its church was in 994, when King Aethelred concluded a treaty with the leader of a party of invading Danes, Olag Trygvasson, and sponsored the latter's conversion to Christianity in the Andover church. Trygvasson subsequently became the first king of Norway after leading a successful revolt against the Danes. The borough gained its charter in 1178, but it was not until 1205 that John I came to the town to present it. The town has seen its share of England's wars, being burnt during civil wars in the 12th and 15th centuries and emerging as a key town in the struggle between King and Parliament.

Andover has expanded dramatically since the end of World War II, due largely to government plans to treble the then population of 16,000 by relocating Londoners. The old heart is now the centre of sprawling housing estates and a set of ring roads that are a traffic planner's delight. Getting into the centre of the town and finding off-street parking present few problems as everything is well signposted. However, leaving Andover in the desired direction requires careful navigation. Visitors should use the car-park, which is only yards from the market place through the shopping mall or along the street at the entrance, as people with local knowledge will have taken the few parking places in the centre.

The **Market Place.** The dozen or so buildings that are more than fifty years old all appear to have been either taverns or coaching inns at one stage in their histories. Two survive as pubs: **The George,** dating from Elizabethan times, and **The Globe,** which is 18th-century. Both have modern interiors, that of the George being the most disappointing. At the bottom of the market is the **Danebury Hotel,** an 18th-century coaching inn with a portico, which still functions as a hotel. Around the other corner is the **Hart Hotel,** which claims to have been founded in the 13th century, though the exterior is pseudo-Regency. If you walk into the car park you will see the old stable, barns and other outbuildings of an extensive and much modified establishment. A tablet above the door states that King Charles II stopped here during the Civil War. The **Guild Hall** dominates the marketplace and has itself been turned into a traditional indoor market. It is an imposing brownstone Regency block.

🍷 The **Angel Inn,** just off the market on the road to the church, claims to be the oldest in Andover and to have a clutch of royal connections. It was founded in 1175 and rebuilt in 1445 after the great fire of Andover in 1435. A tablet claims that King John stayed there while presenting the royal charter in 1205; that Catherine of Aragon stayed in 1501; and that Henry VIII stayed at some point; and that King James II ate here while retreating from the army of William of Orange. It was during his night in Andover that his own army disintegrated and he had to fly to London, Ireland and exile.

[M] The **Norman Arch,** just up the road on the right from the Angel Inn, forms an entrance to the churchyard. It was the old west door of the previous church demolished in 1840 to make way for the current building.

⛪ **St Mary's Church,** built 1840–6, replaced the old Norman church and was the donation of Dr Goddard, a headmaster of Winchester College who had retired to Andover. It is a typical clean, lofty Victorian church built of flint dressed with sandstone. The latter has started to wear alarmingly due to mistakes in the construction and neglect by a previous incumbent. The interior is being repaired. Two early 17th-century memorials, a husband and wife effigy and a brass tablet, are on the right of the entrance. The Victorian stained glass windows are of a high standard.
Tourist Information Centre: *Town Mill Car Park, Bridge St. Tel: (0264) 324320.*

APPLESHAW

Map p.153, F2
4 miles from Andover off the A342

Appleshaw ('apple wood'), on the Wiltshire border, is on the edge of serious horse country. It is built largely on the west side of 'The Street', a road by a stream lined with a long row of walnut trees. The comfortable mixture of houses stretches almost 400 yards from the 18th-century pub to the church, with more recent houses and buildings filling in the gaps between the 16th- and 17th-century thatched cottages and farmhouses. These include an 18th-century vicarage with a portico, a clock with Roman numerals over the road next to the stables, and a pastoral centre. There is a Methodist chapel dating from 1869 opposite the pub. The east of 'The Street' is largely pasture with two large houses and the church. The latter is a white cruciform building of chapel size. Opposite is the Iron Pear Tree, a former pub, with thatch pheasants and a fox on the thatched roof.

ASHLEY

Map p.149, F1 *
6 miles W of Winchester off the A272

This little hamlet consists of a number of handsome houses and cottages, some in flint and brick, some in the Hampshire livery of thatch and plaster, which follow a narrow winding lane as it descends towards the valley of the Test. With a population of only about 60 people it has no inn, shop, or school but nevertheless still has the feeling of a genuine community.

⛪ **Church of St Mary.**** The upkeep of this little gem being beyond the financial ability of the parish, it is now maintained by the Redundant Churches Fund. That is, it remains a consecrated building (usually a service is held at least once a year in such churches) but its costs are met from a centralized fund, partly State-supported.

Built in the early years of the 12th century, St Mary's was simply a chapel of the castle of William Brimvere. The castle has now vanished completely except for its earthworks. The chapel is described as 'Norman' but has many Saxon features, understandably so since it was built only a generation after the Norman Conquest by Saxon workmen in a remote region. In the Saxon manner the chancel is almost entirely separated from the nave by a massive screen. The window on the south side of the chancel has a contemporary painting of a woman, probably a representation of the Virgin Mary. By the door is an immense alms box, probably from the 17th century, cut from a massive oak post. At the west end of the church is a most interesting collection of items relating to local history including a village model.

In early spring it is possible to explore the enigmatic mounds of the castle remains, but by late summer a heavy crop of stinging nettles and other undergrowth bar the path to all but the most dedicated.

ASHMANSWORTH

Map p.154, C2 *

17 miles N of Winchester off the A343

From all directions the approach to Ashmansworth is up steep lanes. The village, which is principally one main street lined by flint, brick, timber and thatch cottages and farmhouses, sits high up on the chalk. Most of the village houses are small and pretty, with an occasional larger house like Flint House by the triangular green, with its Georgian porch.

St James' Church** is a modest building at the end of a short lane off the road at the village's southern end. Outside it is a mixture of flint, brick and render, with a white boarded bellcote. The tombstone beside the little late 17th-century porch commemorates the composer Gerald Finzi, who died in 1956, and his widow Joy, who died in 1991. Finzi was best known for his settings of English poems, and his place in English music is honoured here by the porch's engraved glass window by Lawrence Whistler and the rollcall of English composers carved by Reynolds Stone. The church's simple interior escaped the hand of Victorian restorers; it has a pair of galleries at the west end, and unusually carved bosses on the roof beams. Various medieval wall paintings have been uncovered, particularly in the chancel which is reached through a narrow arch flanked by large squints.

AVINGTON

Map p.150, E1

4 miles E of Winchester off the B3047

Avington is an outwardly untouched example of an estate village. It sprawls along the walls of Avington House on the south side of the Itchen Valley, giving a façade of unspoilt Georgian cottages with new additions sprinkled almost unseen among the trees. The houses, single and two-storey, are simple red brick with slate roofs. In the centre of the village a terrace of these overlook the wall and the old well, now filled with a flowerbed.

St Mary's Church is said to be, and most likely is, the purest example of a Georgian church. It is almost untouched. It was rebuilt in the 18th century by the Marchioness of Carnarvon. The interior is dramatic, with large pew boxes. Overlooking this imposing array of wood is one of the few examples of a domed pulpit. It is also noted for containing a 'Vinegar Bible', a famous 18th-century edition so called because of the misprint which substitutes 'vinegar' for 'vineyard'.

BARTON ON SEA

Map p.135, D2

7 miles W of Lymington on the A337

Following the boundary changes of 1974, Barton now lies in the south-westernmost corner of Hampshire, above the cliffs and beach which are the reason for its existence. It is a quiet small seaside town, with streets filled with bungalows and just a few touches of grandeur in its clifftop hotels. Chewton Bunny, the deep tight valley running up from the sea at the west, was a well-known smuggling route 200 years ago; Chewton Glen Hotel, set in the woods alongside it, is now one of the grandest country house hotels.
It was once the home of Captain Frederick Marryatt, author of the classic Cavalier romance, *The Children of the New Forest* (1847).

BARTON STACEY

Map p.149, C2
7 miles E of Andover off the A303 or A30

This working village is sheltered from the nearby rifle ranges in a small valley above the Dever river shortly before it joins the Test to the west. It has a mixture of house styles dating from the 18th century, with modern red bricks hidden on the outskirts. The Swan Inn, just south of the crossroads, is a square solid 18th-century building. The village's glory, however, is its church.

All Saints' Church stands in a yard which drops rapidly away towards the river. The tower dates from the 16th century and has a row of grinning heads around the top. Inside the chapels and aisles date from the 13th century and there are some 13th- to 14th-century tiles by the altar. The font dates from the 12th century. The panels with Faith, Hope and Charity on the altar are late 17th-century. Keys may be obtained from the Yellow Lodge.

BASINGSTOKE

Map p.155, E4 * *
16 miles NE of Winchester off the M3

Basingstoke is a large, modern town which has grown rapidly since the early 1960s, virtually obliterating its previous history. The population has increased from around 20,000 in 1960 to 100,000 now, many of them moving to the town from London under the overspill policy worked out with Hampshire County Council. The old Hampshire accent is now strangely mixed with a Cockney twang. The growth of Basingstoke is not appreciated by everyone, particularly those older residents who can remember when it was a typical market town where cattle were auctioned in the square once a week. But there is no turning the clock back, and although Basingstoke has become the butt of jokes as being one of the less desirable places on earth, there is no denying that it is the product of booming prosperity and technology.

The tall office blocks can be seen from many miles away, and towering over all is the Automobile Association's building which was among the first to be built when the town was embarking on its new role. The headquarters of papermakers Wiggins Teape are known as the Hanging Gardens of Basingstoke because of the profusion of plants and trees which adorn its terraces and balconies.

With the new offices has come an equally new pedestrianized shopping centre, accommodating all of the well-known high street stores. A new road system has had to be developed, too, which has led to Basingstoke being cruelly dubbed Doughnut City because of the plethora of roundabouts. But it is the road and rail links which make Basingstoke such a convenient centre and which have convinced growing numbers of industrial and commercial concerns that it is the place for them.

Basingstoke has a long history and traces of a Stone Age settlement have been discovered. It is thought the town may have taken its name from a tribe of people called the Basingae but another theory is that it derived from Basing Stakes, a crossing marked by stakes over the River Loddon. The town was recorded in the Domesday Book which mentions the manor of Basingstoke being granted to Queen Edgira in 945. Although most of Basingstoke's history has been buried under concrete, steel and glass, there are still some gems.

The **Chapel of the Holy Ghost.*** The ruins of this chapel date from the 13th century. Adjoining land was used for burials and it was consecrated after King John signed the Magna Carta.

St Michael's Church* is often described as the town's most interesting old building. The church was founded by the monks of Mont St Michel, off the Normandy coast, and traces of Norman architecture can still be seen. The nave of the present building was built around 1500 by Bishop Fox and has a turbulent history. During the Civil War it narrowly avoided being wrecked when explosives being stored by Cromwell's troops blew up. Shortly before World War II part of the roof was destroyed by fire and in 1940

most of the stained glass windows were blown out when German bombs fell nearby.

Church Cottage, next door, is an Elizabethan building which underwent extensive restoration during the 1970s. It was originally part vicarage and part tithe barn and during the restoration seeds of grain were found behind some of the old timbers. A particularly impressive feature is the large open fireplace.

The former **Town Hall,** built in 1832, once had an impressive clock tower presented by Lieutenant Colonel John May in 1887 to commemorate Queen Victoria's golden jubilee. Seventy years later, however, it was demolished as unsafe. The building now houses the **Willis Museum**, named after its founder, George Willis, who was Basingstoke's first freeman. The museum traces the town's development from prehistoric times and also houses examples of the traditional arts and crafts of the region.

Sir James Deane's Almshouses in London St were built in 1608 and are still in use today, though the green in front, which used to be pig market in Basingstoke's agricultural era, now plays a purely picturesque role.

The **Basingstoke Canal** was opened in 1794 as an important link with London. It served its purpose until the coming of the railways in 1840 and then gradually declined. The last canal barge reached Basingstoke in 1913 when, as a token gesture, a load of sand was delivered. Much of the canal has been restored but sadly there is no chance of it being revived here because most of it has been obliterated by modern development.

The **Basingstoke and Alton Light Railway** was built at the turn of the century. Because of the number of unmanned road crossings and tight curves, speed was strictly limited to 25 mph maximum. The line, leading to Alton, ten miles away, was never heavily used and in 1916 the track was torn up for use in the war in France. The Southern Railway was forced, very reluctantly, to relay the line after the war but in the early 1930s it was closed for good. There is still some evidence of the junction with the main line, just West of Basingstoke station, and in the middle of a new road roundabout, built on part of the old trackbed, a token section of track has been laid. The **Haymarket Theatre** is the home of the professional repertory Horsehoe Theatre Company, but the town's amateur dramatic groups also staged productions there. The theatre has recently been given a facelift and is a popular venue with North Hampshire theatre-goers.

The Thornycroft factory, producing a range of lorries, was once the major employer in the town. Now there is an organisation devoted to restoring Thornycroft vehicles and an annual rally is being established. Forklift trucks made in the town by Lansing are exported around the world, and another important company is Eli Lilley which makes a range of medicines.

Queen Mary's College, a sixth form establishment, perpetuates the name of the town's former grammar school. There is also a large technical college which teaches an extensive range of academic and practical skills.

There are plenty of recreational facilities including a new multi-screen cinema complex, an ice rink, a well-equipped sports centre with a swimming pool, and a range of outdoor sporting facilities. Hampshire County Cricket Club have several County Championship fixtures in the town and Basingstoke Town football club play in the Diadora Premier League.

The **Viables Craft Centre,** using converted farm buildings, gives an insight into former rural industries. It includes a gift shop, a restaurant and tea rooms, and a miniature railway runs on occasional weekends during the summer. The centre is open all year except early January.

An attractive park with a boating and paddling pool has been laid out at Eastrop, alongside the River Loddon, and there is a walk to the nearby historic village of Old

The Beaulieu estuary, with Beaulieu Palace and village at the centre.

Basing. The pool at Black Dam, despite its close proximity to the centre of town, is a haven for wildlife.
Willis Museum: *All year, Tues–Fri 10am–5pm, Sat 10am–4pm. Tel: (0256) 465902.*
Viables Craft Centre: *All year exc. early Jan, Tues–Fri 1–4pm, Sat–Sun 2–5pm. Free car park. Tel: (0256) 473634 (24 hours).*

BEAULIEU

Map p.136, C4 * *
8 miles SW of Southampton on the B3054

Beaulieu means 'beautiful place', and it remains so even at its busiest. Its beauty comes from its position at the navigable head of the Beaulieu River, with the woods coming down to the water's edge, the lake formed by the causeway dam, and the remains of the great Cistercian abbey founded by King John in 1204. The abbey, along with Palace House and the National Motor Museum, is now a major tourist attraction (see p.12).

The **Church of the Blessed Virgin and Child**** is usually only accessible from the Abbey ruins. It was originally the Abbey's refectory, becoming the parish church after the Dissolution in 1538. So there is no division between nave and chancel, except for the raising of the chancel end in the 19th century. The finest surviving monastic features are the stone pulpit, reached by a vaulted staircase within the wall, from which books were read aloud during meals, and the 14th-century roof with decorative bosses. There are monuments to the Montagu family, and a new parish hall built in traditional timberwork. The church is frequently used for concerts.

The church is separate from most of the village, which lies in line with the former abbey gate, now Palace House. The Montagu Arms, with its late Victorian red brick and tile, and the former water mill are the most noticeable features, but the small village is also filled with cottages and shops, mostly 18th- and 19th-century. As the busy road climbs to the east, it passes the springs and wells which gave Beaulieu its particular reason for existence.

BENTLEY

Map p.151, B4 *
5 miles NE of Alton on the A31

Bentley found national fame in recent years because the radio programme, *The Village*, was based there and many local personalities found themselves enjoying unexpected recognition. An even better-known resident was Lord Baden-Powell, the founder of the Boy Scout movement. He lived at Pax Hill from 1918 until 1938, when he retired to Kenya. He was mainly responsible for the design and construction of the Memorial Hall, which he opened in 1920, and for the village sign which is in the shape of a large wooden book.

St Mary's Church has an odd entry in its parish records of a meeting in 1774 when the two churchwardens and nine others ruled 'that no relief be given to any of the poor people of this parish who drink tea or frequent the public house'.

Bentley was the junction for the branch railway line to Bordon, closed to passengers in the 1950s, and Station Rd was originally known as Pickling Lane because it was there that the railway sleepers were treated, or 'pickled'.

BINSTED

Map p.151, C4
4 miles NE of Alton off the A31

Field Marshal Viscount Montgomery of Alamein (1887–1976) is buried in the churchyard at Holy Cross Church. Lord Montgomery, the World War II commander, chose to spend his final years at nearby Isington Mill, a tranquil spot on the River Wey, but he kept several mementoes of his wartime years, including his military caravan command centre.

Telegraph House is an unusual, square-shaped building. It was one of a chain of semaphore signalling stations built by the Admiralty during the Napoleonic wars linking London with Portsmouth and Plymouth. On clear days the system worked well and messages could be relayed within minutes, but poor weather often rendered it useless. The building was saved from demolition in the 1970s. It has since been sympathetically restored and is now used as a private residence.

Binsted rock is the name of the local stone, which be seen in several buildings, including a Victorian extension to Wyck Place, built on the site of a Roman villa.

BISHOP'S WALTHAM

Map p.144, C4 * *
6 miles E of Eastleigh on the B2177

Bishop's Waltham has been a victim of changes in social, economic and industrial trends over the centuries, but now it is enjoying a revival as one of Hampshire's most attractive small towns. The building of new homes on the outskirts and the sensitive preservation of the town centre have resulted in a thriving, progressive community which still respects its ancient heritage. The ruins of Bishop's Waltham Palace (see p.33), built around 1136 by Bishop Henry de Blois, are a constant reminder of its influential past.

As a bustling agricultural and market town in the last century, Bishop's Waltham had its own bank, run for several generations by the Gunner family, which issued its own banknotes.

In the middle of the last century there was a thriving brickworks here. Its bricks were used in the construction of London's Blackfriars Bridge and in the building of the Suez Canal.

Close to the palace ruins are the remains of a much later construction, the old railway station. A short branch line from Botley reached Bishop's Waltham in 1863 but it was never widely used and it was closed to passengers in 1933. Goods traffic lingered for another 30 years. The station is now used for industrial purposes and the track bed makes an attractive rural walk.

BOLDRE

Map p.136, E2 *
2 miles N of Lymington off the A337

The 'beautiful views, on the north to the forest, and on the south towards the white cliffs of the Isle of Wight, which are set off by intermediate woods', are still those which William Gilpin enjoyed in the late 18th century. Gilpin was a great promoter of the picturesque tour, and as vicar of Boldre from 1777 to 1804 he loved the picturesque qualities of the New Forest, about which he wrote in *Remarks on Forest Scenery* (1791).

Near Vicars Hill, in one of the scattered parts of Boldre, is Spinners Garden (see p.22)

St John the Baptist's Church** stands alone on a high point so as to be visible from the forest trackways. Gilpin is buried here, and there is a memorial to him inside this rough stone church, to which cut-down box pews and clear glass still give a Georgian air. Boldre church is also notable for its associations with the ill-fated HMS *Hood*, which sank in 1941 with the loss of 1416 lives.

BOSSINGTON

Map p.148, F3
3 miles SW of Stockbridge off the A3057

The landowners of the Test Valley seem unusually intent on keeping their privacy. At this beautiful junction where the little Wallop Brook meets the Test River the area is spattered with 'Private. Keep out' notices. However the view of this meeting of rivers can be enjoyed from the road which the public is permitted to use. Just over the bridge leading to Horsebridge the road runs beneath a majestic avenue of horse chestnuts, singularly beautiful in May with their candelabra of blossoms, refreshing in high summer for the deep shade they cast, and dramatic in autumn with their golden leaves. At the watermeet is Houghton Mill, a handsome three storeyed red-brick building that has been well restored and converted to residential use.

BOTLEY

Map p.144, E2 * *
7 miles E of Southampton on the A334

William Cobbett, of *Rural Rides* fame, was Botley's most famous resident. He wrote in the 19th century: 'Botley is the most delightful village in the world. It has everything in a village that I love and none of the things that I hate.' If Cobbett were to return today he would still find many of the things that he loved, but it is doubtful whether he would approve of the traffic which chokes the village centre, ruining the local authority's efforts to introduce a conservation scheme. Nonetheless, Botley is architecturally well worth a visit.

Botley Mill on the River Hamble is still a prominent feature of the village, having survived a major fire a few years ago. Today it still produces flour and animal feed, though many of its associated buildings have been rented out to other retail businesses.

The **Market Hall** dominates the Square. It was built in 1848, partly from public subscription, and partly through Botley Farmers Club, which was founded by Cobbett and his friend James Warner. Of the 17 hostelries that existed in the last century, only three remain.

BRAMDEAN

Map p.150, F3
8 miles E of Winchester on the A272

Travellers on the A272 may spot an odd pile of flint stones by the roadside. It marks the spot where Colonel George Greenwood, who wrote *Hints on Horsemanship* in 1839, buried his favourite hunter. Tales about the horse having golden shoes have in the past led to more than one attempt to unearth its remains.

Another resident was Field Marshall Sir William Gomm who, it is said, disguised himself as a female match-seller and walked through the French lines to warn the Duke of Wellington of the French attack at the Battle of Waterloo. There is a memorial to him in the church of St Simon and St Jude. Sir William's grandfather was a rector at Bramdean.

The gardens at Bramdean House (see p.18) are open to the public.

The **Church in the Woods*,** hidden away in a woodland glade on nearby Bramdean Common, is a delightful little church. It was built out of corrugated iron in 1883 for the gypsies who in those days camped in considerable numbers on the common land. Services are still held there on occasional summer Sundays.

BRAMLEY

Map p.156, C1
5 miles NE of Basingstoke off the A33

In recent years Bramley has expanded rapidly and is in danger of becoming a dormitory for Basingstoke and Reading. For the moment, though, it retains a certain amount of its village atmosphere. The pond has been rescued from dereliction and is now an attractive feature.

During World War I a large area of land was commandeered for use as a prisoner-of-war camp and it was subsequently taken over by the Central Ammunition Depot. That provided Bramley with a certain amount of prosperity over the years, but the base has now closed and there is speculation about what will happen to the site. One suggestion is that it could become a transport museum or a steam railway centre.

St James' Church, with its brick tower and flint chancel, is reputed to have one of the best furnished interiors in Hampshire. Wall paintings include the murder of Thomas à Becket at Canterbury and another of St Christopher. Near by is the grave of Lise Meitner, a nuclear scientist who fled from Germany at the beginning of World War II.

BRAMSHOTT

Map p.152, E3 * *
1 mile NE of Liphook off the A3

It is difficult to imagine that this quiet corner of Hampshire, close to the borders of Surrey and Sussex, was once a centre of the iron industry. The sound of hammers on anvils and the smell of smelted iron ore filled the air. The iron industry was at its peak in the 16th and early 17th centuries. Henry Hooke, lord of the manor of Bramshott, established a large foundry and built a series of dams across the Downwater stream to form three large ponds and a source of power. Iron ore came from Weavers Down and there was a good supply of timber for the furnaces in the neighbouring forests.

Waggoners Wells, as the ponds are known today , are a National Trust beauty spot (see p.27) and well worth a visit. Industrial archaeologists will be able to identify evidence of the past, though most will simply appreciate the beauty and solitude and the variety of wildlife which has long since returned.

St Mary's Church. The churchyard here has a special burial grounds for Canadian soldiers based on Bramshott Common, known to them as Mudsplosh Camp, who died during a flu epidemic in 1917.

In 1812 a former rector of the parish, the Reverend John Monkhouse, was deeply concerned about the morals of the local people and he wrote: 'The want of honesty and the want of chastity are prevailing defects here'. In his will he left £1850 for the education of children except those whose parents were given to 'whoring, thieving, cheating, tricking, backbiting, over-reaching and extorting'.

BREAMORE

Map p.141, C3 * *
4 miles N of Fordingbridge on the A338

Knots of cottages and farmhouses, many of considerable age with their timber framing and catslide thatched roofs, are dotted around the commons and lanes of Breamore. As the area called Flood Street suggests, many houses and farms lie on the Avon Valley floor, and there are vestiges of the water-meadows which were once flooded every year to produce better grass. At the Shallows, on the other side of the A338, the river is channelled into different courses for the now-disused watermill.

Breamore House (see p.00) is the largest building in the village, and it is visible on the hillside from miles around.

St Mary's Church*** stands just below it, a premier Anglo-Saxon survival. The basic fabric of the church dates to around the year 1000, as does its curious shape, descending in stages from the stubby crossing tower. Its most evocative features are the former carved stone rood, over the south door, and the south transept. The cross and figures of the rood, although mutilated after the Reformation, are still beautifully expressive sculptures, with later medieval wall painting. The exterior of the south transept is the most complete of the pre-Conquest masonry, while inside the arch from the crossing there is an Anglo-Saxon inscription, translated as 'Here the covenant is explained to you'. There are also Norman carvings and doors, internal arches from the 14th century, and many memorials to the Hulse family.

BROCKENHURST

Map p.136, C1 * *
10 miles SW of Southampton on the B3055

As one of the principal settlements in the New Forest, Brockenhurst offers accommodation, shops and restaurants for visitors. Only with the coming of the railway in 1849 did expansion occur, so the village centre is dominated by buildings of the turn of the century, and few older properties survive. Away from the centre, cottages tend to cluster around forest clearings.

St Nicholas' Church** is, like many New Forest churches, set alone on a rise, south of the village and across the railway line. An enormous graveyard occupies the hill below the church, with a huge memorial to New Zealand soldiers from World War I who died in a nearby hospital. Set in line with it is a gravestone depicting 'Brusher' Mills, last of the Forest snake-catchers, outside his turf hut. A great yew tree almost smothers the Georgian brick tower of the 13th-century church, while inside the church there is a Georgian west gallery. The church is only open on summer afternoons.

St Saviour's Church* was built in 1903 close to the village, by the watersplash or ford. The stone for this Edwardian Gothic building was brought from Dorset – but the carving was never finished, so the decorative flourishes are largely missing.

There are many areas of open grazing, like that by the hotel at Balmer Lawn. To the north-west of the village, the ornamental Rhinefield carriage drive of coniferous trees (including redwoods) was planted in the mid-19th century, and the trees are now of majestic maturity. Rhinefield House Hotel (formerly Rhinefield Lodge) sits at the centre of the drive. It was built in the 1880s in a flamboyant 'Jacobethan' style in stone and flint, with grand gardens and capacious wine cellars. The gardens are being returned to their late Victorian splendour.

BROUGHTON

Map p.148, E2 * *

9 miles SW of Andover off the B3084

Until the modern upgrading of the road now known as the B3084, Broughton was served only by a network of minor country lanes. One of the remarkable things about the village as a result is that its population has remained static at around 1000 for the past 100 years. In architectural terms Broughton is a perfect, unchanged survival from the past.

Physically, it more closely resembles a small town than a village, with a relatively dense development of houses and cottages on both sides of the Wallop Brook. The heart of the village, with its mixture of half-timbered cottages and Georgian brick houses, is at a road junction; fortunately the traffic is entirely local.

Church of St Mary.** Unlike most Hampshire churches this is in the very centre of the village. Part of the churchyard immediately flanks the High St, providing a refreshing green note. In the main part of the large churchyard behind, there is an unusual survival, a massive brick dovecot, believed to date back to the 14th century when doves were a major source of food. It was extensively rebuilt in the 17th century and has been recently restored. It is kept locked but a notice on the door gives directions for obtaining the key.

BUCKLERS HARD

Map p.136, D4 * * *

9 miles S of Southampton off the B3054

Unless you live here, you must pay to see Bucklers Hard, since this curious village is entirely a maritime museum. Originally intended as a new port town by the 2nd Duke of Montagu in the 1720s, the village consists of two rows of terraced Georgian brick cottages which face each other across a wide grassed area leading down to the Beaulieu River. The houses mainly date from the 1740s and 50s.

Shipbuilding began in earnest in the 1740s under Henry Adams, and his family built many great ships here, including Nelson's HMS *Agamemnon*, before the firm was dissolved in 1811. In the 19th century Bucklers Hard slumbered, to be re-awakened by modern interest. The maritime museum at the entrance to the village includes reconstructions of cottage and inn interiors, peopled by dummy figures, as well as models of ships built here. Some of the village houses, one converted into a chapel, are also open to public view.

St Leonard's Grange* lies some two miles to the south on the road to Lymington; this was the great barn which belonged to Beaulieu Abbey. Its huge end walls are still

Butser Hill.

standing, alongside the ruins of a little chapel and a 17th-century farmhouse. Narrow lanes lead further south still to the isolated coastal farms and cottages of Sowley, where the pond is the sole survivor of the 19th-century iron industry.

Maritime Museum: *March–Spring BH, daily 10am–6pm; Spring BH–Sept, 10am–9pm; Sept–Oct, 10am–6pm; Nov–Feb 10am–4.30pm. Admission charge. Tel: (0590) 616203.*

BULLINGTON

Map p.149, C3
8 miles E of Andover off the A34

Upper and Lower Bullington are a mile-long straggle of isolated houses and working farms overlooking the River Dever and overshadowed by the A303 just to the north. The area's charm lies in its rambling nature, its setting and its church. This is just opposite Bullington Manor, a rare simple 18th-century two storey farmhouse, the barn of which is within feet of the north wall of the church.

St Michael and All Angels Church dates from Saxon times but almost all of the current church is more recent. It is reached through a small avenue of trees along a flint and tile path. The main construction, with the exception of the recent, squat tower, is flint. It has simple, tracery windows and a size and style which still indicate its Saxon origins. Inside, the chancel is 13th-century and the font a century younger.

BURGHCLERE

Map p.154, B3 *
11 miles NW of Basingstoke on the A34

Proximity to the M4, and the wooded landscape, have made Burghclere a desirable place to live, which is reflected in the number of new houses. Older cottages are dotted around the main village and the Common to its north.

The **Church of the Ascension** is a Victorian building. Originally erected in 1838 when the centre of population had moved away from Old Burghclere two miles to the south, it was extended in 1875 under the supervision of Norman Shaw. Burghclere's main interest lies within another chapel, which is one of the pinnacles of British 20th century art.

The **Sandham Memorial Chapel★★★**, now in the care of the National Trust, stands by the railway at the village's southern end. Outside, it is a brick box flanked by Georgian-style cottages and set amid lawns and trees. Inside, the chapel's walls are lined with a cycle of paintings by Stanley Spencer, executed between 1927 and 1932, showing army life in the Macedonian campaign and in Army hospitals during World War I. The sequence culminates in a great Resurrection painting on the east wall, with soldiers rising from their graves and carrying their crosses towards the risen Christ. The work, moving and comic by turn, was commissioned as a memorial to a young lieutenant, H. W. Sandham, who died following the campaign. Only in the painting called *Map-reading*, however, is an officer depicted; otherwise the pictures show ordinary soldiers going about their business or suffering from the effects of war. There is no artificial light in the chapel, so it is often dark.

Sandham Memorial Chapel: *Winter, Sat–Sun 11am–4pm; summer, Weds–Sun and BHs 11am–5pm. Weds after BHs closed. Adm. charge. Tel: (063527) 292.*

BURITON

Map p.146, C2 *
3 miles S of Petersfield off the A3

Buriton, one of Hampshire's oldest villages, nestles under the western edge of the South Downs. Edward Gibbon, the historian best known for his work, *The Decline and Fall of the Roman Empire*, lived at the manor house and is buried in the churchyard.

St Mary's Church★, standing high above the village, was built between 1150 and 1200 and also served neighbouring Petersfield and Sheet. But times have changed and the vicar of Petersfield now takes Buriton under his wing.

Also buried in the churchyard is John Goodyer (1592–1654), who was one of the first great botanists; he wrote about the value of new species such as potatoes and tobacco which were then being brought back to Britain by the great seafarers.

Devotees of Charles Dickens believe he was referring to Buriton in *Nicholas Nickleby* when he wrote about Nicholas and Smike, on their journey from London, 'turning off the path to the door of a roadside inn, yet twelve miles short of Portsmouth'.

BURLEY

Map p.135, A1 * *
1 mile SE of Ringwood off the A31

Horse-drawn wagonettes provide rides for visitors in and around Burley, which has so many of the varied features of the New Forest. Houses, mainly of the past hundred years but with a fewer older properties interspersed, cluster in the woods. The road running across the undulating heath towards Ringwood is still called Smuggler's Road, and the earthworks on the hill at its eastern end, nearest the village, are an ancient British fortification.

St John the Baptist Church* is a quiet little Victorian brick building hidden among the trees. Crossed hockey sticks in its newest stained glass window commemorate a former resident who brought women's hockey to the USA.

BURSLEDON

Map p.144, F1 *
5 miles SE of Southampton on the A27

Bursledon, built on the banks of the River Hamble, has long been associated with boats and boatbuilding. The forest of masts which dominates the scene today shows that the industry still thrives here, adapting to changing construction methods over the years.

St Leonard's Church contains several memorials to former shipbuilders, including Philemon Ewer, who died in 1750. His epitaph tells how he built seven large ships of war for his majesty's service during the wars with France and Spain. Daniel Defoe, best known as the author of *Robinson Crusoe*, is said to have lodged at Bursledon and worked in one of the shipyards. Several references in his books are thought to relate to the village.

Bursledon windmill, built during the last century and neglected for years, has recently been restored to full working order.

CHAWTON

Map p.151, D2 * * *
1 mile S of Alton off the A31

Chawton, Jane Austen's village, used to be situated on the junction of the busy A31 and A32 roads, but the Alton bypass has changed all that. The village is now tucked quietly away and the comparative freedom from traffic has opened a new and welcome chapter in the village's history.

Jane Austen, who was born at Steventon, near Basingstoke, moved to Chawton in 1809 and it was here that she wrote *Mansfield Park*, *Emma* and *Persuasion*, before moving to her last home at Winchester in 1816, shortly before her death. Jane is buried in Winchester Cathedral but her sister, Cassandra, and her mother are both buried in the churchyard at Chawton. (For Jane Austen's House, see p.14).

Jane Austen's nephew, Edward Knight, who was lord of the manor, established the first school in the village in 1840. It is still flourishing, though of course in a much different form. The Knight family have been in the village for more than four hundred years.

The **Church of St Nicholas** was rebuilt and re-opened in 1872 by the Bishop of Winchester following a disastrous fire. Buried in this imposing church is Sir Edward Bradford who, according to his epitaph, served in India during and after the mutiny, 'suppressing crime, introducing good government and popularising railways'. He also lost an arm when attacked by a wounded tiger. In 1889, at the age of 53, he became Police Commissioner in London, making the force 'a model for the world'.

Clinkers was the house of the village blacksmith and wheelwright, where it is said the mummified remains of a cat and a rat were kept in the roof to protect the occupants from evil spirits. **Clinkers Forge** has found a new role as a gift shop. Another interesting house is **Baigens**, reputed to be one of the oldest in the county, where Elizabethan murals were found behind the plastered walls.

The pub, opposite Jane Austen's house, is called the Grey Friar which is probably a reference to the old Pilgrims' Way which linked Winchester with Canterbury and passed close by.

Chawton Park Woods*, just a drive from the village, are run by the Forestry Commission. There are some splendid, well-marked routes for walkers through conifer plantations established soon after the end of the last war to replenish timber stocks. The trees provide a habitat for a variety of wildlife.

CHERITON

Map p.150, F2
7 miles E of Winchester on the A272

Cheriton is best remembered for a particularly violent and decisive battle during the Civil War in 1644 when it was reported that lanes were running with blood. It has been estimated that the Parliamentarians lost 900 men and the Royalists 1400. Several mounds to the east of the village are said to mark the mass graves of dead soldiers. Occasionally, farmers still plough up relics of the battle.

Today the village presents a much more peaceful scene. The village green is a favourite spot with children, who come to feed the ducks on the infant River Itchen which rises a short distance away. Little wonder it has won Hampshire's Best Kept Village contest for a record three times.

The Flowerpots is the only pub, but in the past Cheriton was a centre for illicit trade in smuggled spirits – Brandy Mount is a reminder of the village's notorious past. It is also reputed to be the last place in England where truffle hunting was carried out commercially.

CHILBOLTON

Map p.149, C1
4 miles SE of Andover off the B3420

Chilbolton meanders along the south bank of the Test in a mixture of houses and cottages of all ages and sizes, many dispersed among the trees. Only half of the houses are thatched, the rest being covered in slate. At the north end of the village by the crossroads and opposite the church is one of the most extensive thatched buildings in the country. Now making up at least five separate houses, it forms a loose 'T' and has been built and joined together in a variety of styles dating from, possibly, the 16th century. Chilbolton Radio Telescope, which resembles an upturned cornet, may be seen from the top of the signed road.

The **Church of St Mary-the-Less** is built of flint rubble and dressed stone with its tower and steeple to one side. This church has a 13th-century nave and oak-pegged tile roof. It still has its original tie beams and an Elizabethan pulpit with moulded and carved panels.

CHILCOMB

Map p.149, F4
2 miles E of Winchester off the A272

Chilcomb was once a vast manor which covered about 15 square miles around Winchester. The Domesday Book records that it included nine churches, but these have long since been absorbed into neighbouring parishes. Today Chilcomb, within a stone's throw of Winchester city centre, lives with the constant background noise of traffic on the M3 motorway.

The **Church of St Andrew** is Chilcomb's most notable feature. It dates from early Norman times. Visitors are warned, incongruously, not to stray into the nearby Army firing range when the red flags are flying. The church is simple and little altered since the days of William the Conqueror and is a good example of Norman architecture.

It was in the fields around Chilcomb that the now famous corn circles were first noticed. No logical explanation has been found for these strange circular patterns in fields of standing corn. A popular theory is that they are caused by visitors from space.

CHILTON CANDOVER

Map p.150, C3
13 miles NE of Winchester off the B3046

Even small places can have their vanished glories. At right angles to the B3046 as it passes through this hamlet there is still a splendid avenue of yew trees, 40ft wide and over half a mile long, which once formed an imposing approach to a house belonging to the Worsley family, torn down two centuries ago. The avenue now constitutes a clearly marked 'private road'. Just to the north, fronting the road, stands an 18th-century rectory with a fine doorway and two pairs of Venetian windows.

The **Buried Church.** The church of St. Nicholas, which stood on a slope opposite the rectory, was demolished in 1878. But in 1927, prompted by a scrap of childhood memory from a village elder, William Spiers, the rector decided to excavate the site, which yielded up a rare Norman crypt over thirty feet long where the aged William once played as a boy. It is now sign-posted as 'the buried church'. Set within the flint wall of the old churchyard it contains a 12th-century font and several stone coffins. The overall effect of the interior is light and eerie rather than light and airy.

CLIDDESDEN

Map p.155, F4
1 mile S of Basingstoke on the B3046

The building of the M3 motorway has effectively prevented Cliddesden being swallowed up by rapidly expanding Basingstoke. The village is just to the south of the motorway which is a formidable barrier to any future growth plans which Basingstoke may have.

Cliddesden now pursues a more leisurely way of life, centred around St Leonard's church which was extensively restored in 1950, and the pub. The village pond has been given a facelift and is a favourite spot with children.

Basingstoke and Alton Light Railway. Industrial archaeologists can still spot evidence of this railway, which ran through the village until its closure in the 1930s. The bridge which crossed the main street has long since been demolished but there are still a few signs of the track bed. The old station was used for scenes in a 1930s comedy film called *Oh! Mr Porter*, starring Will Hay. For the purposes of the film, Cliddesden became Buggleskelly, a fictional village somewhere in Ireland.

COLEMORE

Map p.151, F2 *
5 miles S of Alton off the A32

Although Colemore is little more than a name on the map, there are three very good reasons why it is worth making a short detour off the A32 Alton to Fareham Road. The first is that this really is an unspoiled corner of the Hampshire countryside, but a word of warning – the lanes are narrow and winding and apart from the need to take care, it is not difficult to get lost.

The **Church of St Peter,** the little Norman church where agricultural workers once gave thanks for the harvest, is the second good reason to visit Colemore. It is now redundant but services are held on odd occasions. It is a beautifully tranquil spot and small animals, birds and plants thrive in the churchyard.

The third attraction, if you have enough perseverance to find it, is a splendid pub officially called the **White Horse** but since there are no signs, it is more often referred to as 'the pub with no name'. Because it is unspoiled and remote, it has become very popular in recent years, although the landlord has managed to maintain its original charm.

CORHAMPTON

Map p.145, C1
9 miles N of Fareham on the A32

Corhampton is one of the villages raided by the Danes when they invaded the Meon Valley. Some of the intruders settled on the other side of the river at Meonstoke and it is said that rivalry between the two villages existed for centuries.

One of the first golf courses in the country was built at Corhampton. It was established as a nine-hole course in 1885 and was extended to 18 holes in the early 1970s. It is now a flourishing concern and attracts golfers from a wide area. For others who enjoy outdoor pursuits, the Wayfarers' Walk (see p.39) from Emsworth to Inkpen Beacon passes near by.

Corhampton Church is a small Saxon building which has survived remarkably intact. Inside are a series of medieval frescoes which were for years covered by cement facing. Experts restored them in the 1960s and one that is particularly impressive depicts the miracle, attributed to St Swithun, of the restoration of a basket of eggs which an old woman had broken. In the churchyard is a stone Romano-British coffin dug up many years ago in a nearby field which now serves as an attractive flower planter.

CRAWLEY

Map p.149, D2
3½ miles NW of Winchester off the A272 or B3420

Crawley ('glade of the crows') is a picture-postcard village with a duck pond and a 19th-century pub. The village is regulated by a restrictive covenant established by the Victorian banking family Philippi, which has prevented any development. Now it is largely a commuter dormitory for nearby Winchester. It is a dormitory with a difference, though, with largely red-brick thatched cottages manicured to perfection. Some of the 19th-century estate buildings can be seen at the top of the hill, opposite the gates to the house.

Crawley Court, a 19th-century mansion, was built by the Philippis. In the 1920s, it was a famous sporting country house, but cannot be seen from the road.

CRONDALL

Map p.157, F1 * *
3 miles NW of Farnham off the A267

As attractive a village as any you will find in Hampshire – that is how Crondall has been described. Queen Victoria is said to have visited it after inspecting her troops at nearby Aldershot so that she could admire the views. The village is now a subtle blend of old and new. It is said that there are 83 listed buildings, but villagers are quick to point out that this is no museum-piece. Two council estates and a large amount of infilling have seen the number of homes double since World War II.

But there remains very much a rural atmosphere, which is not surprising since Crondall's heritage is firmly based in agriculture, though modern crops like oil-seed rape and linseed have for the most part replaced traditional hop growing.

The **Church of All Saints** dates from 1170 and was used to billet Parliamentary troops during the Civil War. It was the church which bought the first village fire engine in 1776, but such foresight was not enough to prevent a catastrophe nearly a hundred years later when the great tithe barn burnt down.

CROOKHAM VILLAGE

Map p.157, E1 *
1 mile SW of Fleet off the B3013

Crookham Village just manages to live up to its name despite the dangerous advances being made by the neighbouring conurbations of Fleet. For the most part, though, its residents rely on Fleet, Farnborough and Aldershot for work and shopping.

The establishment of the Army camp at Aldershot in Victorian times has had a major influence on Crookham Village, starting with the building contractors who persuaded agricultural workers with what were considered to be fabulous wages to leave their jobs on the land. Farmers also switched to new crops, and one that flourished for a while was tobacco. This was grown from 1912 until 1937 and sold under brand names including Golden Queen and Blue Pryor.

≋ The **Basingstoke Canal,** which meanders through the parish, is an interesting feature, crossing the River Hart on a high embankment. The site of the former **Crookham Wharf** has been converted into a car park for visiting canal enthusiasts, naturalists and walkers who come to enjoy the rural environment which the canal restoration has opened up.

DAMERHAM

Map p.141, D1 *

3 miles W of Fordingbridge on the B3078

Like its neighbour Martin, Damerham is an outlying chalkland village which was previously in Wiltshire. This pretty village is divided into various areas, with cottages clustering near the stream which runs down to the Avon, and the remains of ancient defensive earthworks on the chalk heights.

The **Terrace★** contains the parish's most unusual cottages (originally called The Barracks), forming three sides of a square with rustic thatched porches, built in 1863 after a disastrous village fire.

St George's Church★ is set a little apart, dominated by its broad tower. The structure is basically Norman, although there has been considerable work done over the centuries, while the church's proudest possession is a Norman sculpture in the porch, of a slayer on horseback, perhaps St George himself.

DEANE

Map p.155, E2

5 miles W of Basingstoke on the B3400

The Deane Gate Inn, at the crossroads on the B3400, was the place where Jane Austen and her family would catch the stagecoach, having walked up from Steventon. The rest of the village lies to the north of the main road, with farms and neat thatched cottages tucked away on one side of the lane, and the picturesque pairing of the big house and the parish church set among lawns on the other.

All Saints' Church★ was built in 1818, in a pretty late Georgian Gothic. The church and its west tower are cement rendered, with the window tracery and tower pinnacles in the artificial Coade stone that was so popular at the time. Apart from fragments of medieval stained glass reset in the porch, the windows are filled with brightly coloured plain glass: vibrant blues, yellows and reds. The church's interior decoration and furnishings are all original.

Ashe★, a mile to the west where the River Test rises in a series of ponds in the fields, is an even smaller village. It too has Jane Austen connections since she often visited the Rectory there; the handsome Georgian brick building remains, at the roadside.

Holy Trinity Church was rebuilt in the 1870s, in flint with decorative stone flourishes and a dainty bellcote. A charming interior feature is the carved robin near the screen, commemorating the bird which nested there while it was being built.

DOGMERSFIELD

Map p.156, D4 *

2 miles NE of Odiham off the A287

In Saxon times Dogmersfield meant 'a field by the lake where the waterlilies grow'.

The **Great House** is set in splendid parkland on the site of a 13th-century bishop's palace. Henry VI was a regular visitor and Henry VII accompanied Prince Arthur there to meet Catherine of Aragon from Spain. Her marriage to Arthur, the heir to the throne, took place soon afterwards but he died before long and his brother, Henry VIII, was crowned king. Catherine became the first of his six wives.

A new manor house was built in 1728 by the first Baronet St John and enlarged by his

son, Sir Henry, who, in the pursuit of privacy, demolished most of the village and turned the green into Tundry Pond. He also made sure that the builders of the Basingstoke Canal made an inconvenient and expensive detour around his land so his peace would not be disturbed.

His regimental way of life extended to the village which he rebuilt in such a fashion that critics called it The Barracks.

DROXFORD

Map p.145, C1 *

8 miles N of Fareham on the A32

Droxford was once an important centre in the Meon Valley, with its own police headquarters, magistrates' court and rural district council. In recent years, however, much of its influence has been eroded. The police station is now little more than a token presence, the court has moved to Fareham, and municipal decisions are taken at Winchester. Nevertheless, Droxford still supports a thriving, rural way of life and the fire station is a closely guarded asset.

The infamous Droxford Union was a workhouse which during the last century kept up to 200 inmates in extremely harsh conditions, with wives, husbands and children segregated. The building was demolished in 1971.

In the 17th century, a regular visitor was Izaak Walton, of *Compleat Angler* fame, who considered the Meon the best trout river in England. During the last war the village was shrouded in secrecy when Winston Churchill and General Eisenhower used a special train tucked away in a siding at Droxford station to plan the D-Day invasion of Europe.

DUMMER

Map p.155, E3 *

3 miles S of Basingstoke off the M3 and B3046

This largely thatched and half-timbered dormitory and retirement village for Andover stretches along both sides of its main street from the village shop to the notable church at the crossroads. The Queen Inn, a modernized 18th-century cottage, claims to be the home of Fergie's Fizz, invented for a royal wedding.

The Old Rectory, a magnificent 19th-century flint and stone building, stands opposite the church and is many times its size. Two 17th-century joined cottages overlook the crossroads. The single track road to the south gives magnificent views over the Candover Valley through gaps in the large hedgerows.

All Saints' Church** is listed in the Domesday Book, but the oldest visible part of it is the 12th-century doorway of the nave. Sir John Betjeman described it as having 'rustic, cottagey interest, with gallery and 15th-century rood canopy' and featured it on a television programme. This small church has a number of notable and rare features including one of the few virtually intact medieval rood canopies, a gallery, and one of the oldest pulpits in the country (1380). Other points of interest are the modern laid-up standard of the Lifeguards, several memorials dating as early as the 15th century, a benefice board, a rare palimpsest brass, 13th-century chancel and arch, and 16th-century bells. For its size, this church is over-blessed.

DURLEY

Map p.144, D2

5 miles SE of Eastleigh off the B3335

Durley is a blend of the old and the new, most apparent at the village hall where recent brick extensions to original corrugated iron make a rather odd partnership. At the school, too, the original Victorian building has been augmented by modern classrooms Durley Mill is a reminder of activities gone by. Many of the farms in the area have some splendid old buildings, too. The Farmers' Home pub has retained its old-fashioned charm while adapting to its modern role.

The **Church of the Holy Cross** stands on high ground on the edge of the

All Saints' Church, East Meon.

village. In the churchyard is the grave of Louis Leopold Jenner, research student at the Lister Institute of Preventative Medicine who died in 1904. His epitaph tells how he 'devoted his gifts and his energies to the advancement of science and the lessening the suffering and sorrows of mankind and finally sacrificed his life in his labours for those ends, dying of enteric fever in the thirty-ninth year of his age'.

EAST MEON

Map p.145, B3 * *

6 miles W of Petersfield off the A272

The infant River Meon, which rises just half a mile away, gurgles through the village beside the High Street. It used to cause problems with flooding but it has now been channelled along a concrete course, crossed in many places by small bridges. The result enhances a village which is already particularly charming.

All Saints' Church has been described as one of the best Norman churches in the south of England. Inside the church, a tombstone with the inscription, 'Amens Plenty', is said to have covered the grave of four Parliamentary soldiers who were killed prior to the battle of Cheriton and were buried in a vertical position.

To the south of the village is HMS Mercury, the Royal Navy communications school. It occupies Leydene House which was constructed in 1924 and was probably the last stately home to be built. It was the home of Eleanor Countess Peel and when she died in 1949 it was bought by the Admiralty. Large numbers of Wrens have passed through HMS Mercury over the years.

EAST STRATTON

Map p.150, C1

6 miles S of Basingstoke off the M3 or A33

The crossroads of this village is dominated by the brick and flint of the barn of a working farm and the Victorian church. To the south, past the entrance to the farm, there are a half-dozen well lived-in two-storey thatched houses and a very simple 18th-century village pub opposite the green. Fifty yards north of the pub is the remains of the village well.

The Plough is one of the few examples of a virtually unchanged village pub, but it does boast a skittles alley, food and parking. Down the hill to the north of the crossroads in Baileys End are a clutch of ideal brick and half-timbered and plaster and half-timbered thatched cottages. Past this are a cross in a field giving the location of the original church (1308) and the boarded up 19th-century village school. Beyond is a water-meadow with public footpaths and the columns which are all that remain of the Palladian Stratton manor.

All Saints' Church was rebuilt in 1888 by Lord Northbrook with Thomas Jackson as architect. It has a clean and lofty interior, the hallmark of what was nicknamed the 'Anglo-Jackson' style. Windows in the chancel, taken from the previous church, commemorate Lord and Lady William Russell. He was beheaded in 1683 for his part in the Rye House Plot against Charles II.

EAST TISTED

Map p.151, E2 *

6 miles S of Alton on the A32

East Tisted owes its existence to the nearby Rotherfield Park estate. Apart from the traffic using the main Alton to Fareham road, it might still be in the last century. Rotherfield Park (see p.14) is the home of the Lord Lieutenant of Hampshire, Sir James Scott Bt, and is a fine example of romantic Victorian Gothic architecture with furniture and other contents that have remained unchanged for more than a hundred years. The neatly kept village, with cottages originally built for estate workers, is very much in the same mould.

East Tisted was once a station on the former Meon Valley Railway line which was completed at the turn of the century and closed in 1955 before it became fashionable to campaign to preserve rural routes. The station became a private residence.

The story is told of Isaac Bone, who was born in East Tisted in 1787 and reached the fine old age of 105. It is said that he celebrated his 100th birthday by ringing three of the church bells together – one with each hand and the third with a foot.

EAST TYTHERLEY

Map p.148, F2 *

16 miles NW of Southampton off the B3084

In this tiny village, many of the neat cottages were once part of the estate of the now-demolished manor house or of nearby Lockerley Hall.

St Peter's Church★, although basically 13th-century, was extensively restored in the 19th century, when an idiosyncratic north tower with stepped outline and sweeping pyramid roof was added in 1897. A huge Wellingtonia was planted in 1887. Inside, there is a modern wall painting of St Peter against the tower wall, and a Tudor wall monument incongruously placed on the floor.

EAST WELLOW

Map p.142, B4 * *

9 miles NW of Southampton off the A27

Settlement is sparse and scattered in East Wellow and the neighbouring parishes. But many visitors make the journey here to see the grave of Florence Nightingale.

Church of St Margaret.★★ There are frequent signposts leading to this church where, under a steeple-topped tomb in the churchyard, inscribed only 'F.N.1820–1910', Florence Nightingale is buried. Her life is commemorated inside the little 13th-century church, which is also distinguished by a prodigious amount of surviving wall painting, including St Christopher and St Thomas à Becket, as well as architectural decoration.

Florence Nightingale's connection with East Wellow arose from her family's ownership of nearby Embley Hall, which they used as a retreat from their Derbyshire home. The hall, which was largely rebuilt in 1895 in brick, in an Elizabethan idiom, is now a private school.

West Wellow. In contrast to the scattered farms and cottages of East Wellow, the settlement of West Wellow is mainly new, and clusters alongside the main A36. The village's most notable new feature is the Wellow Vineyard, on Tanner's Lane, which is open to the public for viewing and tasting.

EAST WORLDHAM

Map p.151, D3 *

2 miles SE of Alton on the B3004

It is worth going to East Worldham just to enjoy the magnificent panorama from the top of the hill. The heathlands of North Hampshire and Surrey beyond are laid out in a patchwork which only nature can produce. Hop growing used to be the main agricultural activity in these parts, but while some hop gardens are still maintained, many growers have switched to other crops.

St Mary's churchyard is said to contain the mortal remains of Philippa Chaucer, wife of the poet Geoffrey Chaucer. The lid from her coffin is kept in a niche in the church. Chaucer's son was lord of the manor at Worldham. An interesting geographical feature is King John's Hill which is reputed to be the site of a royal hunting lodge.

The twin village of **West Worldham** is situated a short distance to the south. At one time the area supported two schools, but numbers dwindled as people drifted away from the land and now they are both closed. The Three Horseshoes pub on the main road at East Worldham represents a lasting, established way of life.

EASTLEIGH

Map p.144, C1 * *

5 miles N of Southampton off the M3

Eastleigh is trying, with a good deal of success, to shake off its image as a grimy, industrial railway town. While the town owes its existence to the London and South Western Railway, which established its locomotive and carriage works there at the end of the last century, times have moved on and today Eastleigh relies less and less on the railway for its prosperity.

The **Swan Centre,** an attractive covered shopping precinct, is the centrepiece of the new Eastleigh. And in an imaginative urban regeneration exercise, the shops in the adjoining streets which have served the town for so long are being linked to the centre in a pedestrianization scheme.

Another important step forward will be the rebuilding of the airport, known as Southampton-Eastleigh but wholly within the Eastleigh boundary. This is being promoted as a regional gateway to Europe.

The railway works, while employing nowhere near as many people as in times gone by, continue to be important to the town. Until the 1880s, when the LSWR decided to move its works from Nine Elms in London, there was little here except the railway junction.

Now the railway's influence is everywhere, not least in the town centre where the park, with its bandstand, was a gift to the town in 1896. Traditional railway workers' cottages abound, and there are names evocative of the past, such as the Locomotive Engineers Club and the Railway Institute. Some of the best steam locomotives were built at Eastleigh, including the Battle of Britain and Merchant Navy class engines which were used to haul glamorous express trains such as the Golden Arrow, the Bournemouth Belle and the Devon Belle. Today the expertise of Eastleigh men is sought to repair engines on many preserved railway lines.

The other big employer in the town is the Pirelli General cable works. The factory was built in 1921 on land previously owned by the Air Ministry. Work continued through World War II and you can still see traces of the doors and windows which were painted onto the walls so that from the air the factory looked like a row of houses. Since the war there has been a rapid expansion in light industry which provides a diversity of employment.

Because of the town's comparatively brief existence, there is little architecture of note here. The Church of the Resurrection, built in 1868 with the help of Charlotte Yonge, the novelist, was badly damaged by a fire in 1985.

The **Eastleigh Museum★** in High St is the best place to trace the town's history. Among the many fascinating exhibits is the reconstruction of a locomotive footplate. There are also documents relating to the establishment of Eastleigh as a borough and a pictorial record of changing times.

Eastleigh has good recreational facilities. The **Fleming Park** leisure centre has swimming pools, squash and tennis courts and health and fitness suites. There is also a bowling green and an 18-hole golf course. Exhibitions and shows are held at Fleming Park during the course of the year. The Town Hall Centre, the old council offices, is also used for arts events, exhibitions and other entertainment.

EASTON

Map p.149, E4
3 miles NE of Winchester off the B3047

The Elizabethan poet Sir Philip Sidney was once Lord of the Manor of this well-kept village which meanders along the south bank of the River Itchen. There are many fine houses from every century between his time and the present.

St Mary's Church. The 13th-century building, set in a strikingly beautiful churchyard, attracts attention by its western tower, modified in the 1860s to achieve an effect variously described as 'tent-roofed', picturesque, outlandish, peculiar and French. Its interior features include a 13th-century piscina, a 17th-century pulpit and a monument to the remarkable Agatha Barlow, a triumphant survivor of the turbulence of the Reformation. An ex-nun, she married an ex-monk who became a bishop. He was disgraced and exiled and then restored to favour and a bishopric again; she lived to be 91 and had the signal satisfaction of seeing every one of her five daughters married off to a bishop. Her son served as Rector here for 48 years.

ELING

Map p.143, E2 * *
4 miles W of Southampton on the A326

A toll bridge protects Eling from the pressure of the nearby built-up area at the head of Southampton Water, and preserves it as a pleasant backwater.

Eling Tide Mill.** The toll bridge crosses the causeway which forms the dam to operate this, the only remaining tide mill in operation. The tidal flow operated the mill wheels, and sea-going grain vessels were able to tie up in the creek. Most of the machinery dates from the 1890s, and since 1980 it has been working again as a museum with explanatory displays and a shop selling the flour.

St Mary's Church** sits on a low hill surrounded by Georgian houses around. The church's harshly restored Victorian exterior hides a well-preserved 13th- and 14th-century interior, with a wide and tall chancel arch. The altarpiece is a mid-16th-century Venetian painting of the Last Supper, and the church is filled with good Georgian memorials.
Eling Tide Mill: *Wed–Sun 10am–4pm. Charge. Tel: (0703) 869575.*

ELLINGHAM

Map p.141, F2 *
2 miles N of Ringwood off the A338

This tiny hamlet, dwarfed by the great piles of sand and gravel extracted in the nearby pits, sits on a short dead end off the A338.

St Mary's Church** is a well-preserved gem. The gable of the south porch is filled with a Georgian sundial against a splendid blue background, while inside there is a wealth of woodwork: the 15th-century screen, with the space above filled with 17th-century painted texts, and an hourglass fixed beside the Jacobean pulpit which faces a huge, enclosed family pew. At the west end, which was rebuilt in the 1740s, stands the former reredos, an exuberant example of baroque wood-carving of the late 17th century, framing a 16th-century German painting of the Last Judgement.

Ellingham has two big houses, although neither is open to view. **Somerley,** near the church, which is a large yellow brick house of the 1790s, occasionally opens its gardens. A mile east, on the forest edge and encircled by footpaths, the mid-Stuart brick-built **Moyles Court** (now a school) was the home of Dame Alicia Moyles who was hanged for sheltering rebels in Monmouth's rising in 1685 and is buried near the church porch.

EMERY DOWN

Map p.142, F3 *
1 mile NW of Lyndhurst off the A35

There are oak trees everywhere in this pretty New Forest village, where brick and thatch cottages cluster beneath the hills. **Christ Church*** on the hillside was designed, along with the almshouses opposite it, by William Butterfield in 1864 in his characteristic polychrome brick style. Twenty-five years later, Sir Arthur Conan Doyle lived here, writing his New Forest-based historical novel *The White Company* (1891).

EMPSHOTT

Map p.151, E4 *
6 miles S of Alton on the B3006

It is worth making a quick detour off the main Alton to Petersfield road at Empshott to see the charming church, set in one of the most beautiful parts of Hampshire.

The **Church of the Holy Rood*** is an architectural gem. The flock of white doves perched on the roof set the scene splendidly and it is difficult to imagine the violent incident that took place in the 1500s. Robert Aske, the lord of the manor of Empshott, paid a terrible price for defying Thomas Cromwell. He was taken to York and hanged in chains for six days before all sign of life ceased.

While the church dates back to Saxon times, it has been considerably rebuilt and restored over the years; but the most striking feature, the unique wooden lantern tower belfry, topped by a shingle spire, was built in 1624. In the churchyard is the grave of Thomas Russell Horner (1914–1970), described on his tombstone as an idealist, sportsman and farmer, and adding: 'He sowed that others might reap.'

EMSWORTH

Map p.139, B2 * *
2 miles E of Havant on the A27

Emsworth, nestling against the Hampshire border with Sussex on the edge of Chichester harbour, is a delightful village with interesting old buildings, narrow streets and a good selection of pubs and restaurants. While the fishing and boatbuilding industries now play a minor role, Emsworth still has an unmistakable maritime atmosphere. P. G. Wodehouse is said to have based his characters and locations on the people and places of Emsworth. He wrote the first of his novels while he was living at a preparatory school in the village.

There are several attractive walks in the area. Favourites are around the two tidal millponds which support a wide range of seabirds. The mills, two on each pond, still stand, although they have now been converted. Emsworth is also at one end of the Solent Way (see p.38).

Emsworth Museum★★ in North St is not to be missed, with exhibits retracing the village's history to the times when it was a flourishing seaport famed for its oysters.
***Emsworth Museum:** Easter–Sept, Sat 10am–4pm, Sun 2–4pm. Tel: (0705) 480024.*

EVERSLEY

Map p.156, B4 * *
4 miles NE of Hartley Wintney on the A327

This northern outpost of Hampshire is best known for its association with Charles Kingsley, who was the rector of Eversley from 1844 to 1875. It was here that he wrote *The Water Babies* and he also founded the village school which is named after him. His best known character, Tom, has been incorporated in the design of the gates both as a chimney sweep and a water baby.

St Mary's churchyard contains the grave of Kingsley and his wife. It is marked by a white marble cross with the epitaph, 'Amavimus, Amamus, Amambimus', which translated from the Latin means 'We loved, we love, we shall love'. The Old Rectory where the Kingsleys lived is now a private residence.

Eversley has an excellent network of footpaths and bridleways, and easy access to hundreds of acres of the **Royal Forest of Eversley** which is now administered by Hampshire County Council and the Forestry Commission. Nearby is Bramshill House, a large Jacobean building which now houses the Police Staff College and is unfortunately not open to the public.

EVERTON

Map p.136, F1 *
2 miles W of Lymington on the A337

The thatched cottage just by Everton's parish church is said to have been the original for the keeper's house in Captain Marryatt's *The Children of the New Forest.* Everton has a number of these older houses, but, like many villages around Lymington, also has a lot of new development.

Hordle, the village a mile north-west, has even more new housing estates, together with a variety of plant nurseries. Its box-like church of 1872 is in the harsh red brick in which many Forest churches were then being built. Nearby Sky End Lane gives Hordle a touch of whimsy, its smuggling past some glamour, and the existence of a community of Shakers, the intriguing American religious sect, in the 1870s and 80s, provides curiosity value.

The harbour at Emsworth.

THE OLD FLOUR MILL
QUEEN STREET
EMSWORT

FAREHAM

Map p.138, B1 *

10 miles E of Southampton off the M27

The name Fareham was originally spelt Fearnhamme, but according to local legend, when Queen Elizabeth I visited, she exclaimed: 'Oh what a fair town', and since then it has been known as Fareham.

The town is situated on a creek in the north-west corner of Portsmouth harbour. It did not begin to prosper until the 18th and 19th centuries, when the Royal Navy made use of the shipyards. Admiral Lord Nelson and the Duke of Wellington both established links with the area and Fareham grew into a pleasant town with many large houses which were the homes of high-ranking naval officers.

The shipbuilding and related industries, along with the importance of horticulture inland, put Fareham on a firm footing for the future. At the beginning of the century, the town was still fairly compact but since the war housing and industrial development have boomed, so that today there is little open space to separate Fareham from its neighbouring parishes.

The town itself has acquired a large, covered shopping precinct in the process, and thanks to a combination of pedestrian and traffic management schemes the town centre is no longer used for through traffic. Holy Trinity Church in West St, which dates from 1830, is of particular interest, and Westbury Manor, the former headquarters of the local council, has now been converted into a town museum.

The **High St,** with its Georgian and early Victorian buildings, is considered one of the best examples of a country town street in southern England. Set back from the High St is the **Church of St Peter and St Paul** which has been extended and rebuilt so many times that it shows traces of architecture from Norman times to the present day. The tower was built in 1742.

Fareham Creek*, a short walk from the town centre, is still used by sizeable commercial dredgers but is mainly a centre for yachts. Since being designated a conservation area it has become an attractive spot for people visiting by land and by water.

Fareham still retains close links with the Royal Navy, and on the outskirts of the town is HMS Collingwood, one of the most modern training establishments in the country. It was established in 1940 for training recruits but it is now the Royal Naval Weapon Engineering School, employing around 2000 service and civilian personnel.

An important development in recent years has been the electrification of the railway lines to Southampton, Portsmouth and Eastleigh, connecting the town with other electrified lines so that now, for the first time since before the war, Fareham has a direct train service to London.

Tourist Information Centre: *Westbury Manor, West St. Tel: (0329) 236100.*

FARLEIGH WALLOP

Map p.155, F4

3 miles S of Basingstoke off the B3046

High on the hills separating Basingstoke from the Candover Valley, Farleigh Wallop really owes its existence to the Farleigh Estate.

Farleigh House was built in 1731, the seat of the Earl of Portsmouth. Today most people look to the estate for employment, and to some extent for recreation as well. There is a special estate club housed in a neat little thatched building which in other surroundings might be mistaken for a village hall.

The tiny church is isolated in the middle of a field down a leafy track. A winding, concrete path across the field tempts the casual observer towards it, only to disappoint because the door is firmly padlocked and there are obvious signs of neglect. Things must have been different in 1949, for a notice in the porch tells how parishioners paid for electricity to be laid on in that year, which must have been quite an achievement in the austerity of the post-war years.

At the other end of the church lane, opposite a group of houses, a pond has been restored and a house built for the ducks.

FARLEY CHAMBERLAYNE

Map p.149, F1 (Farley Down) *
6 miles W of Winchester off the A3090

A network of deep, narrow lanes criss-crosses this parish of scattered farms. Of the original manor and village, only the parish church and Farley Farm, and a few bumps in the fields, survive.

St John the Baptist Church★★ is one of Hampshire's loveliest small churches, being secluded and peaceful. A Norman structure with a fine doorway, it has Georgian round-headed windows, monuments to the St John family, Jacobean panelling and communion rail, and a king-post trussed timber roof. The support for the belfry at the west end is a marvellously intricate piece of braced carpentry. The careful restoration in 1910 left much untouched, and the church is still lit by gas

FARNBOROUGH

Map p.157, D3 *
14 miles E of Basingstoke off the M3

Like Aldershot, Farnborough was a sparsely populated area of heathland until the 1850s when Queen Victoria's military advisers bought 25,000 acres to build a new base for the British Army. A few years later the military ballooning base was transferred from Woolwich and that was the modest start of Farnborough's aeronautical connections. Now the town is internationally known for its biennial air show, when a quarter of a million visitors from all over the world come to see the latest in aero and space technology. It is a far cry from the day in 1908 when pioneer pilot Samuel Cody, a Texan, made Britain's first aeroplane flight at Laffan's Plain, which has long been swallowed up in the airfield's development. Since then Farnborough has been at the forefront of aeronautics and many of Britain's top military and civilian aircraft have made public debuts here.

Scientists, technicians and engineers at the base have also been involved in investigating air disasters. One of the biggest projects in recent years was painstakingly to piece together the fragments of the jumbo jet which was blown up by a terrorist bomb over Lockerbie, killing more than 250 people.

Farnborough, now officially linked with neighbouring Aldershot under the umbrella of Rushmoor Council, is dominated by the airfield and the work that goes on there, but there is another side to the town. The town centre has evolved since the early 1960s and is built around the impressive Queensmead and Kingsmead shopping precincts, with another development of new shops at Southwood Village Centre.

The **Church of St Peter**, although much enlarged and restored, dates from Norman times. Buried in the crypt are five Earls of Anglesey whose seat was Farnborough Place. That is now occupied by St Peter's School.

Farnborough Hill is a remarkable mansion built in 1860 in the form of a vast chalet-type building. It was bought in 1880 by the Empress Eugenie, wife of Napoleon III who fled to Britain following his defeat in the Franco-Prussian war. She lived at Farnborough until her death in 1920, aged 95. On an adjacent site she built St Michael's Abbey as a memorial to her husband and her son. It is built in typically French Gothic style with the flamboyant use of flying buttresses.

Knellwood War Memorial Home was established in 1947 as a tribute to those who died during World War II. It accommodates 54 residents who have connections with the area. Devereaux House was originally the Farnborough and Cove War Memorial Hospital and now offers a wide range of medical services.
***Farnborough Hill:** Aug, Mon, Weds and Fri (tours only). Tel: (0252) 545197.*

FARRINGDON

Map p.151, D2 *
4 miles S of Alton on the A32

Farringdon is technically made up of two parts – Lower Farringdon, which sits astride the A32, and Upper Farringdon just to the east.

Massey's Folly★, a curious red brick building built by the eccentric rector Thomas Massey, is the best-known feature. He spent thirty years on it, only for it to be described by critics as 'a most appalling horror of scarlet brick and tile... a suburban palace of varieties'.

Massey's Folly subsequently served a useful purpose as a village hall and a school, now closed, but in recent times it has found a new lease of life as, oddly enough, headquarters of the Royal Institute of British Architecture which says the unusual style has certain merit.

In the churchyard is the grave of Mary Windebank who died in 1785 at the age of 75. Her tombstone shows an old lady in a four poster bed with a row of money bags beneath it. A thief is seen climbing the stairs and behind him is a figure thought to portray the Devil. The true significance has been lost in time but it is widely thought that Mary was murdered for her money.

FAWLEY

Map p.137, C2 *

5 miles S of Southampton off the B3053

For most visitors to Southampton Water, Fawley means one thing: the Esso oil refinery, its tall flare stacks shooting flames into the air. The present refinery was begun in 1951, and extends over 3000 acres. There is still a country village at the heart of the modern sprawl of Fawley, with a small knot of older buildings and pubs, and the parish church of All Saints, standing beside one of the main entrances to the refinery. The church was bombed in World War II, and part was reconstructed, but the Norman west door and 12th-century nave escaped damage.

Fawley power station, close to Calshot Spit to the south, has a 670ft high chimney which dominates this landscape. Calshot village largely grew up to house the RAF Flying Boat Squadron; the great hangars on the spit itself are now used as an activity centre by Hampshire County Council. A modern coastguard tower stands beside Henry VIII's Calshot Castle (see p.16), all still guarding the entrance to Southampton Water, and sometimes the flying boats come back to Calshot on a demonstration flight.

The coastal marshes between Fawley and Calshot, and the old creek quay at Ashlett with its former tide mill, offer a striking contrast to the industrial scenes on either side. Quieter still is Eaglehurst, on the coast behind Calshot village down a private road, where the Georgian folly tower in the grounds has been restored as a holiday home by the Landmark Trust. The tower, which Marconi used for some of his early wireless experiments, is clearly visible from the Calshot shore.

FLEET

Map p.157, D1 *

12 miles E of Basingstoke off the M3

Fleet was a sparsely-populated area of marsh, heathland and forest surrounding a large lake, until the construction of the London to Southampton railway in 1840. Situated only forty miles from the capital, it was an obvious spot for cheap day trips from London for families seeking a brief respite from city life. They were enthralled by the pond, set among birches and pines, and some who could afford it decided to set up homes nearby. Over the years Fleet has grown dramatically and is now part of a spreading urban area adjacent to Aldershot and Farnborough.

The **Hart Centre** is a modern covered shopping precinct with fifty shops, a café and a bar. Linked to it is a large car park. A new 26-acre industrial site is being developed at Ancells Park to the north of the town and there is a weekly market held next to the Hart Council Offices.

Fleet Pond★★ is still the main attraction for most visitors. It was recorded in Saxon times as Fugelmere and supplied fish to the monks at St Swithin's in Winchester, which was the forerunner of Winchester Cathedral. Public use is very much encouraged by Hart Council which issues licences for angling and boating. But the area, which comprises 135 acres of varied countryside, is also a nature reserve and is home to a wide range of animal and plant life. Up to 180 different species of birds have been recorded, 26 types of butterflies, 21 dragonflies and 400 wild flowers.

FORDINGBRIDGE

Map p.141, D2 *

6 miles N of Ringwood on the A338

This little town was originally called Forde, but its name was extended when the 13th-century bridge over the River Avon was built. The seven-arch bridge is still there, widened in 1841 in the original style. It and the parish church are the town's only surviving early features.

St Mary's Church★, to the south of the town's main centre, is large, mostly dating from the 13th century, with tall lancet windows. Its great porch was added in the 15th century, when the beautiful hammerbeam angel roof was also built over the north chapel. These roofs are more common in East Anglia than the south.

The centre of the town consists of Bridge St, High St, and Salisbury St. The 17th-century former manor house stands on Salisbury St, with the Regency Gothic Burgate House at the old town's end; otherwise, there are few buildings of note, except for a group of thatched cottages on Church St. Shering's Museum stands to the east of Church St, displaying local artefacts. (It is open on application to a nearby house.)

Fordingbridge is a centre for anglers, since the Avon is renowned for coarse fishing. Beside the river, just downstream from the bridge, is a rugged sculpture of Augustus John (1878–1961), the artist and lover of many women, who is buried in the cemetery on the Stockton road out of the town. He lived at Fryern Court, a mile to the north. The house is private, but it and some of the artist's studios may be glimpsed from the lane.

FOUR MARKS

Map p.151, D1 *

4 miles SW of Alton on the A31

Four Marks has grown up in comparatively recent years around the spot where the boundaries of four other parishes joined – hence the name. Clues to the village's origins are still to be found. The house at the doctors' surgery is known as The Boundaries and the garage on the other side of the A31 is called Chawton End.

The village sits on 700ft ridge that divides north and south Hampshire. Generations of railwaymen said it was like crosssing the Alps, especially during the winter when the stiff gradient and icy conditions often tested the skill of engine drivers to the limit. Four Marks still has its railway (it shares the station with neighbouring Medstead) but it is now part of the restored Watercress Line (see ALTON). The sight of a steam locomotive battling its way to the summit is still something to relish.

Because of its lofty situation, Four Marks was the site of one of the Admiralty's telegraph stations linking London with Portsmouth and Plymouth (see also BINSTED). Telegraph Lane and Semaphore Farm are reminders of this.

FRITHAM

Map p.142, D2 *

11 miles W of Southampton off the B3078

The hamlet at Fritham is an enclave of animal pasture and cottages in the north of the New Forest. Most houses are 20th-century, with the exception of the plain Georgian buildings of Fritham Farm. Between 1865 and 1923, however, this quiet place was bustling: Schulze's Gunpowder works was established here, originally using New Forest charcoal. The most significant relic of the industry is the tree-fringed large pond at **Iron Wells★** to the west, which had originally been a chalybeate spring where lepers came to be cured in the Middle Ages.

Only a mile or two to the east are the twin forest settlements of Brook and

Bramshaw, with extensive commons; the end of the M27 is only a short distance away.

The **Rufus Stone**,** between Brook village and the A31, marks the spot where William II, the Conqueror's son, was killed (supposedly by accident) while out hunting in 1100. It became one of the earliest tourist attractions in the New Forest, probably because access to it was easy, and the 18th-century marker stone had to be encased in cast iron in 1842 to protect it from souvenir hunters.

St Peter's Church, Bramshaw, stands, like many Forest churches, on a rise and surrounded by trees. Most of the church is brick and early 19th-century, although 13th-century work remains in the nave. The county boundary ran through this church until reorganization in 1895.

FROYLE

Map p.151, B4 *
4 miles NE of Alton off the A31

Froyle has been called the 'Village of the Saints', thanks to Sir Hubert Miller, a former lord of the manor who was in the habit of bringing back Italian statues of saints from his villa near Venice. Many of these have found a place above doorways of village homes. The Miller family were lords of the manor for around 200 years and clearly made a big impact on village life. The school was founded by Sir Charles Hayes Miller in 1867. Froyle, consisting up of Upper and Lower, is tucked off the busy A31 and the most obvious sign for travellers is the Hen and Chicken pub beside the road. The village is the home of the Lord Mayor Treloar College for disabled youngsters.

The Church of St Mary of the Assumption has a chequered history but the tower, built of Crondall bricks, was constructed in 1722 and replaces a steeple.

A group of houses known as The Barracks housed French prisoners of war in Napoleonic times and before that they were almshouses. Brecklands, opposite the village hall, was the workhouse.

FYFIELD

Map p.148, A2 *
3½ miles W of Andover off the A342

Fyfield remains a small and rural village overlooking a water-meadow and Pillhill brook despite the addition of a scattering of new houses to the east. It is surrounded by pastures and grazing sheep. The village is best known as the home of the British Thoroughbred Racing and Breeding plc stables, which occupy the previous manor house, but it also has an interesting church.

Fyfield is an active village with an 18th-century pub, Highland Wedding, renamed in honour of the 1969 Grand National winner bred at Fyfield Manor. The rest of the village consists of a handful of thatched cottages (17th- and 18th-century) and newer houses with the two large 18th-century houses, the Rectory and the Grange, both now private residences. The path to the church is lined with two impressive rows of beeches, most of which on the south side of the path have had to be cut down.

St Nicholas' Church has flint and stone walls which are at least 700 years old as well as an open belfry with a single bell. The font, carved with quatrefoils, has been tentatively dated as 15th-century.

GOSPORT

Map p.138, D2 * *
5 miles S of Fareham on the A32

Legend has it that the town was named in the 12th century when Henry de Blois, the Bishop of Winchester, arrived back from Normandy in a dreadful storm. He was so pleased to get ashore that he decreed it should be called God's Port.

Whatever the truth, Gosport's links with the sea and the Royal Navy across the harbour at Portsmouth go back centuries and represent an important element of the town's continuing prosperity. The future of the HMS Dolphin submarine base, however, is giving rise to concern following an announcement by the Navy that in future submarines will be based in Plymouth. While the loss of jobs and prestige will be a blow to the town, Gosport is fortunate in having a diversity of other industries to help cushion the blow, and the **Royal Naval Submarine Museum**, where visitors can board a submarine for a guided tour, will remain.

Gosport, on the western entrance to Portsmouth Harbour, has always played an important part in the defence of the fleet. Consequently there are several massive fortifications around the town and at one time ships could be prevented from entering the harbour by huge chains stretched across the entrance to Portsmouth's Round Tower. Boatbuilding remains an important industry. The marina is an asset for local yachtsmen and an attraction for visiting sailors from other parts of the south coast.

The Royal Navy Aircraft Yard at Fleetlands on the outskirts of the town employs large numbers on the maintenance and repair of helicopters in particular, and in the same area there are several other large factories engaged in a variety of work ranging from medicines to computers. However, a setback in recent times was the closure of the television factory with the loss of 700 jobs.

Holy Trinity Church★, one of the oldest buildings in the town, was built as a garrison church in 1696. Handel is reputed to have composed some of his music on the organ when he was director of music to the Duke of Chandos. After the Duke's death the organ was auctioned and Holy Trinity Church bought it. The nave has two rows of huge columns, each beautifully made from the trunk of a single oak tree.

Another interesting old building, now sadly neglected despite being officially designated as of special architectural interest, is the former railway station, last used by passengers in 1953 and for freight in 1969. It was built in 1840 to a design by Sir William Tite who was famous for his Italianate style. Gosport had a railway long before Portsmouth, and Queen Victoria regularly used the branch line on her way to Osborne House on the Isle of Wight. She had a special spur line built to Clarence Pier where she boarded her ferry.

The **17th-Century Village★** is a recreation of a woodland hamlet of those times which provides a unique insight into how people existed then. Unfortunately opening times are limited to a few days each year; details from **Gosport Museum★**. The museum itself is packed with fascinating displays recording local history.

Royal Naval Submarine Museum: *April–Oct, daily 10am–(last tour) 4.30pm; Nov–Mar, daily 10am–(last tour) 3.30pm. Admission charge. Tel: (0705) 529217.*

Gosport Museum: *Tues–Sat 10am–5pm. Free. Tel: (0705) 588035.*

GRATELEY

Map p.148, B1 *

4 miles SW of Andover off the A303

Although Grateley still retains its railway station and thus is a commuter centre for people working in Andover or Salisbury, it is remarkably unspoilt, its half-timbered, thatched, or brick houses set in a delightful tangle of lanes. It is not easy to find by road, but well worth the search.

Church of St Leonard.★★★ In the 1790s the architect James Wyatt lived up to his nickname of 'The Destroyer' when he got to work on Salisbury cathedral. Among the victims of his 'restoration' were the superb early 13th-century stained glass windows. He simply smashed them, throwing the fragments, with other 'rubbish' into the town ditch. Some time later somebody – presumably a resident of Grateley – salvaged some of these fragments and had them placed in this 12th-century church. They depict the stoning of St Stephen, and though they form only part of a small window on the south wall it is impossible to miss them for, seven centuries after they were made and despite their cavalier handling, they glow with beauty and colour. There is much else in the church, small though it is. The font was probaby Roman in origin, recut and consecrated to Christian purposes. A bracket for an hourglass near the pulpit must have given fair warning of the length of sermons in the post Reformation period.

HALE

Map p.141, C4 *

5 miles NE of Fordingbridge off the A338

Sitting between the River Avon and the forest edge, Hale is memorable for its triangular green, flanked by thatched cottages, and especially for its little church beside the big house. Thomas Archer, the great baroque church architect, rebuilt the original house and church for himself in 1717. The grand porticoed front of Hale House (which is private, and was considerably altered in the 1790s) is reached via a long lime avenue; the path then turns right towards the church.

St Mary's Church* is set on a steep slope above the valley floor. The church is a cruciform classical temple, with over-sized details on the doors, and although gothicized to some extent in the 19th century, it still retains baroque charm. The enormous classical monument to Archer himself, in the south transept, contributes to its appeal.

The steep path continues to a footbridge over the River Avon, a tranquil scene but the site of the great battle of Cerdic's Ford in 519 in which the Saxons conquered the British and were able to establish Wessex.

HAMBLE

Map p.137, B2 * *

6 miles SE of Southampton on the B3397

This is the centre of *Howards' Way* country, that part of the south coast made famous by the television series about a boatbuilding company and the people behind it. Hamble undoubtedly embraces some of the glamour of very rich people and their floating gin palaces, but it is still a workaday village.

Hamble has also had a long association with the aeroplane industry, and the British Aerospace factory makes parts for civilian and military aircraft. The Harrier pub is named after Britain's revolutionary jump-jet. Many of the world's top airline pilots trained at Hamble but it was the victim of economies and the airfield now seems destined for housing and industry.

The village is also a link in Britain's oil industry. Oil from the Wytch Farm field in Dorset is piped here for distribution, much of it by tanker from the marine terminal on Southampton Water.

HAMBLEDON

Map p.145, D2 * *

8 miles N of Portsmouth on the B2150

Hambledon is best known as the birthplace of cricket. Apparently the game was not actually invented here, but the foundation of the rules of the game we know today were standardized by Hambledon Cricket Club. They played on Broadhalfpenny Down using a curved bat and two stumps and the village team's finest hour was in 1777 when they beat an All England side by an innings and 52 runs.

This delightful Georgian village has played its part in defending king and country over the years. At the beginning of the 19th century the Hambledon Volunteers were raised to fight Napoleon, and their colours now hang in the Church of St Peter and St Paul. During World War II the village was packed with troops and equipment in readiness for D-Day. King George VI paid a visit to the village to inspect the forces and although it was supposed to be a secret, he was given an enthusiastic greeting.

HANNINGTON

Map p.155, D1

6 miles NW of Basingstoke

Situated on a hilltop high up on the chalk, Hannington has a classic village green at its centre, with the old communal well, farms and cottages around it, and the parish church marked by an avenue of trees.

All Saints' Church incorporates almost every architectural style from Anglo-Saxon,

The ruins of Netley Abbey, near Hamble.

in part of the nave, to the Victorian bell-turret and spire. The 20th century's main contribution has been two engraved glass windows by Lawrence Whistler.

The ancient **Portway**, a prehistoric track taken over by the Romans as their road between Silchester and Sarum, runs diagonally through the parish and on to skirt the nearby mass of Watership Down (see p.27). Although most of the track is a footpath, certain sections are metalled road.

HARTLEY WINTNEY

Map p.156, C4 * *
9 miles NE of Basingstoke on the A30

The construction of the M3 motorway must be the best thing that has happened to Hartley Wintney. For while the village prospered and grew because of its situation on the A30, one of the main routes from London to the West Country, in later years the ever-increasing traffic was in danger of choking the village altogether.

The A30 is still an important lifeline, but the worst of the traffic now roars by on the M3, a couple of miles to the south. Now visitors have a long-awaited chance to appreciate this village, which has won awards for its upkeep and appearance, without the menace of speeding cars and lorries.

Early records show that the village was originally Hertleye Wynteneye, meaning 'the clearing in the forest where the deer graze by Winta's island'. To some extent the character of the place has not altered too much for it is still a series of commons and greens. The houses around the edges are obviously later additions, but they have been built in keeping with their surroundings.

It is said that cricket has been played on the green since 1770 and on a quiet summer afternoon it is not difficult to imagine the scene when the first match was played. Standing over the central common are the Mildmay Oaks which were planted after the Battle of Trafalgar to provide wood for the nation's future shipbuilding requirements.

West Green House, a large 18th-century building owned by the National Trust, was recently badly damaged by a terrorist bomb and it is now being rebuilt. A former resident was Lieutenant General Henry Hawley who rose to fame during the Jacobite rebellion of 1745 and was noted for his ruthlessness. According to local legend, on 16 April each year, the anniversary of the battle of Culloden, the skirl of bagpipes and the battle cries of the Highland clans echo around the gardens.

At Hartley Grange Sir Douglas Bader, later to become the wartime Spitfire hero, learned how to walk on his artificial legs after an horrific plane crash in the early 1930s. Within a few months he had mastered his disability and was playing golf on the nearby course.

HAVANT

Map p.139, B1 *
5 miles NE of Portsmouth off the A27

Havant is at the centre of a large borough which includes some of the most heavily populated areas of south Hampshire. The town originally grew up around the freshwater Homewell spring which wells up in the centre of the town. By the 15th century there was a weekly market and two fairs were held annually. The town later became well known for the high quality parchment that was made here.

Then in 1761 a disastrous fire destroyed a large part of the town. Consequently most of the old buildings date from just after that time; only the pub, the Old House at Home, remains as an example of what the town must once have looked like.

Havant continued to rebuild and thrived during the Victorian era, helped by the coming of the railway from London in the 1850s and the completion of the south coast route, giving easy access to Portsmouth and Southampton to the west, and Chichester and Brighton to the east. The old trades have now given way to a wealth of high-tech industries.

St Faith's Church*, built in the 12th century but extensively restored in the 19th, has been at the centre of Havant's development. Of much later origin, but still interesting, is the ornate gas lamp standard erected in the churchyard a hundred years ago. Inside is a tattered banner of a group of volunteers who banded together when an invasion by Napoleon seemed imminent.

Homewell is a pleasant street of 19th-century houses leading to the spring and the buildings to the south were those of the old parchment factory. It was an industry in Havant for centuries and it is reputed the Magna Carta was written on parchment made in the town. Certainly the parchment for the Treaty of Versailles in 1919 came from the town.

In South St the Old House at Home has always been a popular meeting place and in Victorian times had its own dancing bear. The post to which the unfortunate creature was tethered can still be seen. Across the road are the premises of a former brewery which benefited from the constant supply of pure spring water.

At the end of Grove Rd an embankment crosses the track of the former Hayling Island branch railway which closed in 1963. The Hayling Billy is still fondly remembered by many residents who conveniently forget the traffic delays it caused at level crossings. The track now forms part of a nature trail through an otherwise built-up area.

The Bear Hotel is one of many which claim to have had Queen Victoria as a guest. Whether or not it is true, there is no doubt that The Bear was an important staging post and an important venue for social and business meetings.

Havant's long and varied history has been conveniently condensed at the **Museum★** in East St. As well as examples of the town's former industries and its social life, it has an important collection of firearms given by the Hampshire inventor, Cecil Vokes. The museum also mounts a variety of temporary exhibitions which change every seven weeks.

Havant Museum: *Tues–Sat 10am–5pm*
Tel: (0705) 451155.
Tourist Information Centre: *Park Rd South.*
Tel: (0705) 480024.

HAYLING ISLAND

Map p.139, D2 * *
4 miles S of Havant on the A3023

Hayling Island is known as a holiday resort, but away from the beach and the seaside entertainments there is a wealth of interesting places and buildings which are seldom noticed. The island, covering ten square miles, is bordered by Langstone harbour to the west, Chichester harbour to the east and the open sea off Spithead to the south. It is linked to the mainland by a concrete road bridge opened in 1956 to replace a wooden toll bridge built in 1824.

Watching the stream of cars flooding over it today, it is interesting to note that when the first motor car crossed the old toll bridge a bewildered gatekeeper had no idea what to charge. When told the car was 8½ horsepower he decided to charge one penny per horse and forget about the foal!

It was when the first bridge was built that the attractions of Hayling Island became more widely known to the rest of the country, and before long there were plans to develop it into a resort rivalling South Coast neighbours Bognor and Brighton. It was then that the two large seafront hotels, the Royal and the Norfolk Terrace, were built.

The opening of the railway in 1867 brought the island within easy reach of the large towns and cities. The railway had its own bridge, built of timber on concrete piles, but when the bridge reached the end of its life in the 1960s it was decided it would be too expensive to replace it. The branch line from Havant was closed, leaving the Hayling Billy to be lamented by residents and holidaymakers alike. Part of the track is now used as a footpath.

Another link to the mainland is by passenger ferry to Portsmouth from the end of Ferry Rd at West Town. Although there have been occasional scares about its future, the service has been running for 200 years. The Ferry Boat Inn, once called the Norfolk Arms, is one of the island's oldest pubs.

St Peter's Church★ at North Hayling is claimed by many to be the island's loveliest building. It was built in 1140 and escaped the great fire which swept the village in 1757. The peal of three bells is said to be the oldest in the country. **St Mary's** is the parish church of South Hayling. The yew tree in the churchyard is 30ft around and about a thousand years old.

Hayling is good for all watersports and is a mecca for board sailing. Indeeed, the island claims to be the birthplace of the sport: in 1958 Peter Chilvers, a boy of 12, used a sheet of plywood and a tent flysheet attached to a pole with curtain rings to sail up an island creek. The claim has since been upheld by a High Court ruling. Nowadays the annual round the island windsurfing marathon is a colourful spectacle attracting more than 500 entries.

Many of the holiday camp and caravan sites have their own sporting facilities, but there is a good range of public amenities as well. Hayling Golf Club, founded in 1883 and one of the first in the country, is noted for its fine sea views and exhilarating air.

Apart from farming, the holiday trade and boat repairing, there is little industry, but new oyster beds are being established in former saltings, reviving a business abandoned last century.

Tourist Information Centre: *Seafront. Tel: (0705) 467111.*

HEADBOURNE WORTHY

Map p.149, E3 * *

2 miles N of central Winchester off the A3090

The village is one of those which circle England's ancient capital like a diadem or necklace. Modern traffic conditions have rather spoilt its homogeneity but there are a number of pleasant buildings and private houses tucked away among the greenery of Hampshire. Headbourne Worthy, however, possesses one building which Pevsner, not usually given to superlatives, correctly describes as 'a treasure of international value'. This is the Saxon church of St Swithun, situated on the northern side of the unumbered road from Kings Worthy.

Church of St Swithun.** It is only too easy to miss the church for not only does it not have the customary board identifying it but it is screened from the world by a thick bank of trees and shrubs. This, however, increases the sense of delight and surprise as you step through the screen and find yourself in a setting which could figure in one of the Grimm fairy tales. Crossing a little bridge you see before you a green dell, surrounded by trees, through which a sparkling stream, the Hyde Bourne, meanders with its banks a profusion of comfrey. In spring, the whole dell (you cannot really call it a churchyard though there are graves) is a blaze of daffodils. In the centre is the church. Its main body was built at least thirty years before the Norman Conquest and though there have been additions and alterations down to our own time it is still essentially a Saxon church. The massive little tower with its conical roof of shingle like a gnome's cap, was built about 1250 – but the handsome glass door leading into the nave was hung in 1987. The font is 13th-century, but its wooden cover was lovingly carved by the rector at the turn of the 20th century in eight triangular sections, each depicting some local flora – blackberries, holly, hazelnuts, wild strawberries, acorns, grapes and oak leaves. On the north wall of the chancel is the famous John Kent brass, commemorating a Winchester scholar dressed in the sober costume of the period (he died in 1434). The outstanding feature of the church is tucked away in the vestry at the west end. This is an immense rood, carved in stone some time in the 11th century, and though it was savagely mutilated by the fanatics of the Reformation it is still a majestic piece of work, an almost life-sized representation of Christ on the cross, flanked by Our Lady and St John, and with the hand of God coming down out of a cloud. Originally this magnificent sculpture would have been on an exterior wall (like the rood still to be seen at Romsey Abbey) until this porch was built over it in the early 16th century for its protection.

HECKFIELD

Map p.156, B2 *

8 miles NE of Basingstoke off the A33

It is a sign of the times that two large country houses at Heckfield have been converted into conference centres for international businesses. The change has been welcomed locally since the houses have been preserved in good order and new jobs have been created. A traffic management scheme has been introduced in the picturesque village centre which means that only local traffic is allowed.

Stratfield Saye House (see p.15), home of the Dukes of Wellington, has its main entrance at the north of the village and the tall column bearing a statute of the first Duke of Wellington is a well-known local landmark.

St Michael's Church has a memorial tablet to former Prime Minister Neville Chamberlain ('I have here a piece of paper from Mr Hitler') who died nearby at Highfield House. Novelist Anthony Trollope's parents were married in the church in 1809. The vicar was William Milton, the bride's father, who was better known for designing devices to stop wheels falling off horse-drawn coaches.

HINTON AMPNER

Map p.145, A1

8 miles E of Winchester off the A272

The impressive Georgian-style Hinton Ampner House (see p.13), set in superb undulating Hampshire countryside, has had a lively history. The house, bequeathed to the National Trust by Sir Ralph Dutton in 1984, was rebuilt in the 1960s following a disastrous fire. A blaze broke out in the library and despite the efforts of more than 100 firemen the house was wrecked. When the restoration was complete Sir Ralph invited the firemen to a party to celebrate.

In 1793 a previous manor house was demolished when a poltergeist made life intolerable. A small skull was found under floorboards which villagers claimed was that of a murdered lovechild.

The church contains many memorials to the Stewkeley family who at one time lived at the manor house. The village school, now closed, was one of the earliest schools in the county, dating from 1730, and was endowed under the will of William Blake, a groom who married one of the Stewkeley daughters.

HOLYBOURNE

Map p.151, C3 *

1 mile NE of Alton off the A31

Holybourne has done well to avoid being annexed by its large neighbour, Alton. Although the green belt between the two has been eroded over the years and is now just a token represented by playing fields, Holybourne has managed to retain its own identity. The village is said to take its name from a spring believed to rise under the 12th-century church of the Holyrood. It flows under the main road before joining the River Wey at Neatham.

The Lawn is the house bought in 1865 by the Victorian novelist Mrs Elizabeth Gaskell, as a retirement gift for her husband who was a Unitarian church minister in Manchester. Unfortunately she died suddenly at the house, leaving the last few instalments of her best known novel, *Sons and Daughters*, still unfinished.

Holybourne Theatre was built by the local drama group which stages some ambitious productions there. Thomas Andrews, who died in 1719, left money in his will to build a school at which children by the name of Andrews were to have preference.

HORSEBRIDGE

Map p.148, F3 *

1 mile SW of King's Somborne off the A3057

Just south of this pretty little hamlet, the River Test goes through one of its most confusing phases with no less than four branches, all claiming to be the main stream.

The Roman road from Winchester to Old Sarum crossed the river at exactly this point, although there are no indications of any remains of the possible Roman bridge. Just beyond the present bridge is the track of the now disused railway which has been turned into a footpath, the Test Way (you can follow it from here nearly 30 miles to the north to Inkpen Beacon; see p.39).

The hamlet has a mill and a pub, the John of Gaunt, where you can get an excellent pub lunch. The pub's name is derived from the fact that it sits on the southern edge of John of Gaunt's Deer Park which runs between King's Somborne and the river. John of Gaunt (1340–99) was the fourth son of Edward III and father of Henry IV. Through his marriage with Blanche of Lancaster he acquired the deer park which was then part of the manor of King's Somborne. Part of the enclosing banks of the park and its yew trees still survive.

HOUGHTON

Map p.148, E3 * *

2 miles NW of King's Somborne off the A3057

An outstanding characteristic of Hampshire villages, and one in which they differ from their neighbours in Surrey and Sussex, is that they tend to develop along roads. They are in fact an early form of 'ribbon development' though, happily, their architecture is usually attractive and interspersed with greenery.

Houghton is an excellent example of this kind of development. As you drive north from Bossington, again and again it seems as though you have finally passed through the village, only for another clump of cottages and houses to tell you that this is not the case. Then, abruptly, the heart of the village appears at its very end. On the right-hand side, by the river, is an inn; opposite it a spur road leads to an enchanting group: the late 13th-century Church of All Saints, with a most beautiful roof of warm red tiles sweeping low down, the elegant 18th-century brick Rectory, the manor house and an open parkland behind handsome wrought iron railings.

On the eastern side of the main road a footpath marked Clarendon Way (see p.38) leads within a few yards to a section of the Test river which the general public is permitted to use. This is an idyllic spot, perfectly suited for young children as the ford beneath the footbridge is barely a foot deep with shingle underfoot. On the far side, a footpath meanders along the river bank through a rich natural garden of wild flowers and water shrubs.

HURSLEY

Map p.143, A4 *

6 miles SW of Winchester on the A3090

All Saints' Church** is an important monument to the early Victorian Anglican revival. (The key is available from the post office opposite.) It was rebuilt in 1847–8, and only the west tower survives of the medieval church. John Keble (after whom Keble College, Oxford is named), vicar of Hursley from 1835–1866, funded the new church from the royalties of his books of hymns and prayers. Of note are the craftsmanship in its furnishings and stained glass, the clerestory dormers and braced collared-rafters in the nave roof, and the monument in the tower to the Cromwell family, headed by Richard, who briefly succeeded his father Oliver as Lord Protector in 1659. He was buried at Hursley, like Keble, of whom (in the vestry) there is a photograph in the last year of his life.

The churchyard has largely been cleared, although some graves remain, including Keble's and the brick mausoleum of the Heathcotes, 18th-century owners of Hursley Park.

Hursley Park* is set above the linear village. The early 18th-century house, enlarged in the Edwardian period, has in recent years become a main centre for IBM, and the computer firm has built extensively in the Park's grounds, in an idiom resembling a new Oxbridge college.

The rustic bus shelter beside the back drive to Hursley Park sets the tone for the picturesque village, set mainly along the

A3090, with older half-timbered cottages interspersed with Victorian Tudoresque brick cottages.

HURSTBOURNE PRIORS

Map p.149, A2 * *
I mile SW of Whitchurch on the B3400

The village stands at the junction of two of Hampshire's rivers, the Test and the Bourne. (The ballad 'Where the Bright Waters Meet', very popular in Edwardian times, was inspired by this watermeet: its author, Harry Plunket Green, is buried in the churchyard). The Roman road, the Portway, runs to the north of the parish but even this is a newcomer compared with its neighbour, the Harrow Way which, running from Kent down through Hampshire to the Salisbury Plain, was in use at least 4000 years ago. Hurstbourne Priors is therefore in an area of great antiquity, its first (Saxon) church having been consecrated in the year 802. In the manner usual in Hampshire, the village developed along a road, its centre being marked by a crossroads and a comfortable inn and, unusually for Hampshire, a large green used as a playing field. Hurstbourne Park, to the north of the village, was the seat of the earls of Portsmouth. Its Victorian mansion was demolished in 1965 but there remains a statue of a Roman emperor on the drive to Whitchurch and the so-called Andover Lodge.

Church of St Andrew.★★ This is well outside the main body of the village, its creeper-covered tower just visible in a protective belt of trees. A handsome avenue lined with lime trees leads to the West Tower, built in a pseudo-Norman style in the 19th century but with a genuine Norman door. The North Chapel is Elizabethan. The most striking feature of the church is the splendid Oxenbridge Altar Tomb, built in 1574. Buried in it are Sir Robert Oxenbridge, at one time Constable of the Tower of London, and his wife. Their three sons and four daughters are shown in profile on both sides of the tomb. It has recently been restored with the original colour scheme carefully refurbished. On the south side of the church is an immense yew tree believed to be between 700 and 800 years old and on the east side, between the church and the river, a 250-year-old horse chestnut which is claimed to be the second largest of its kind in England.

HURSTBOURNE TARRANT

Map p.154, D1 * *
5 miles N of Andover on the A343

William Cobbett, writing his *Rural Rides* for 1821, thought Hurstbourne Tarrant was one of the finest places he knew. His description of its 'very nice country' still holds good: 'To stand upon any of the hills and look around you, you almost think you see the ups and downs of sea in a heavy swell… The undulations are endless, and the great variety in the… little hills has a very delightful effect.'

Cobbett used to stay at **Rookery Farm**, close to the crossroads at the foot of the steep hill leading down into the village. It is but one of the many handsome buildings in Hurstbourne Tarrant; the finest is **Parsonage Farm**, alongside the parish church. Its brick gate-piers are dated 1685 and a thick yew hedge opens onto the house's grand brick front, while thatched timber barns and outbuildings surround the huge yard beside it.

The bourne which gives the village its name is an often dry river, with little bridges crossing it from the main road to timbered and thatched cottages. The steep-sided river valley defines the lines of the main street.

St Peter's Church★★ is a low, spreading building in flint, with a weatherboarded bell-turret topped by a spire. The main body of the church dates from the late 12th and early 13th centuries, with the carved Norman south door its grandest feature. The most notable element inside is the amount of surviving wall painting, with medieval work like the Three Kings and Three Dead Men, which had been overpainted after the Reformation with scriptural texts.

IBTHORPE

Map p.153, D4 * *
6 miles N of Andover off the A343

Like its near neighbour, Hurstbourne Tarrant, Ibthorpe is one of Hampshire's prettiest villages. It lies further up the Bourne valley, contained by rough steep slopes beside the river which usually flows only in winter and spring. Larger houses are to be found among the timber, plaster, flint, brick and thatch of the cottages and smaller farms. The impressive Georgian Ibthorpe House, built in chequered brick, is the largest; Jane Austen stayed there quite frequently, attending services in Hurstbourne Tarrant.

ITCHEN STOKE

Map p.150, E2
1 mile W of New Alresford off the B3047

St Mary's Church.★★ If there is such a thing as a mini-cathedral St.Mary's (1866) is it, tall and narrow in the French style and complete with a rose window, blind arcading and a painted wooden ceiling. Alas, the last regular service held here was in 1971 and it is now in the care of the Redundant Churches Fund, an ironic comment on the generosity of the munificent incumbent, the Revd Charles Conybeare, who stumped up no less than £7000 and entrusted the task of construction to his brother, H. Conybeare, apparently exhorting him not to cut any corners. Conybeare H. accordingly set to with a will. The font, of enamel, gilt bronze and black Californian marble, was inspired by the colour-scheme of a tomb in Bourges; the apse floor 'maze' was modelled on that of Chartres; the pulpit and bench-ends were inset with cast-iron ends; a profusion of rich carving was installed; the walls were prodigally diapered and the windows enriched with stained glass still dazzling in its brilliance. Alas, this riot of aesthetic self-indulgence was overshadowed by personal tragedy – the death of the architect's ten-year-old daughter. Inscribed around the font is an echo of the resultant parental anguish:

Oh! for the touch of a vanished hand
And the sound of a voice that is still.

KIMPTON

Map p.148, A1 *
4 miles W of Andover off the A342

Tucked away in a tangle of narrow lanes, the hamlet of Kimpton dreams on, seemingly untouched by time. Church and manor house share sovereignty over the village, companionably side by side. The manor, surrounded by the cob wall characteristic of this part of the country, seems a self-contained community in its own right.

St Peter and St Paul's Church.★ The church tower is dated 1837 but the main body is 13th–14th century. Inside is a 17th-century wall-monument decorated with a remarkable grim death's head.

KING'S SOMBORNE

Map p.148, F4 * *
8 miles W of Winchester on the A3057

At the heart of the village is a grim reminder of the problem which is increasingly facing much of Britain: water shortage. Until 1990 the pretty little stream called the Som added a gracenote to the village, flowing through like a sparkling thread. Today it is simply a grassy track with only the footbridges to indicate that here was once one of the Test Valley's many streams.

King's Somborne has two focal points: one around what was the stream, and the other a broad, handsome open space with a war memorial in front of the church. With an inn on one side, the church on the other and ancient houses around it, this could be the equivalent of the French *place* or Italian *piazza*, a place where the villagers could naturally gather. Unfortunately it is marred by the heavy traffic pounding through on

The Grange, Northington.

the A3057, the price King's Somborne pays for being an important road junction. (The Roman road from Winchester to Old Sarum runs just south of the village: see HORSEBRIDGE). In the field behind the church a number of enigmatic bumps and hollows in the turf indicate the remains of some large stone building. It is possible that this formed part of a royal palace of the Saxon kings which gave the adjective to the village's name.

Church of St Peter and St Paul.** In the chancel of the church is one of Hampshire's oldest monuments, that of a priest, William Bristowe who was vicar from 1305 until his death in 1327. The head is missing. Curiously, it does not seem to have been hacked off in deliberate mutilation but removed with almost surgical precision. On the chancel floor are brasses, dated around 1380, which are believed to represent two of John of Gaunt's stewards. (He was the fourth son of Edward III and acquired the manor of King's Somborne on his marriage to Blanche of Lancaster). The church was substantially 'restored' in 1886, the then vicar remarking that 'The Norman pillars go down like a pack of cards'. Despite this cavalier treatment the church is still full of atmosphere.

KINGSCLERE

Map p.155, C1 *

8 miles NW of Basingstoke on the A339

Showing many signs of having once been a more important place than it is today, Kingsclere sits in the wooded valley beneath the great chalk downland. Swan Street, running south from the parish church and the former market place, is the best-preserved of the older parts of the village. It is lined with many Georgian brick houses and cottages, with the broad brick frontage of the Swan Hotel half-way along. Elsewhere in Kingsclere there is further evidence of its well-to-do past as a market and coaching town, especially grander Georgian porches on houses. Even the almshouses have four-square porches set on classical columns. The main road twists around the complex of brick buildings of the former mill, maltings and brewery by the river, remnants of another former trade.

St Mary's Church* is a substantial building at the heart of Kingsclere, a large Norman flint structure with a squat crossing tower which was effectively rebuilt in the late 1840s. Some parts, like the tiny high nave windows and the north doorway, are Norman, and many fine monuments inside were preserved, but most of the building was renewed with a heavy hand.

KNIGHT'S ENHAM

Map p.148, A4

3 miles N of Andover off the A343

Knight's Enham is probably only a fragment of the size it once was: a church, the substantial Manor Farm and the Georgian rectory almost make up the whole settlement. It is a quiet, tree-shaded enclave.

St Michael's Church* is a charmingly muddled building set within a quiet churchyard filled with fine Georgian and Victorian tombs. Its simply furnished and whitewashed interior has an unusual rood screen, with a single main opening beneath a moulded beam, and three arched openings above that. The neatly painted royal arms above add a final flourish.

Enham Alamein* to the north was established as a centre for ex-servicement after World War I, and got its unusual name to mark the battle of World War II.

LASHAM

Map p.151, B1 *

4 miles NW of Alton off the A339

On the face of it, Lasham is a typical English village with a church, a pub, and ducks on the village pond. Time might well have stood still for a couple of centuries. But all is not quite what it seems, because half a mile away from the village centre is a former wartime airfield where modern passenger jets are serviced. The site is also used by the world-renowned National Gliding Centre. To avoid too much disturbance, jet movements are strictly limited.

Church Farm, which dates from the 17th century, is the site of a minor revolution. The farmhouse and farm buildings have been converted into modern homes but the exterior appearance has been virtually unaltered.

On the outskirts of the village can be found the old station buildings which were part of the Basingstoke and Alton Light Railway. Close to the station there was a dramatic crash when a passenger train collided with a steam lorry on a level crossing. No one was hurt– it was a stunt for a film called *The Wrecker*.

LAVERSTOKE

Map p.154, F4 *

2 miles E of Whitchurch off the B3400

From the 1720s to 1950 Laverstoke was noted for the manufacture of water-marked paper for the Bank of England's notes. The industry was started by Henri de Portal, a Huguenot refugee who, as a child, is said to have escaped massacre by hiding in an oven when Louis XIV's troops ransacked his Toulouse home. The Georgian red-brick Mill House survives and the Portal name is still omnipresent.

Laverstoke House was built by Joseph Bonomi (1796/8) for Harry Portal, and the **Parsonage** by G. E. Street (1858) for Melville Portal. Both win the approval of Professor Pevsner. The thatched almshouses built in 1939 for the then current Portal must bear his scorn. Portal, however, redeemed himself by going on to win the Battle of Britain.

The **Church of St Mary** by J. L. Pearson (1896) has an unusual reredos copied from a medieval painting. The tiny **Church of St. Nicholas,** shared with the adjoining village of Freefolk, has a monument to twice-married Sir Richard Powlett, surmounted by his helm (1614). (The key is held at nearby Batts Cottage.)

LECKFORD

Map p.148, D4 * *

2 miles NE of Stockbridge on the A3057

Early in the 19th century the two clubs which controlled the fishing in (and, hence, much of the access to) the River Test were formed. One was the Leckford Club, the other the Houghton (See STOCKBRIDGE). Fishing on the Test has always been a rich man's hobby and access to its most attractive areas north of Stockbridge (attractive both for angler and walker) is strictly controlled by the Leckford Estate. A source of irritation to the ordinary non-fisherman, it must be admitted that the Estate keeps one of the finest of England's trout streams in good heart.

The village and its neighbour Longstock form a delightful pair, one on each side of the river. A main road, the A3057, divides Leckford, but it is still compact with houses of thatch and plaster set in gardens all along the High St.

Church of St Nicholas.* This 13th-century church is built of much-repaired flint, one of Hampshire's characteristic building materials. Inside is an 11th-century font.

LEE-ON-THE-SOLENT

Map p.138, D1 *

4 miles S of Fareham on the B3385

A new chapter in the history of Lee-on-the-Solent is about to be written with the closure of the large HMS Daedalus Fleet Air Arm airfield as part of the defence cuts. As well as providing a certain amount of local prosperity, the airfield has also ensured an open space, albeit slightly artificial, between Lee-on-the-Solent and neighbouring Fareham and Gosport. The future of the land is causing some concern to many who fear that it could be developed with housing or industry.

Lee has had mixed fortunes over the last century, never quite becoming the important seaside resort which was envisaged when watering places were becoming popular during Victorian times. Development began in 1894 when a three-mile railway branch line was built from Fort Brockhurst, near Gosport, and a 750ft pier was opened four years later.

But just as the resort was getting established in 1935, with the addition of a tall viewing tower and a heated salt water swimming pool, the railway closed down. With the depression of the pre-war years and then the war itself the odds became stacked against Lee. During the war part of the pier was blown up as a precaution against enemy invasion and has never been rebuilt. The pier and the tower with its accompanying complex, which included a cinema, have now been demolished.

The Fleet Air Arm base brought most recognition to Lee, particularly through its evaluation of hovercraft for military purposes; during the 1960s and 1970s the activity attracted many sightseers. The base is also home of the Coastguard search and rescue helicopter and that will remain when the Navy moves out.

LIPHOOK

Map p.152, E2 *

8 miles NE of Petersfield on the A3

Six roads converge on the Square at Liphook, but it is to one, the A3 from London to Portsmouth, that the village chiefly owes its existence. This has been an important route for centuries and in the days of the mail coach Liphook became a significant resting place for weary travellers. Samuel Pepys recorded in his diaries: 'So by coach to Lippock. Here good honest people; and after supper, to bed.'

Just south of the village centre along the A3 is Bohunt Manor (see p.18), whose fine gardens are open to the public.

The **Royal Anchor Hotel,** which dominates The Square, was used by most travellers. Notable guests included George III, Admiral Lord Nelson and the Duke of Wellington, who were grateful for good food, ale and a comfortable bed. But for some, the convicts being marched to Portsmouth before being transported to Australia, the night would be spent chained up in the cellars with a bed of straw if they were lucky.

The **Hollycombe Steam and Garden Collection** at Midhurst Road is a unique mixture of steam-powered paraphernalia ranging from large and small railway engines to a magnificent carousel.

Hollycombe Steam and Garden Collection: *Apr–Oct, Sun and BHs 1–6pm. Tel: (0420) 474740.*

LONG SUTTON

Map p.151, A3 *

5 miles N of Alton off the B3349

The Harrow Way, one of the oldest roads in the country, runs through Long Sutton. Times have changed, for it is now very much off the beaten track, although that is undoubtedly the reason why it retains its rural charm.

Lord Wandsworth College was originally founded to educate the orphan sons of agricultural workers but it has since become a public school with around 400 pupils. It is believed that the gates to the 1200-acre college estate are based on the design of memorial gates in Belgium which commemorate men and women who died in World War I.

All Saints' Church dates from the 13th century and was extensively restored in 1961. Nearby is the village pond, home to a variety of waterfowl, where two seats have been placed in memory of Madge Stratton who was lady of the manor for many years.

The **Four Horseshoes**, situated on the road to Well, is a pleasant stop and affords fine views over to Basingstoke where the high rise buildings are a comparatively recent addition to the landscape.

LONGPARISH

Map p.149, B2 * *
3 miles SW of Whitchurch on the B3048

There can be no doubt as to how this village got its name, for it ambles along for over a mile in length. As you approach it from the north, the road takes a dog-leg round the grounds of Longparish House, a textbook example of the fact that 'the rolling English road' was not made by the 'rolling English drunkard', as G.K.Chesterton claimed, or even by topography, but more prosaically by property rights. Nevertheless, a footpath runs through the grounds of the elegant 18th-century mansion.

It seems that every house, every cottage in Longparish is a jewel, thatched with whitewashed plaster walls, or elegant in 18th-century brick, each with its flower-bright garden. The River Test runs a few yards to the west, but apart from a stream which penetrates to the centre of the village one is not aware of the river's proximity. The long-distance footpath known as the Test Way (see p.39) actually passes through the pub garden and then through the churchyard.

Church of St Nicholas.** At the end of the village the road takes another dog-leg around the church. Built in the early 13th century, it escaped the heavy hand of the Victorian restorer; a major restoration took place in 1956 when work was limited to making good. The east window is by Burne-Jones. The remains of the village stocks can be seen by the lych gate.

LONGSTOCK

Map p.148, D3 * *
2 miles N of Stockbridge off the A3057

The village lives in intimate association with the River Test, watermeadows stretching from eastward of its high street to the river itself. Unlike Leckford, its neighbour across the river, the road that passes through it is still a country road, ambling north to Goodworth Clatford and south to Stockbridge, so the pretty little village is still a peaceful place.

The **Church of St Mary**, high on its elevated churchyard, looms over the narrow street. The church was entirely rebuilt in 1880 with only a handful of artefacts preserved in piety from the old church: some odds and ends of sculpture, a 14th-century font.

Where a small lane darts off to the east to cross the watermeadows and join up with the A3057 is an attractive inn. Not far from the inn, towards the Test and alongside an arm of it, is a series of earthworks which, modest in appearance, have a unique history so far inland. They form the remains of a dock built by the Danes for their flat-bottomed long-ships. The whole structure is 130yds long and 30yds wide, separated from the river proper by the bank of earth excavated during the construction of the dock, and was very possibly destined for the fleet of Canute himself. By the side of the church a rough footpath climbs steeply to another great earthworks, Danebury Ring (see p.35), associated by name at least with the same marauding seamen.

LYMINGTON

Map p.136, E2 * *
12 miles SW of Southampton on the A337

Lymington, situated on the short broad stretch of the Lymington River as it enters the wide waters of the Solent, is known throughout the sailing world as a great centre for boating and boat-building. Much of the little town has a raffish nautical air. It was founded in 1200 as a harbour, since it provided the shortest crossing to the Isle of Wight. The Lymington-Yarmouth ferry runs still.

The **High Street*** is the spine of the town, climbing steeply from the buildings on the river's edge towards the parish church on top of the hill. Only half-way up does the church, with its jaunty white cupola on the old stone tower, come into view. The broad High St is lined with a variety of shops and houses, a great many of them 18th-century, and the street is filled with market stalls on Saturdays.

St Thomas' Church* has, despite its medieval fabric, an 18th-century air, with plasterwork ceilings and galleries on three sides, carried on Tuscan columns. Even at the east end, where the medieval work is more apparent, gilded putti look down from the coved ceiling above. The churchyard is criss-crossed with paths, and is clearly a popular thoroughfare. St Thomas' St continues the line of the High St past the church, but it is more domestic in scale.

Monmouth House*, a grand red-brick late 17th-century house (now a nursing home), stands on the corner of Church St which runs at right angles from the top of High St. Some 18th-century cottages and grander houses with doorcases run down the left-hand side, and two of the gardens have crinkle-crankle, or serpentine, walls. A number of these gardens, like that at **South End House*** (a 'philosopher's garden') are open occasionally for charity.

Quay Hill* at the bottom of High St exemplifies the town's maritime atmosphere. Boats from the public slipway offer trips into the Solent, and houses with porthole windows abound. The river continues past boatyards and sailmakers and the open-air sea water swimming baths (in existence since 1833) on the way downstream. The club-houses of the Royal Lymington Yacht Club, the homelier Lymington Town Sailing Club, and the yacht havens and marina, mark the point where the town ends and the sailing begins.

LYNDHURST

Map p.136, B1 * *
8 miles SW of Southampton on the A35

Lyndhurst was originally, and remains, the only settlement of any size within the New Forest. William the Conqueror made it the administrative centre when he created the forest in 1079. The narrow streets, organized into a complicated one-way system, can be a traffic bottleneck at holiday times.

St Michael's Church** stands above the town on a high mound. It was rebuilt, to designs by William White, in the period 1858–70. What distinguishes it is the polychrome brickwork, the crowning spire, the unusual, almost wilful, window patterns, and the interior paintings and stained glass. The best windows, at the east end, are by Burne-Jones, and the reredos mural of the Wise and Foolish Virgins was painted by Frederick, Lord Leighton. Mrs Hargreaves, the original Alice in Lewis Carroll's books, is buried on the south side, and there are many Hargreaves memorials inside the church.

The **Queen's House and Verderers' Court**** to the west of the church has been the administrative centre for the forest since the 13th century. The oldest part is the 17th-century Verderers' Courtroom, open only when in session some six Mondays a year. The court polices the foresters' rights and adjudicates on disputes. The Forestry Commission, which now controls much of the forest, is based in the adjacent large grey Queen's House, dating back to 1700 though much restored.

The **New Forest Visitor Centre*** is housed in a new purpose-built block beside the town's main public car park. It provides a good introduction to the forest, its history and its peculiar ways, in a series of tape-slide displays and models, as well as a shop and tourist information desk.

The overriding impression of Lyndhurst is late Victorian and Edwardian, since so much reconstruction took place when the New Forest became a fashionable resort. Most prominent is the exuberantly tile-hung and half-timbered Crown Hotel opposite the church. Lyndhurst is filled with gift shops.

The forest landscape begins immediately outside the town, with little greens grazed by ponies, and then the trees. Many of the earliest inclosures, begun in the 17th century to encourage the growing of timber for shipbuilding, are to be found near Lyndhurst.

The **Knightwood Oak*** is probably the oldest tree in the forest. It stands at the end of the

The salt marshes near Lower Pennington, looking across to the Isle of Wight.

Bolderwood Ornamental Drive, a 19th-century carriage drive planted with specimen trees, close to the main A35 Lyndhurst–Brockenhurst road. This great oak was probably an acorn in 1600, and was pollarded before that practice was stopped in the later 17th century, so it has many main trunks. The Queen planted new oaks around it in 1979. ***New Forest Visitor Centre:*** *Daily 10am–6pm. Tel: (0703) 282269 or 283914.*

MARTIN

Map p.140, C4 * *
5 miles NW of Fordingbridge off the B3078

Much has changed for this downland parish in the furthest corner of the county, where Hampshire meets Wiltshire and Dorset, since the celebrated naturalist W. H. Hudson wrote *A Shepherd's Life* (1910). 'I cannot think that any person for whom it had no association, no secret interest, would, after looking at this village with its dried-up winterbourne, care to make his home in it... [or] wants to see it...' Hudson himself brought fame to Martin, since it was the home of the shepherd around whose stories he wove his famous book, while restoration and prosperity have transformed its variety of brick, tile and thatch cottages and farmhouses lining the single main street into desirable homes. The winterbourne, the chalk-country stream, still dries up, and sheep continue to graze the green sweep of Martin Down (see p.) as well as the grass of the churchyard.

All Saints' Church*, with its 15th-century tower and spire, set back from the main street, sits behind a huge, ancient apple tree. The Victorians laid a heavy hand upon the church, but there is evidence still in its fabric and furnishings of almost every century since the 11th.

MATTINGLEY

Map p.156, C3 *
9 miles NE of Basingstoke on the B3349

Mattingley is a small, scattered village set among the leafy lanes of North Hampshire. The best known feature is the unusual church which 600 years ago was converted from a barn to a chapel-of-ease of St Michael's church at neighbouring Heckfield. That would account for its rather unusual construction consisting of a timber frame infilled with herringbone brickwork.

The bus shelter on the main A33 road doubles as a war memorial and consequently is rather more elaborate than most. It includes delicate wrought iron work and the names of those who perished in the defence of their country are recorded on a carved wooden plaque.

Mattingley Green and **Hound Green** are the area's two commons, but commoning rights have long since lapsed, and without cattle to graze they are now overgrown. Industrial archaeologists would recognize traces of old brick workings, though they are mostly overgrown and go unnoticed except to a trained eye.

MEONSTOKE

Map p.145, C1 * *
9 miles N of Fareham on the A32

Meonstoke is a pleasant village with a striking Georgian high street, set in the valley of the River Meon. The ducks which waddle across the road from the river for their titbits from customers sitting in the gardens of the Bucks Head pub present an idyllic scene. And hand in hand with this tranquil way of life is a thriving community. Children at the village school have recently celebrated its 150th anniversary, paying tribute to its founder, Charles Hume, a former rector who is buried in the churchyard.

St Andrew's Church looks out across splendidly kept lawns and gardens. In 1830 the dedication was changed to St Andrew from St Mary, but the reason seems to have been forgotten with time. Two stone coffins near the altar rails are interesting. They are probably 14th-century and are believed to have originally been buried in the chancel, having been lifted when the floor was retiled in the 19th century.

MICHELDEVER

Map p.150, C1 *
6 miles NE of Winchester off the A33

Micheldever Station, opened as Andover Road in 1840, is a very early example of railway architecture and was designed by William Tite, who also rebuilt the Royal Exchange in London. Its iron-columned canopy gives it the look of a Victorian vicarage surprised wearing a crinoline at half-mast.

The sprawling village, some two miles to the south, contains some very fine white-washed half-timbered cottages and an imposing Victorian primary school with a splendid clock-tower.

St. Mary's Church, while retaining its early Tudor tower and gargoyles, bears the unmistakable imprint of another London architect, George Dance the Younger who, between 1808 and 1810, replaced its nave with an uncompromising brick octagon. The London theme continues within where there is a group of three related monuments to members of the Baring banking dynasty, by Flaxman, no less. As befits descendants of a Protestant pastor and pillars of City rectitude they illustrate themes from the Lord's Prayer – Thy Will be Done; Thy Kingdom Come; and Deliver us from Evil. In the churchyard lies the grave of Henri de Massu de Ruvigny who, having served as aide-de-camp to the formidable Turenne, was hounded from his native France for the sake of his Protestant faith and so came to serve England for a quarter of a century, losing an arm and an eye in exchange for the title Earl of Galway. In an unmarked grave lies a teenage ploughboy hanged during the agrarian riots of 1831 for allegedly daring to strike a Baring.

MIDDLE WALLOP

Map p.148, D2 * *
7 miles SW of Andover on the A343

This is one of the three closely related villages which owe their odd name to the little Wallop brook (the other two are Over Wallop and NETHER WALLOP). Middle Wallop lies on the main A343 road to Andover and so lacks the tranquility of its two neighbours but still has some interesting vernacular architecture. Just outside the village is Middle Wallop airfield whose fighter aircraft played a vital part in the defence of Britain during World War II, particularly during the so-called Battle of Britain in 1940. It is still a highly active military airfield. A little further along the road towards Andover is the **Museum of Army Flying**, open to the public with its displays of historic aircraft.

Over Wallop is virtually a continuation of Middle Wallop, running to the north, but most of it is situated around a network of small lanes. It is therefore relatively traffic free and the visitor can enjoy its changing vistas with less fear of being mown down.
Museum of Army Flying: *All year, daily 10am–4.30pm. Admission charge. Tel: (0264) 384421.*

MILFORD ON SEA

Map p.135, E3 *
4 miles SW of Lymington on the B3058

As a seaside resort, Milford developed from the late 1880s onwards, under the auspices of Major Cornwallis West, and it is that aspect of the town's history which is most striking today. Large Victorian and Edwardian villas set within gardens are Milford's hallmarks, and it continues to breathe an air of gentility in its narrow shopping street and the little park with a stream at the centre. New flats have begun to sprout, especially on the outskirts, and some of the older houses have been demolished to make way for them, while older hotels stand empty. Milford, however, had an earlier importance, the best evidence of which is provided by the parish church.

All Saints' Church**, down a lane on the hill which leads into Milford, is a particularly complete example of a 13th-century church, with fragments of the Norman building which preceded it.

The proud rebuilding took place when Milford flourished with the sea salt industry which operated along this stretch of coast. The curious lean-tos on either side of the west tower accommodated the priests from Christchurch Priory who came over to serve the church, and there are fragments of medieval carving preserved which show how fine a display the church could then put on. The ceilings, especially that at the crossing with its curiously carved boss, date from the mid-17th century.

MINSTEAD

Map p.142, E3 * *
9 miles W of Southampton off the A31

A knot of narrow wooded lanes and sharp inclines south of the busy A31, Minstead is a dispersed parish with small clusters of houses, many of them thatched and weatherboarded. Pasture and woodland alternate, and horse-riding is popular. The village centre has two main features – the church and the pub.

All Saints' Church** is one of the hidden treasures of the county. A lane leads up to the lych-gate, complete with a coffin rest, beyond which lies the well-kept graveyard and the unusual huddle of brick and stone walls of the church. The many gables and dormers give the church an oddly domestic air, offset by the Georgian brick tower. The interior of the nave is stuffed with galleries, one upon another, fitting closely under the moulded contours of the roof. The large south transept is filled with cut-down box pews, one of which is made extra comfortable with plush cushions. Off the chancel, there are two more gentry pews, one with a fireplace. The church also retains its three-decker pulpit, by the chancel arch, with a 13th-century font (dug up in the rectory garden) in front of it.

Sir Arthur Conan Doyle (1869–1930) is buried under a large cross in the churchyard, which also boasts one of the fine ancient yew trees common in Hampshire.

The village pub beside the main road is almost as worthy of note: called **The Trusted Servant***, the inn has a sign depicting a hybrid animal – part pig, part ass, part domestic – which is based on a 16th-century painting at Winchester College.

MONK SHERBORNE

Map p.155, C3 *
3 miles NE of Basingstoke off the A340

Monk Sherborne gets its name from a combination of features, one natural and one man-made. Sherborne means a clear, bright stream and Monk comes from the old Benedictine Pamber Priory which was founded nearby in the 12th century. All that remains of the priory today is the chancel with its massive tower.

The **Church of All Saints** dates from around the same time. Inside there is a brass tablet in memory of Thomas Simpson who, in 1674, left £15 a year to the poor of the six adjoining parishes 'so long as the world shall endure'.

The location called Court Corner perpetuates the old Court Leet which met in the open air; the proceedings were recorded on a piece of wood called a tally.

While all the village shops have long since succumbed to competition from supermarkets in Basingstoke, the pub called **The Mole** provides welcome sustenance. Spring is a spectacular time to visit Monk Sherborne because large fields have been given over to the growing of bulbs.

MONXTON

Map p.148, B2 * *
2 miles SW of Andover off the A303

For reasons best known to themselves the postal authorities have changed the spelling of this village's name by spelling it with an 'X' instead of a 'K', a fact which not only irritates the locals but disguises the origin of the village. The original spelling of the name means 'monks's farm'. It is almost overwhelmingly picturesque with its meticulously thatched and whitened cottages, most with roses round the door, set at odd angles to each other so that the village has a comfortable, intimate look. Behind the public appearance is a lot of private hard work and expense. The ridge of a thatched roof has to be renewed every ten years and the entire roof every twenty years or so, an expensive operation.

The village has a charming little green with a stream running through it. Beyond, almost entirely hidden in a copse, is the Church of St Mary, built in 1854 by the ubiquitous Henry Woodyer.

MOTTISFONT

Map p.143, A1 *

11 miles NW of Southampton on the B3084

Even the telephone box is painted a discreet grey in this well-kept village, most of which is owned by the National Trust as part of the estate of Mottisfont Abbey (see p.14). The village takes its name from the 'moot font', the spring where the Anglo-Saxon moot or meeting took place. The spring wells up in the grounds of the abbey, ten feet deep and never known to have dried up. The gardens of the village post office are popular, serving teas for parched visitors.

St Andrew's Church* stands beside the narrow road. Recently restored, its main fabric is 12th-century, consisting of a simple nave and chancel with a square, pyramid-roofed slate-hung belfry over the west porch. The windows are of varying shapes and sizes, and those beyond the Norman chancel arch contain 15th-century stained glass.

NETHER WALLOP

Map p.148, D2 * *

8 miles SW of Andover off the A343

Nether Wallop is one of the most beautiful but also one of the strangest villages in a county which does not lack strange and beautiful villages. It comes as little surprise to learn that it has a well authenticated, if somewhat pointless, ghost story from the 18th century, with a ghost known to have rattled the latch of a cottage door under observation. The mile or so which separates the village from its neighbour, MIDDLE WALLOP, also separates it from the main road so that the village is tranquil. It is perhaps best to drive straight through it to the churchyard and, resisting the temptation to go into the church at this stage, climb the steep hill behind it. From there you can get an overall picture of the village as it lies in the shallow Wallop valley, its many houses buried among the trees and bushes.

The village falls into two halves, separated by the brook. A little bridge takes you over this to the western part, past a watermeadow which doubles as the village green. This is the more social area, with the inn and a shop and narrow lanes winding between the cottages. Although it is only a matter of a hundred yards or so to the church area, the rich vegetation gives this area an enclosed, detached feeling. On the eastern side of the brook a narrow lane will take you up to Chattis Hill with its tumuli and view of Danebury (see p.35).

Church of St Andrew.** This is one of the most puzzling of ancient churches. Almost every century for the past 700 years has left its mark upon it, successive builders not bothering to harmonize their work with that of their predecessors, so that the church is virtually a sampler of architectural styles. Over the chancel arch, for instance, a Saxon wall-painting has been almost destroyed where the Normans widened the arch simply by hacking away the work of their predecessors. In the 1930s a remarkable series of wall paintings was uncovered, including one of St George in armour fighting the Dragon, an unusual representation in a church. It has been suggested that it is a representation of one of the miracle plays which took place in the village in the 14th century. In the churchyard is yet another oddity: a tomb in the form of a pyramid with stone flames emerging from the apex. The inscription today is unreadable but records show that it commemorates an 18th-century 'Doctor of Physick', Francis Douce, who died in 1760.

NETLEY

Map p.137, B2
4 miles SE of Southampton off the A3026

Cistercian monks from Beaulieu founded an abbey at Netley in 1239, but that was laid in ruins at the Dissolution; nothing else much happened here until the middle of the 19th century, when the Royal Victoria Hospital was built. This was a massive building, campaigned for by Florence Nightingale after the Crimean War had demonstrated the inadequacies of military hospitals. It had its own pier on the edge of Southampton Water so that casualties could be landed by ship, and a specially built branch railway ran to the centre of the complex. It could accommodate 1400 patients in its 138 wards. The hospital closed in 1955 and was demolished in 1966, following a fire. Only the chapel and the former officers' mess, used as a police training establishment, still remain. The grounds have become a country park.

Netley itself grew up in Victorian times around the hospital, although in recent years much residential building has taken place.

NEW ALRESFORD

Map p.150, E3
5 miles E of Winchester on the A31

Like adjoining Old Alresford, this bustling town predates the Norman Conquest although it was substantially redeveloped around 1200 by Godfrey de Lucy, bishop of Winchester, to become one of the ten greatest wool-markets in England. The project included a dam which was one of the largest feats of civil engineering attempted in the Middle Ages; it simultaneously improved the navigation on the River Itchen and created a 200-acre reservoir, now shrunk to some 30 acres. Tree-lined Broad Street still deserves its name and leads down to a 14th-century bridge. Neville Chamberlain used to stay at a nearby house when he came here for fishing holidays.

Frequent fires brought repeated devastation, most recently in 1689, so the best older buildings date from the 18th century, with good examples at no. 5 East St., no. 9 West St. and beside the Methodist church of 1825.

The Church of St John the Baptist incorporates a tower dating from the 14th and 17th centuries with a small Saxon crucifix, but is substantially the work of Blomfield (1898).

Mary Russell Mitford, born at no. 27 Broad St, won a £20,000 lottery at the age of ten and was obliged to watch her doctor father squander the lot. She restored the family fortunes and achieved literary success with her account of 'Our Village' (1824–32), although the village in question was Three Mile Cross, near Reading.

Watercress Line.** The Mid-Hants Railway, also known as 'the Watercress Line' in deference to a local speciality, runs ten miles to ALTON. Opened in 1863, closed in 1973, it is now manned by volunteers at weekends from March to October.

Old Alresford lies just over the River Alre. Its handsome **Church of St Mary** is built of brick and flint and dates from 1753. It houses numerous memorials, including an extravagant confection in pink, white and black marble to the memory of Mrs. Rodney, the great admiral's first wife. There is also a memorial plaque to Mary Sumner, wife of a former rector who established the first ever branch of the Mothers' Union here in 1875. The churchyard has a modern sundial and commands a fine view.

Watercress Line: *Easter–Oct, Sat and BHs; mid June–mid July also Mon–Fri; mid July–Aug, daily; Jan–Easter, Sun only. Trips approximately ½-hourly. Tel: (0962) 733810.*

THE NEW FOREST

Map p.134, A4, to p.137, C1 * * *
Bounded by Woodgreen, West Wellow, Blackfield and Ringwood

Visitors to the New Forest are often surprised to find that it is not dense woodland. Some 30,000 acres, or about a third of the forest, is covered with trees. As much again is open heathland, grass and bog, and almost as much is now in private hands as farms and gardens. However, the New Forest is still a forest in the technical sense, as a royal preserve, and it is perhaps the most enduring legacy of the Norman Conquest .

'Preserve' is the key word: the forest has been managed ever since its foundation in 1079. William the Conqueror's royal hunting ground covered the entire south-western corner of Hampshire. Draconian forest laws prevented the inhabitants from hunting, on pain of death, so as to preserve the deer for the king's sport. In return. the commoners were given extensive rights: of turbary (cutting turf), pannage (feeding their pigs on the acorns in autumn), and grazing. These rights are still jealously preserved by those with commoners' rights, and the legacy can be seen in the numbers of ponies and cattle which roam freely.

By the later Middle Ages the forest was seen more as an important asset for timber, and the process of 'inclosure' began, to manage woodland in demarcated areas. Timber was originally important for house-building, later for ship-building. The dockyards at Portsmouth and the slipways at Bucklers Hard are built of New Forest oak. James II (1633–1701) was the last monarch to hunt in the forest; in Queen Anne's reign (1702–14) a programme of rolling inclosure was set up to provide timber by felling old areas and planting new ones, which lasted until wooden shipbuilding ceased in the 19th century. The present areas of Ancient and Ornamental Woodland, of which the best-preserved are at Bolderwood near Lyndhurst, are mainly the survivors from that era of management.

In the late 18th century the introduction of evergreens further changed the face of the forest, while enthusiasts for the picturesque like William Gilpin, rector of Boldre and the famous author of *Tours* in search of picturesque landscape, praised the forest's natural beauties. The Deer Removal Act of 1851 was designed to rid the forest of its original *raison d'être*; happily, it was not entirely successful, and the 1877 New Forest Act ensured the permanent preservation of the woodlands. Many had come to see how important an asset the New Forest was, not least as a place of recreation. Settlements like Nomansland and Canada sprang up on the forest edge, and the late 19th century saw the expansion of building, settlement, and visitor numbers which still continues.

The extent of the New Forest is not as great as it was when William the Conqueror established it, and the boundary has been redrawn to exclude the built-up areas on the coast and near Southampton, but there are still 148 square miles, which have been designated both an Area of Outstanding Natural Beauty and a National Nature Reserve. Many visitor amenities provide an introduction to the varied flora and fauna.

Since 1924 the New Forest has been controlled by the Forestry Commission, who tread a delicate line between providing access to the forest and preserving its character. The rights of commoners are preserved by the Court of Verderers, which meets regularly at Lyndhurst, and by the agisters who oversee the 5000 ponies and cattle which graze in the forest. Visitor numbers continue to swell – ten times as many staying overnight in the New Forest in the late 1980s as in the mid-1960s – and access by car is strictly controlled. Visitors are encouraged to walk. Parking and camping are permitted only in designated areas, and a 40mph speed limit is being introduced throughout the Forest.

The New Forest Museum and Visitor Centre, Lyndhurst: *Daily, 10am–6pm. Tel: (0703) 283914 or 282269.*

NEW MILTON

Map p.135, D2 *

5 miles W of Lymington on the B3058

When the railway arrived in the 1880s, Milton mushroomed to become the town it now is, joining its southern neighbour Barton on Sea. Previously, it had been a small forest-edge village, in the part now known as Old Milton around the parish church down a little lane. Apart from the church, New Milton is a post-1900 town, boasting a castellated water tower as one of its central features.

St Mary Magdalene Church* has a mid 17th-century stone west tower, with a nave built in brick in 1831 which was extended to the east in a modest Georgian

style in 1928 and again thirty years later. The plain interior sets off a florid and faintly ridiculous monument to Thomas White, who died in 1720.

The **Sammy Miller Museum★,** to the west of the centre, displays well over a hundred different motorcycles, from the earliest models until the present day, including the trials bikes ridden by the 1920s star after whom the museum is named. ***Sammy Miller Museum:*** *All year, daily 9.30am–4.30pm. Tel: (0425) 619696.*

NORTH STONEHAM PARK

Map p.143, C4 *

4 miles N of Southampton off the M27

Set among Southampton's sprawling satellite towns, North Stoneham Park is a rural bastion, relic of an estate with a proud church which once served an enormous parish.

St Nicholas' Church★★, unusually for Hampshire, is built of dressed ashlar stone, and was built around 1600 in a Gothic style. Its nave and aisles are the same size, giving it a triple-gabled east end, while inside there is a wealth of monuments. The most curious is that to Adriatic oarsmen of the late 15th century who plied the Venetian galleys which traded with Southampton in its medieval heyday; the proudest is to Admiral Hawke, the hero in the 18th-century French wars.

Park Farm, north of the church, is the last vestige of the former Big House, built in 1818. The farm is built in yellow brick, the same material as the late Georgian rectory by the church.

NURSLING

Map p.143, D2 *

4 miles N of Southampton on the A3057

Most people see Nursling from the motorway, since the M27/M271 junction bisects the village. The church spire is clearly visible from the motorway, and there are few places in the village which are free of the sound of traffic. Yet there are little pastures and pretty woods throughout Nursling, and a sense of its former tranquillity by the old mill on the River Test.

St Boniface's Church★ forms part of a group with the Georgian former rectory and a line of cottages. St Boniface set out from here in the 8th century to convert the Germans, so it has an important place in the history of European Christianity. His church is now mainly a 14th-century building, with a fine Jacobean pulpit and tomb monuments inside.

Grove Place★, the Elizabethan brick manor north-east of the church, is now a school, and can only be glimpsed up its drive. In the early 19th century it was a pioneering mental hospital.

ODIHAM

Map p.156, E3 * *

7 miles E of Basingstoke on the A287

The occasional clatter of a Chinook helicopter overhead and the cars parked in the main street are about the only reminders that Odiham is in the 20th century. This historic small town has managed to avoid the widespread development which has overtaken most others in Hampshire.

The helicopters come from the RAF base a mile to the south which provides welcome employment for residents, and revenue for some of its business people.

The RAF has maintained a discreet presence while gradually becoming part of the town's history, a fact emphasized by the Royal Air Force window in the parish church. This was dedicated on Battle of Britain Sunday in 1989 and depicts the golden rays of the sun spreading out from the centre, surrounded by a ring of gold said to be reminiscent of a revolving

Portchester Castle.

Spitfire propeller. Panels in the window depict the various activities of RAF Odiham over the years.

Odiham Castle (see p.36) is some distance from the town on the banks of the canal. All that remain are the ruins of the keep but the setting makes a visit worthwhile.

≋ The **Basingstoke Canal★★**, when it opened in 1794, provided an important trade link for Odiham. The Great Wharf saw shipments of grain, coal, timber and building materials, and in Edwardian times rowing boats were hired out to visiting pleasure-seekers. Commercial traffic ceased shortly after World War I but the canal has been restored for the greater part of its 32-mile length and the first section to be reopened was between Odiham and Winchfield.

John Pinkerton, the barge named after the contractor who built the canal, was launched at Odiham in 1978 and is operated by volunteers taking people for pleasure trips from the Great Wharf. Rowing boats are for hire once more and the Waterwitch pub nearby is a typical canal-side hostelry which enjoys new found trade from enthusiasts and sightseers.

Thanks to a new bypass the High Street, designated a conservation area more than twenty years ago, is free from through traffic. However, this architecturally rich area is marred by the cars parked both sides of the road, despite the provision of car parks nearby.

The Odiham Society, custodians of the town's heritage, have produced a splendid booklet giving detailed descriptions of the High Street buildings.

All Saints' Church, mentioned briefly earlier, dates back to the Domesday Book but the brickwork tower was built in 1649 and the four pinnacles were added in the 19th century. The Bury, the square in front of the church, still has its stocks and whipping post. Opposite is a pub, aptly named The Bell.

The White House and **Orchard House,** built in the 1800s, are roofed with Welsh slates brought by barge on the then newly-built canal.

The **Pest House** was built in 1665 to isolate victims of the Great Plague but it has now been converted to a small museum. The Library occupies part of the 18th-century Bridewell which was a house of correction and forerunner of the police station.

Palace Gate Farm is thought to be built on the site of a former royal mansion where Queen Elizabeth I held Privy Council meetings in 1576 and 1591.

The George Hotel in the High Street was first licensed in 1540 and is one of just a few hostelries now remaining from a total of nearly 30 at one time.

OLD BASING

Map p.156, E1 *

2 miles E of Basingstoke on the A30

Peaceful Old Basing, with thatched cottages lining narrow village streets, has its roots in much bloodier times. Although best known for the siege of Basing House (see p.33) during the Civil War, which ended when Oliver Cromwell personally led his men at the final storming of the stronghold, the village was also the scene of a much earlier conflict. In 871 King Alfred led a battle against the invading Danes at Old Basing.

Despite the proximity to Basingstoke and a certain amount of post-war development, Old Basing is for the most part a well preserved village and has now been designated a conservation area. Even the railway embankment carrying trains from the South Coast to London does not detract too much from the atmosphere.

St Mary's Church is an obvious focal point, as are the two pubs, the Crown, and the Bolton Arms – which takes its name from the times when the village was the seat of the Dukes of Bolton. The church is large by village standards and is a reminder that Old Basing was an important place when neighbouring Basingstoke was little more than a hamlet.

Traces of the old **Basingstoke Canal** can still be seen and adjacent to Basing House there is a well preserved canal bridge. But while the bridge provides access to Basing House, no water runs beneath it. Most of the 32-mile canal has been restored to working order but this section is isolated by the collapsed Greywell tunnel and the M3 motorway, so it can never be restored to full working order. Nevertheless, the village is set on the River Loddon and there are some pleasant riverside walks.

OLD BURGHCLERE

Map p.154, C3
10 miles NW of Basingstoke off the A34

Some two miles south of the present village of Burghclere, the older settlement is dominated by the mass of Beacon Hill (see p.33) on the far side of the fast A34. The main focus is the manor house, its Georgian brick walls encasing a medieval timbered house, and the parish church, which stand together beside the footpath from the road.

All Saints' Church* is a long, low building; its walls demonstrate the decorative uses of flint. The main walls are of unadorned flint, the north transept has coursed stone and flint surrounding a large, early 14th-century window, and the east end is in a flint and stone chequerboard pattern. A weatherboarded bell turret tops the church, and the south and north doorways are both Norman, each with a carved tympanum. Many of the monuments inside are to the Herbert family, owners of nearby Highclere Castle (see p.13).

OVERTON

Map p.155, E1 * *
8 miles W of Basingstoke on the B3400

Overton is a medieval new town, founded in the early 13th century by Bishop Lucy of Winchester, as were New Alresford, the now almost deserted Newtown in the very north of the county, and Downton, Wiltshire. The new towns were founded to provide cash rents for the bishopric, and often had fairs or markets established with them.

Overton's planned origins are to be seen in its small grid of streets, with bridges over the River Test to the old original village on the north bank. The parish church and its neighbour, the grand Court Farm, are to be found there. The broad river plain was the site of the great annual sheep fair which lasted until the early 20th century; now the ducks have the young river to themselves.

St Mary's Church* is the only evidence of the medieval town, although its external appearance is entirely Victorian and Edwardian. The ancient 14th-century doors open into the aisle arcades, which are mainly 12th-century except for the early Tudor western bays and tower arch. In the chancel, 13th-century plate tracery windows remain, with an unusual inscription on one window sill commemorating a medieval rector. An unusual modern commemoration is found in the inner porch: portraits of the Queen and Prince Charles in bank note watermarks. Paper mills on the River Test here and at nearby Whitchurch specialized in making bank note paper, and some production continues.

A number of old watermills stand by the Test and beside the large ponds at Quidhampton, the hamlet just to the north. Overton's oldest survival is also to be found at Quidhampton – a tiny Norman stone chapel which is now an outbuilding in the farmyard on Station Road.

PAMBER

Map p.155, B3 and C3
5 miles N of Basingstoke on the A340

This straggling parish is made up of Pamber Heath, Pamber Green and Pamber End and has grown considerably in recent years, providing homes for people who work at the nearby Atomic Weapons Establishment at Aldermaston.

Pamber Forest was an ancient woodland where King John is reputed to have hunted deer. Although the forest has diminished over the years, nearly five hundred acres owned by the Benyon Trust have now been designated a nature reserve, noted for rare insects and flowers. Butterflies that can be found there include the purple emperor and the white admiral. A policy of coppicing has allowed light to penetrate the leaf cover, encouraging the growth of orchids, anemones and primroses.

Pamber Priory (see also Monk Sherborne) was founded in the 12th century by Henry de Port and its ruins are an interesting feature. In its time it was one of the most important monastic establishments in Hampshire. The name of the pub at Pamber End, the Queen's College Arms, is a reference to the fact that the college was responsible for the administration of the priory.

PENNINGTON

Map p.136, F4
17 miles SW of Southampton on the A337

Pennington is now largely an extension of Lymington. The **salt marshes***, which lie between the A337 and the sea, are the parish's most distinctive feature. Until the late 19th century they were a principal centre of the salt industry. The old salterns, or saltwater pools, still exist in some parts, reached from the leafy narrow lanes by a network of footpaths and used by wading birds and paddling children.

PENTON MEWSEY

Map p.148, A3
3 miles NW of Andover off the A342

Although Andover is very close, Penton Mewsey and its neighbour Penton Grafton are quiet rural settlements of farms and thatched cottages. Some village houses mix Georgian sophistication with rustic details; the mature parkland of Penton Lodge is now the grounds of St Benedict's Convent. The roads running through each village continue into open countryside and narrow twisting lanes bordered by high hedges. Some of the isolated farmsteads are substantial, evidence of good farming country, like the former barn (sensitively converted into a house) with its enormous thatched roof at Pigeon House to the north of the Penton villages.

Holy Trinity Church, Penton Mewsey, is reached along a short, shady track beside the ornate many-gabled Victorian rectory. The church is a Victorian recasing, in flint, of the original medieval fabric which is still to be seen in the chequerboard patterning on the east wall. The interior is dominated by the unusual curved bracing of the timbers in the barrel-vaulted roof, while there is a variety of handsome Georgian tombs in the churchyard, one in the form of a sarcophagus, like two others at nearby Knight's Enham.

PETERSFIELD

Map p.146, B2 * *
16 miles N of Portsmouth on the A3

In recent years the road from London to Portsmouth, which originally brought trade and prosperity to this attractive market town, has been threatening to choke Petersfield to death. But now, with the building of the new A3 bypass, Petersfield is about to enter a new chapter in its long history.

Petersfield was one of the first 'new towns' in the country, having been established in the 12th century when a great many lords founded new settlements to increase the revenue from their lands and in some cases to strengthen their defences. It is likely, however, that work on the church of St Peter which gave the town its name had already been started by then.

In later times Petersfield was one of the centres for the wool industry – the nearby South Downs were ideal for keeping sheep. Leather was another flourishing industry and several tanneries were established.

But it was the increasing importance of Portsmouth and the Royal Navy which put Petersfield on the map. A great many VIPs on their way from London to the South Coast stopped here and hotels, inns and alehouses sprang up to cater for the new business. Charles II is said to have stayed at the Old White Hart in the High St, and Samuel Pepys wrote in his diary that he lay in a room used by the Queen Mother.

By 1830 as many as thirty coaches a day would pass through the town. The Market Place was well established by this time but many new shops and businesses were also established nearby. The coming of the railway twenty years later put paid to the coaching business, but it brought the town within easy reach of many large centres of population.

Today Petersfield is a pleasant and thriving residential area with modern light industry and commercial businesses. A new covered shopping precinct is under construction in the town centre, opposite the church and The Square. But care has also been taken to preserve the best of its old architecture.

The best known landmark is the statue of King William III in The Square, which dates from 1753, although Petersfield has no particular connection with William. It was erected under the will of Sir William Jollife, the MP from 1734 until 1741, and was restored by the town council in 1911.

The Square★**,** now an attractive pedestrianized area, was the site of a weekly cattle market until the 1960s and some of the old railings where animals were tied up have been retained. Sheep St, leading off it, is particularly rich in 16th- and 17th-century architecture. The Folly shopping area is a new collection of small shops which fit ideally into Petersfield's personalized style.

♣ The **Heath**★**,** just a stone's throw from the town centre, is the town's great natural asset. It covers more than 80 acres and includes a large lake, golf course, cricket pitch, tennis courts and a children's play area. The lake is used for boating and fishing and a delicate balance is maintained between leisure activities and the wildlife which abounds there. Further down the road is the leisure centre with facilities for squash, badminton and keep fit.

The **Flora Twort Gallery**★ is the former home and studio of the local artist whose delightful paintings and drawings form her personal record of Petersfield between the wars. Flora Twort, who died aged 81, bequeathed her cottage and her works to Hampshire County Council in 1985.

Flora Twort Gallery: *Mar–Jan, Tues–Sat 9.30am–5pm. Tel: (0730) 260756.*

Tourist Information Centre: *County Library, 27 The Square. Tel: (0420) 88448.*

PORTCHESTER

Map p.138, C2

3 miles E of Fareham on the A27

Portchester is a place of contrasts. The two features for which it is best known are the massive, well-preserved castle (see p.17) which was established by the Romans, and the modern crematorium which serves a wide area of southern Hampshire.

These two features apart, Portchester is a large, residential area which has grown considerably over the years, filling the gap between Fareham and Portsmouth. There is a comprehensive pedestrianized shopping precinct and other facilities such as a library and a health centre.

Castle St leads from the post-war part of Portchester to an area of complete contrast where, in the vicinity of the castle itself, traditional cottages with attractive gardens still give some semblance of a country village. The parish church, **St Mary's,** which dates from Norman times, is built within the castle walls.

On the foreshore, maintaining the tradition of the boatbuilding industry, is the large, modern Vosper Thornycroft yard which builds fast patrol craft for the British and foreign navies.

PORTSMOUTH

Map p.138, D3 * * *

18 miles SE of Southampton on the M275

Portsmouth, for years famous as the home of the Royal Navy, is now taking on new roles as the size of the fleet diminishes in the wake of the 'peace dividend'.

A few years ago the city was quick to take advantage of industrial strife in neighbouring

Southampton to rob that port of its cross-Channel ferry traffic, and now claims to be the gateway to Europe. The Continental ferry port is easily accessible by road and the crossing to France is about an hour quicker than from Southampton. It is also the port for the Channel Islands.

Consequently Portsmouth has become a focal point for national and international trade and commerce, a feature which the city council is quick to emphasize. But perhaps most obvious of all is Portsmouth's determination to exploit its rich history to become the heritage centre of the South.

Portsmouth's first royal charter was granted by Richard Cœur de Lion in 1194. His brother, King John I, commanded that 'our docks at Portsmouth be enclosed with a good and strong wall lest in the ensuing winters our ships and galleys should suffer any damage'. The city has seen many fortifications since then but their defensive role is now less important than their role as tourist attractions. The ships, too, which defended our shores are now increasingly important for the visitors they bring.

Maintaining the balance between ceremony and tradition, and a positive attitude to the city's future and the people who live there, is a challenge of which the council is only too aware. But it is a task which is being tackled with a mixture of imagination and responsibility.

🏛 **HMS *Victory******, Nelson's flagship, is still at the top of the agenda for most visitors, along with the ***Mary Rose*** exhibition and **HMS *Warrior***, Britain's first iron-clad warship. They are displayed in an historic area of the dockyard where modern warships are an additional and free attraction and the **Royal Naval Museum** provides a background to all this, with displays on five centuries of seafaring. While all three have their own unique merits, it is the reconstruction of the *Mary Rose* which is particularly fascinating, especially as the nation watched on television as the wreck of Henry VIII's flagship was raised from the sea-bed.

A walk through **Old Portsmouth High St** is like turning the clock back. Over the centuries it has waved farewell to sailors going off to war and welcomed them home victorious. A commemorative stone marks the site of the Old George Hotel where Nelson spent his last night on English soil before setting off for the Battle of Trafalgar.

Camber Docks, still busy with modern ferries and cargo ships, is where Sir Walter Raleigh landed the first potatoes and tobacco after his expedition to Virginia. The **Round Tower*** is a familiar landmark to generations of sailors and their families since it is the traditional vantage point for sad farewells and joyous greetings. The Square Tower was originally the official residence of the city's military governor. Later it became the main gunpowder magazine and then a meat store. **Sally Port** is an ancient sea gate through which passed thousands of manacled convicts being transported to Botany Bay, among them the Tolpuddle Martyrs from Dorset, sentenced in 1835 for trying to organize Britain's first trade union among agricultural workers.

Many of the historic architectural features of the shoreline are best seen from the water, and there is a waterbus service as well as regular boat trips. Walking tours through Old Portsmouth are conducted by guides who miss no opportunity to tell their audience that the area was once described as 'a stew of debauchery and corruption'.

⛪ **Cathedral of St Thomas of Canterbury.**** The cathedral has had a long and chequered history and is only just at the stage of completion. It began as a chapel in the 12th century dedicated to St Thomas à Becket after his murder at Canterbury Cathedral. The building was extended in the Cromwellian era but plans to complete it were interrupted by World War II. The finishing touches now being made offer visitors the rare opportunity to see a cathedral in the making. In the Navy aisle are buried the remains of an unknown member of the crew who perished on the *Mary Rose*.

🏠 🏛 **Charles Dickens' House.** No. 393 Old Commercial Rd is Charles Dickens's birthplace. The house, where he was born in 1812, has been restored and furnished in the style of the early 19th century, and stands in a cobbled street typical of the times. It contains personal relics of Dickens as well as several first editions of his novels. Dickens's father worked in the dockyard and is said to have been the inspiration for Mr Micawber in *David Copperfield*.

Much of Portsmouth's history is recorded and displayed in a variety of museums around the city. The **City Museum and Art Gallery*** includes a comprehensive 'Story of Portsmouth' display. The **Royal Marines Museum**** at Eastney includes an audio-visual display on the Falklands campaign, a chilled arctic display and an outdoor junior assault course. The **Cumberland House Natural History Museum and Butterfly House*** has as its star attraction a life-size model dinosaur called Emily. Southsea Castle (see p.17) and the **D-Day Museum**** between them span 400 years of history. It is said that the castle is built from stones rifled from Beaulieu Abbey during the Dissolution of the Monasteries and that Henry VIII witnessed the sinking of the *Mary Rose* from here. The D-Day museum recreates the dramatic events leading to the Normandy invasion during World War II, much of which was planned at HMS Dryad at SOUTHWICK, a few miles inland, and features the magnificent 272ft Overlord Embroidery.

But Portsmouth is far more than the museums and the past. The beach at Southsea (see p.41) is an obvious natural attraction, as are the gardens nearby and the Sea Life Centre (see p.32). A new development is the **Pyramids Centre**, described as a complete indoor resort, featuring a fun pool with waves, waterfalls and whirlpools. The Mountbatten Centre is a new sports complex on the harbourside which caters for a wide range of activities.

Entertainment, too, is an important feature and the King's Theatre at Southsea presents top line productions, including a perennially popular Christmas pantomime. In the city centre there is the New Theatre Royal, and the Guildhall, one of the country's leading concert venues, stages everything from Haydn to heavy metal.

A brief look around Portsmouth must end with the sea, and there is no place better than the newly established Port Solent and Eastney marina developments. The marinas have shops, bars and restaurants and even those with no strong nautical interests will find them a fascinating place to visit. There has been some controversy about whether the marinas are destroying natural habitat. That may or may not be, and the sailors who use them are unlikely to equal the exploits of the great seafarers. But they are at least maintaining a tradition.

HMS Victory: *March–Oct, daily 10am–6pm; July–Aug, till 7pm; Nov–Feb 10.30am–5.30pm. Admission charge. Tel: (0705) 839766.*
Mary Rose: *As HMS* Victory. *Tel: (0705) 812931.*
HMS Warrior: *As HMS* Victory. *Tel: (0705) 291379.*
Royal Naval Museum: *As HMS* Victory. *Tel: (0705) 733060.*
Portsmouth Cathedral: *Tel: (0705) 823300.*
Charles Dickens' House: *Easter–Oct, daily 10.30am–5.30pm. Tel: (0705) 827261.*
Portsmouth City Museum and Art Gallery: *All year, daily 10.30am–5.30pm. Tel: (0705) 827261.*
Royal Marines Museum: *June–Aug, daily 10am–5.30pm; Sept–May, daily 10am–4.30pm. Admission fee. Tel: (0705) 819385.*
Cumberland House Natural History Museum and Butterfly House: *All year, daily 10.30am–5.30pm. Tel: (0705) 827261.*
D-Day Museum: *All year, daily exc. 24–26 Dec, 10am–5.30pm. Admission fee. Tel: (0705) 827261.*
Pyramids Centre: *All year, daily exc. 25 Dec. Tel: (0705) 294444.*
Tourist Information Centre: *The Hard. Tel: (0705) 826722 (24 hours).*

PRESTON CANDOVER

Map p.150, C3 *
6 miles S of Basingstoke on the B3046

This is the largest of the villages in the Candover Valley, between Basingstoke and Alresford, the others being Chilton Candover and Brown Candover. The attractions of this attractive Hampshire valley for the most part go unnoticed since the B3046 is used mainly by local traffic, but that is probably why it maintains its charm. The stream which flows

through it is one of the main tributaries of the Itchen trout river which eventually flows into Southampton Water.

The Purefoy Arms and St Mary's Church, at the village centre, face each other across the semblance of the village green where the war memorial is situated. The church, with its impressive steeple, was built in 1845 and replaced most of a much earlier building. There is a general stores nearby.

In the past Preston Candover was on the route for shepherds and herdsmen driving their stock from Wales to markets in London, Surrey and Kent. They rested in woodland near Preston Candover and it is now known as Bangor Wood.

QUARLEY

Map p.148, B1 * *
5 miles W of Andover off the A303

Even though Quarley is barely half a mile from a major highway, the A303, it is in a world of its own, a compact village of thatched cottages set around a crossroads.

Church of St Michael.★★ It is easy to pass by the church, for it has no tower or belfry to announce its presence, simply a low building like two sheds joined together. But it is one of the most interesting in the county for here Saxon and Norman influences met, not long after the Norman Conquest, in a single building. The bells hang in a wooden frame in the churchyard in lieu of a belfry.

Hill Fort. Leading out to the west of the village is a road which terminates, according to the road sign, in a dead end. In fact it continues as an unmetalled track to the base of Quarley Hill. On the crest of the hill is one of the most impressive Iron Age hill forts in the country. A signpost indicates a footpath but curiously, for so important a feature, there appears to be no clear public right of way. There is no alternative but to make one's way through a series of barbed wire fences until at last the fort is gained at a height of nearly 600ft. It occupies the entire crest of the hill, some 8 acres in all. At the centre is a plantation of trees but the oval rampart that surrounds the fort, broken by four causewayed entrances, forms a perfect footpath. Although prehistoric in origin, the site may well have been used by the Romans: the course of their great road, the Portway, is less than a mile to the south. Apart from the interest of the fort itself, it provides a series of marvellous views as you follow the course of the rampart.

RINGWOOD

Map p.134, A4 *
18 miles W of Southampton on the A31

The A31 roars past Ringwood, within sight and sound of the parish church, but from the main road the town appears filled with trees, over which the church tower peeps. The bypass has preserved some of Ringwood's small town charm. The most peaceful part of the village is beside the two bridges and the gardens on the River Avon.

The **High St★** is filled with Georgian brick houses, mainly converted into shops and pubs, while the mid-Victorian classical corn exchange has become a new shopping precinct. Little alleys run off the main streets, with the most substantial Georgian houses around the triangular Market Place and the parish church. The grandest house is Greyfriars, a late Georgian red brick house of five bays, situated on the Christchurch Rd leading away from the town centre.

SS Peter and Paul Church★ was entirely rebuilt in the 1850s, in a plain but pleasing 13th-century style. Inside the sizeable building, many 18th-century monuments were retained from the previous church, while the chancel floor is covered in very colourful deep pile carpets made by the then vicar in 1905. Behind the altar in the south transept hangs a new example of local craft, the New Forest tapestry composed of woven squares and tree shapes, made in 1985.

Ringwood Meeting House★★ is to be found among the delivery area to the main

Old Portsmouth.

shops, behind the High St. It was built in 1727 as the Unitarian chapel, and is now preserved as a museum, with brick pilasters and pediment outside and all its original furnishings, a very complete early Nonconformist chapel.

ROCKBOURNE

Map p.141, C1 * *
4 miles NW of Fordinbridge off the B3078

This is one of the prettiest villages in Hampshire. The Allen Brook flows down the eastern side of the street, little bridges connect the houses with the road, and the houses themselves are a charming variety of brick, flint, timber, thatch and tile. A small lane crosses the brook to the Manor House, an irregular house behind a whitewashed Georgian brick front. From its forecourt a grass path, sheltered by a thick yew hedge and guarded by a topiary bird, climbs to the parish church. The churchyard looks down onto picturesque and ancient flint farm buildings.

Rockbourne's great attraction is the Roman Villa (see p.36), which was only uncovered in 1942.

St Andrew's Church** has many Norman features. The west end is crowned by a 17th-century timber bell-turret, and a 16th-century Flemish triptych painting of the Last Judgement stands in the north aisle on the old communion table. The chancel contains many monuments to the Coote family, and there is a special display on General Sir Eyre Coote, one of the 18th-century heroes in British India. A 100ft high column on West Down, beyond the village near the Roman villa and visible for miles around, was erected in his memory in 1828.

ROMSEY

Map p.143, B2 * *
10 miles NW of Southampton on the A3057

William Cobbett, on his *Rural Ride* in 1826, described the River Test at Romsey as 'a large and very fine river, famous all the way down for trout and eels'. Romsey grew up in the marshy margin of the Test, which flows in various courses (some cut for water mills) to the west of the town. Its great importance was first as a religious centre, and then as a market town, with a particular fame in fulling cloth and later malting and brewing. The series of market places by the abbey stand at the heart of the town.

Romsey Abbey.*** The main parish church, dedicated to SS Anne and Aelfleda, is one of the proudest statements of Norman architecture in southern England. The great church, 260ft long, was the centre of a Benedictine nunnery, originally founded by Aelfleda in 907. Although all the convent buildings were demolished at the Dissolution, the church was saved for £100 by the townspeople (who previously worshipped in its north aisle). The overwhelming impression is of Norman might: huge round piers, and lofty rounded arches, in the arcades and windows. The building we see was begun around 1120, but traces of its predecessor remain, especially two beautiful Anglo-Saxon rood sculptures: one in the chapel in the south chancel aisle, and the life-size Christ crucified outside the south transept. Both from *c.*1000, they are among the finest English carvings of that date.

Carved Norman capitals, medieval paintings, modern tapestries, and St Aelfleda's own hair are among the adornments and treasures of the Abbey, while Earl Mountbatten's pew under the tower crossing and simple monument in the south transept are poignant reminders of Romsey's most famous former inhabitant.

The **old market area*** has been encroached upon over the centuries, and now has two distinct parts. The Market Place is now a square, with a statue of Lord Palmerston, the Victorian prime minister and owner of Broadlands, at the centre. The National Westminster Bank, with a curved front of mathematical tiles, the oddly-proportioned 1860s town hall, and the fake half-timbered Conservative Club, mark the main corners. The flint walls of the church on the west side belong to the handsome 1880s Congregational (now United Reform) church; the abbey itself is obscured by a line of early 18th-century houses and shops, some with original fronts. The corn market stands back to back with the Market Place; the Victorian corn exchange with its Corinthian columns is now Barclays Bank. The Dolphin Hotel, opposite it, is graced by two large semi-circular bays in its white-rendered late Georgian front; a few doors further along, the **Tudor Rose Inn**★ was once the town's guildhall, with substantial timber beams, a great fireplace and an upper hall surviving behind its unremarkable front.

Romsey is a town of quiet delights to be discovered at leisure: Georgian houses tucked away on side streets, the carefully rebuilt 18th-century bridge over the Test, the rambling Tudor manor house – now a restaurant – on Palmerston St (which leads to the lodge gates of Broadlands, see p.12), gardens and meadows by the river, almshouses, and – amazingly, still surviving – the 13th-century King John's House (see p.14), on Church St.
Tourist Information Centre: *Bus Station Car Park, Broadwater Rd. Tel: (0794) 512987 (summer); (0703) 620555 (winter).*

ROPLEY

Map p.150, E4 *
9 miles SW of Alton on the A31

Most visitors to Ropley will probably be heading for the station, on the Watercress Line (see ALTON). In contrast to its days under British Rail, Ropley station is now an important feature of the line which runs from Alresford to Alton. An engine shed has been built to restore and service locomotives and a picnic area overlooks the station complex. Steam enthusiasts will always find something of interest going on.

The village itself is widely spread but the centre, with the parish hall, recreation ground, school, church and pub, is situated just to the south of the A31. Two other pubs and garages are on the main road. The Hampshire Hunt kennels have long been an integral part of the village.

Archbishop's Cottage takes its name from William Howley (1766–1848) who became Archbishop of Canterbury. His father was the rector at Ropley and Howley is said to have been fostered by a woman who lived in the cottage. As Archbishop, Howley crowned William IV and Queen Victoria.

ST MARY BOURNE

Map p.154, E2 *
12 miles W of Basingstoke on the B3048

The village takes its name from the river, dry for many months of the year, which flows for some ten miles to join the River Test upstream from Longparish. The valley contains most of the habitation, in contrast to the open downs; the clear fresh water from the chalk feeds the vibrant green of the huge watercress beds just south of St Mary Bourne. Walkers on the Test Way (see p.39) up above enjoy the downland views and glimpses into the valley.

St Peter's Church★★ (curiously, not St Mary's) stands within a shady churchyard filled with tombs and edged by the thatched catslide roofs of neighbouring houses at the heart of the attractive village. The flint-built church is a delight, with wistaria over the porch. The church's interior is equally attractive, with the huge Norman font in black Tournai marble a rare and distinguishing feature. The nave, with oddly misaligned columns, is filled with cut-down box pews facing the broad round-headed chancel arch and the rare 17th-century four-sided lectern. Like its near neighbour Hurstbourne Tarrant, the church has wall paintings which have been uncovered: post-Reform texts in cartouches and Charles II's royal arms. The best-preserved text is in the south aisle, which also contains an impressive crusading knight's effigy within a decorated wall opening.

The village, following the line of the valley, contains a great variety of building materials in its houses, ranging from timber and plaster through flint to hard Victorian brick. Some are small, rounded cottages, others grander houses of knapped flint, with Victorian almshouses and a few suburban-style 19th-century terraces.

SELBORNE

Map p.151, E3 * *
5 miles S of Alton on the B3006

Selborne has an international reputation thanks to a clergyman who was born in the village nearly 300 years ago. Gilbert White, who later became curate at neighbouring Farringdon, wrote *The Natural History of Selborne,* which is recognized as a classic of its kind.

White was born in his grandfather's vicarage in 1720 and would have been familiar with The Plestor, the open space in front of St Mary's church which was a meeting point for young and old. Apart from the traffic and a few more recent houses, White would not find the village much different today. And it will probably stay that way, too, for much of the land around is protected by the National Trust, and residents take great care to protect their charming environment.

♣ **Selborne Hanger★,** a beech-clad hillside, is a favourite spot for outdoor types and the zig-zag path to the top which White knew is still well used today. The view from the Common at the top is breathtaking, assuming that you have any breath left after the climb.

🏛 **The Wakes★★,** White's home, is now a museum which traces the naturalist's life and work as well as the history of the village itself. The manuscript of *The Natural History of Selborne* is a prized exhibit. The Wakes also incorporates the **Oates Museum** in recognition of Captain Lawrence Oates, who perished while on the ill-fated expedition to the Antarctic led by Captain Robert Falcon Scott in 1912. A second exhibition is dedicated to the Victorian naturalist, Frank Oates.

Opposite The Wakes, in front of a building which was once a butcher's shop, are two of four lime trees planted by White to hide 'the sight of blood and filth from ye windows'. White himself is buried in the churchyard in a simple grave marked by a stone with just his initials and the date of his death.

🏛 The **Mallinson Collection of Rural Relics★★** has been assembled over the past 25 years by Anne Mallinson. Most of the exhibits have come from cottages, sheds and barns in the neighbourhood and others from workshops which have closed down, including the blacksmith, the carpenter and the undertaker.

🏛 The **Romany Folklore Museum and Workshop★★** is a fascinating collection of traditional gypsy caravans and memorabilia; but if you want a pleasant horse-drawn ride around the area, an enterprising business called Horse Power can oblige.

On the Petersfield side of the village there is a splendid drinking fountain in the form of a lion's head flanked by two windmills. The water flows from the lion's mouth into a drinking trough. It is a reminder of Victorian times when it was the main water supply for the village.

Selborne has a thriving community life. The village hall has recently been renovated with many thousands of pounds being raised by enthusiastic villagers. It has managed to keep its two pubs, three shops and a post office, and the sports ground is well used in summer and winter.

The Wakes: *Mar–Oct, Wed–Sun and BHs 11am–5.30pm; July–Sept, Tues–Sun. Tel: (042050) 275.*
The Mallinson Collection of Rural Relics: *Mar–Oct, Sat–Thurs 10.30am–1pm, 2–5.30pm, Sun 2–5.30pm. Tel: (042050) 307 or 505.*
Romany Folklore Museum, and Workshop: *All year, daily 10.30am–5.30pm. Tel: (042050) 486.*

SHERBORNE ST JOHN

Map p.155, D4 *
3 miles N of Basingstoke on the A340

Although within shouting distance of rapidly expanding Basingstoke, Sherborne

St John retains its rural village atmosphere. It has a stream, three duck ponds, and deer are occasionally spotted on the village outskirts. The best known building is The Vyne, a great Tudor house bequeathed to the National Trust (see p.15). The village also has a rare Wealden house, usually found in Kent and Sussex, which dates from 1450.

🍷 **The Swan,** attractively thatched and more than 500 years old, is the village's remaining pub – parish records show that at one time there were seven alehouses. A house called Cleeves was once the brewhouse but it is now a picturesque home.

⛪ Parts of the **Church of St Andrew** date from 1150 but in contrast in the churchyard there is a stone memorial to Henry Briggs who was involved in pioneering work with jet engines. There is also an intriguing memorial to George Hickson who, according to his epitaph, 'lived above 20 years in the service of William Chute Esq as whipper in and huntsman and continued after he died in the family as coachman.'

SHERFIELD ON LODDON

Map p.156, C1 *

5 miles NE of Basingstoke on the A33

The tall spire of St Leonard's church emerging through the tree tops is an early indication that you are approaching Sherfield on Loddon. In fact there is some mystery surrounding the church's location since it is on the outskirts of the village, rather than in the centre where it might be expected. A possible explanation is that during the Black Death, when whole villages were wiped out, surviving inhabitants decided to move to healthier ground.

The old mill, which is a focal point of the village, was recently badly damaged by fire but a restoration programme is now in hand. The village green has also been tastefully restored in recent years to cater for a wide range of sporting and recreational activities. The village has twice been judged the best kept in Hampshire.

In surroundings that can only be described as idyllic, many residents reach a grand old age, and there is a local saying: 'You live as long as you wish in Sherfield on Loddon'.

SILCHESTER

Map p.155, B4 * * *

7 miles N of Basingstoke off the A340

Silchester is best known as the Roman town of Calleva Atrebatum (see p.37), but it was an important place even before the arrival of the Romans. It was the capital town of the Belgic tribe called Atrebates who dominated an area which included most of Surrey and Berkshire as well as northern Hampshire. Under the Romans it became a key military and commercial centre and several important roads radiated from it.

Today Silchester is a peaceful village just inside Hampshire's border with Berkshire. Evidence of its Roman connections is everywhere, including the archaeological remains of the old Roman town, and the vast amphitheatre where ten thousand Romans gathered to their holiday feasts and to watch entertainment which was probably of a bloodthirsty nature.

🏛 The **Calleva Museum**★★ displays many Roman relics, although most of the treasures discovered during forty years of excavations are in a museum in Reading. The pub is called, not surprisingly, the Calleva Arms. Worth seeking out is the Impstone, an Imperial Roman milestone on the Hampshire/Berkshire border reputed to have been thrown from Silchester by a giant.

⛪ The **Church of St Mary**★**,** 700 years old, is easily overlooked amid all the Roman influences. But even here, Roman bricks are incorporated in the walls and buttresses and there is a chair made from wood originally used to line a Roman water culvert. Church records show that in 1349 the parish had six rectors, an indication of the ravages of the Black Death in this corner of the world.

Near the pub is **Silchester House** which has a clock tower with painted clock-jacks striking the hours. **Dial House** has an old sundial and a brass plate explaining that a dial post was first erected there in 1716.

SOPLEY

Map p.134, C4 *

4 miles NW of New Milton off the A35

Sitting on the very edge of the Avon Valley and also on the Dorset boundary, Sopley has a concentration of 18th-century cottages, many of them thatched, and a narrow bridge carrying the main traffic over the river.

St Michael's Church* stands slightly apart on a mound, a building of a bewildering variety of dates. It is built in the brown stone which was dug from the nearby heaths. Purbeck marble effigies of a man and a woman dating from the 13th century flank the entrance, and a new embroidery showing the village decorates the organ.

The large Italianate Victorian house, **Sopley Park,** has now become Moorlands Bible College, entered by the lodge gates just to the south of the main village centre.

SOUTHAMPTON

Map pp.143–4 * * *

18 miles NW of Portsmouth on the M27

Southampton has ridden the switchback of economic fortune in its 1000 years of settlement. In the Middle Ages it was one of the most important, and wealthiest, towns in England. Then followed a long period of low economic fortunes until the 19th century, when the modern docks were developed. Today Southampton and neighbouring Portsmouth have grown together to make the largest urban area on the south coast.

Enough survives to give some sense of Southampton's wealthy past, especially within the uncommonly well-preserved walls of the Old Town, situated on the spur of land where the Rivers Test and Itchen meet to form Southampton Water. The old town of Hamtun gave its name to Hampshire, and came to be called Southampton to distinguish it from Northampton. The city has spread far beyond its walls; but remarkably, enormous areas of green space have been preserved in the heart of the city, remnants of the original open fields and commons which survived.

Southampton was heavily bombed in World War II, and has acquired an intricate network of roads designed to speed freight to and from the docks, so some of its historic character has been lost. Yet much survives, often to be sought out by the visitor on foot, and there is a variety of well-displayed museums to illustrate all the aspects of Southampton's past.

The **Town Walls.***** As an important port town, and often in need of defence against the French, medieval Southampton was walled, and considerable sections of the high town walls survive. Footbridges and walkways give easy access to many stretches of the wall. The most impressive is the western section, below the site of the castle, where the fronts of houses were blocked up and incorporated into a massive defensive wall following French attacks in the mid 14th century. The plain west gate survives.

Bargate is the most impressive of the gateways, standing alone in the middle of one of the main shopping streets at the north end of the Old Town. Punctuated by many openings and guarded by great lions rampant, with a classical statue of George III gazing down onto the High St, the town's former guildhall was in the Bargate's upper room. Free guided walking tours of the Old Town begin here every Monday.

The wartime bombing obliterated parts of the **High St**, which runs down from Bargate to the old Town Quay, but some buildings survive, notably the Georgian Dolphin Hotel, with huge semi-circular bay windows on the first floor, the Red Lion pub with its galleried Tudor hall, and the

The old Roman wall at Silchester.

ruins of the medieval Holy Rood Church, which have been preserved as a memorial to the Merchant Navy, with a great anchor in the roofless nave.

The **Old Town***,** with its grid pattern of streets, is still very residential, with some new housing, Georgian and Victorian houses, some surviving Tudor buildings, and a striking 1960s block of flats on the former Castle mound. Everywhere there are remnants of the medieval town: vaulted cellars, castle or wall towers, archaeological digs in progress.

St Michael's Church* on Bugle St is the only proper survivor of Southampton's medieval churches. Its tall elegant spire is still a landmark, while within the broad, incense-smelling building the Norman crossing tower and a marble Norman font survive, together with two rare medieval brass lecterns, under a delicate early Victorian roof. The church fronts onto its own little square, once the fish market.

Tudor House Museum** stands opposite. Although heavily restored at the end of the last century, this proud merchant's house with its close-set half-timbering and jettied upper storeys retains much of its 15th- and 16th-century fabric, especially in the great hall. Rooms are furnished to show a variety of historical periods, some with costumed figures, while on the first floor there is an enchanting series of bird's eye views of Southampton painted 150 years ago. At the rear a **Tudor Garden** has been planted, with access to the so-called **King John's House**, the stone walls of a great Norman house which was later incorporated into the town defences.

The **Medieval Merchant's House**** on French St represents a different tradition in restoration. Opened by English Heritage in 1988, it has been turned back into a 14th-century shop and house, with unpaved dirt floors, glassless windows, curtained-off sleeping areas, and reproduction furniture of a surprising gaudiness, all undertaken using traditional techniques. There is a personal soundtrack tour around this rare survival.

The **Maritime Museum**** is housed within the Wool House, an enormous medieval stone warehouse beside the former Town Quay, featuring displays of the development of the docks, and of the ocean-going liners which brought such prosperity to modern Southampton. Above is the magnificent carpentry of the roof which once covered the wool that was the most valuable of medieval exports.

God's House Tower** on Winkle St, just to the east, contains displays of the archaeological work which has been carried out in the town, from the Roman period to the early modern. The excavation and publication record has made Southampton one of the best-researched medieval towns. The tower itself was part of the defensive wall (of which a well-preserved section stands to the north), and the group of buildings behind it is the **Hospital of St Julian**, a 12th-century hostel and almshouse. The hospital's residential buildings are mainly Victorian, but the interior of the church of St Julian (once the French church) is still partly Norman.

The sea once came right up to the town walls, but land reclamation has considerably extended the depth of the waterfront. To the west lie the modern docks (mainly inaccessible), but the Town Quay and the pier are still located below the Old Town. The Town Quay has recently been turned into a shopping and office complex, with decking floors, weatherboarding and skylights to preserve the waterside image. A ferry travels frequently from the Town Quay to Ocean Village, a similar redevelopment in the first of the docks, to the east, and across Southampton Water to Hythe. The ferry to the Isle of Wight leaves from beside the pier, Brightonesque with its white, Edwardian onion dome.

The site of the Saxon town of Hamwic lay to the east of the later centre, and the Church of St Mary remained the mother church of Southampton despite being outside the walls.

St Mary's Church* itself was gutted in the blitz and then suffered from uninspired rebuilding after the war in a pale version of G. E. Street's 1870s Gothic which had been there before. The tower and spire survived, and are the church's most distinctive feature.

Southampton's first expansion was into this area north and east of the walls. Above Bar, now a 1950s shopping precinct (where Tourist Information is located), extends north from Bargate towards the sprawling Civic Centre, which was built in the inter-war years in a mixed classical and modern style. The tall, asymmetrically placed bell tower dominates the composition.

Southampton City Art Gallery** in the north wing of the Civic Centre, which re-opens in 1993 after considerable refurbishment, is a provincial art collection with an international reputation, with especially fine holdings in the early 20th-century work of the Camden Road School, and works by Monet, Renoir, Spencer, and many old masters.

Around the Civic Centre there are almost continuous parks to the north and east, each with a statue of a local worthy at its centre: Lord Palmerston, a local merchant, or Isaac Watts, the 17th-century hymn writer. There are many survivors of the late Georgian and early Victorian houses which were built when Southampton had a temporary renaissance as a watering place and seaside town, before the docks were developed: Portland Terrace and one side of Portland Square, west of Above Bar, are the most elegant examples, followed by the streets around Queen's Park to the south-east.

Ocean Village Marina* further to the south-east occupies what was Southampton's earliest dock, built in 1842 hard on the heels of the railway. Hundreds of yachts are now moored where great ships once berthed, and shops and offices stand in the place of warehouses. The SS *Shieldhall*, last of the working coastal vessels, is open to the public, and is in steam on summer weekends, and the former lightship from Calshot Spit is also moored at the marina. The entrance to Ocean Village is from Canute Rd: the fanciful Victorian King Canute Hotel opposite the entrance bears a plaque stating that it stands on the site where Canute 'reproved his courtiers' by unsuccessfully ordering the waves to go back.

The **Hall of Aviation****, located in a great hangar and glass atrium just to the north, on Albert Rd South by the Central Bridge, is an excitingly-presented aircraft museum. Southampton played an important part in early aviation, and it was here that R. J. Mitchell designed the Spitfire and the S6 Seaplane, which won the Schneider Trophy. Many of the exhibits offer hands-on experiences, like sitting at the controls of a supersonic jet, while the centrepiece of the museum is the Sandringham Flying Boat, which occasionally flies to Calshot, the flying boats' former base.

Outer Southampton

Since Victorian times, Southampton has grown at an unprecedented rate, with the docks and now high-tech industries. A town of 8000 people in 1801 had grown to 180,000 a century and a half later. Since the mid-1950s, when Southampton had recovered from its wartime devastation, there has been considerable residential expansion, continuing the pattern of the late 19th and early 20th centuries.

Southampton Common** is one of the most striking features of the pattern of the city's growth. An area of trees and grass extending over 400 acres, this wedge through the northern area of the city has been preserved as common land since the 13th century, and used for recreation since the 18th century. The wide, tree-lined road appropriately called The Avenue is the main road out from central Southampton, and skirts the common. At its southern end are The Dell, home of Southampton's football club, and the Hampshire County Cricket ground. Large mid-19th-century brick villas line The Avenue and the approaches to the common, typical of the houses which arose during the era of Victorian expansion as rough forest country was transformed first into separate estates and then into suburbia. Some of the most interesting examples of the latter are the 'garden suburb' estates developed by Herbert Collins, notably in Highfield just east of the common.

The **University of Southampton's campus**★★ lies north of the common, on either side of University Rd and bounded by residential areas. The original pre-war brick buildings have been eclipsed by the huge expansion of the 1960s, masterminded by Sir Basil Spence. He designed the Nuffield Theatre, with its verdigris copper-sheathed sculptural roof, and the main new buildings. Few of the university buildings are high; rather, they are linear, with rows of large windows and grey wall panels, set amid mature gardens with streams, twisting pathways and steps, and modern sculpture. The theatre, as well as the concert hall and gallery, are all open to the public.

Although Southampton's outer suburbs are generally undistinguished, there is always something of note. The Old Farmhouse pub in the Bevis Valley (named after the legendary giant Bevis of Hampton) is a genuine 17th-century brick house swallowed up in modern development. At Portswood, a recently restored 18th-century Gothic fortified lodge pops up on a dull roadside. The reeds still grow in the river at Redbridge (originally Reedbridge) over to the west, and are now protected. At Shamrock Quay in Northam on the west bank of the Itchen, boat repair yards continue their trade.

South Stoneham★ is an old settlement now encompassed by Swaythling, where many of the University's halls of residence have been built. One of them incorporates South Stoneham House, which was designed in the early 18th century by the great Nicholas Hawksmoor; South Stoneham parish church is mainly medieval, and contains a wealth of monuments, including a grand one by Hawksmoor and a self-aggrandizing one to the Clerke family who were clerks to the Privy Seal for four generations until 1632.

Tudor House Museum: *All year, Tues–Fri 10–12am and 1–5pm, Sat 10–12am and 1–4pm, Sun 2–4pm. Tel: (0703) 224216.*
Medieval Merchant's House: *Oct–Mar, Tues–Sun 10am–4pm; April–Sept, daily 10am–6pm. Tel: (0703) 221503.*
Maritime Museum: *All year, Tues–Fri 10am–1pm and 2–5pm; Sat 10am–1pm and 2–4pm, Sun 2–5pm. Tel: (0703) 224216.*
God's House Tower: *All year, Tues–Sat 10–12am and 1–5pm; Sat 10–12am 1–4pm; Sun 2–4pm. Tel: (0703) 220007.*
Southampton City Art Gallery: *Closed for refurbishment until April 1993. Tel: (0703) 832330.*
Hall of Aviation: *All year, Tues–Sat 10am–5pm, Sun 12am–5pm. Admission charge. Tel: (0703) 635830.*
Tourist Information Centre: *Civic Centre. Tel: (0703) 832330 or 832712.*

SOUTHWICK

Map p.138, B3
6 miles N of Portsmouth on the B2177

The wind of change is blowing through this normally quiet village. For years the estate, which includes Southwick itself, was owned by Mrs Eva Borthwick-Norton, a maternal character who liked the old-fashioned stability of times gone by. When she died in 1988 it was inherited by a nephew and although many of the old values are retained, some villagers are concerned that their way of life is bound to change.

The village, with its oddly named Church of St James without the Priory Gates, and its two pubs, the Red Lion and the Golden Lion, has a certain uniformity because, under the ownership of the estate, the same coloured paint is used for all buildings. At the same time, though, there is an interesting variety of architecture.

The Royal Navy's HMS Dryad shore-base at Southwick Park is where Operation Overlord, the D-Day invasion of France, was masterminded while Winston Churchill and General Eisenhower supervised from a special train at nearby Droxford.

STEVENTON

Map p.155, F1 *

6 miles W of Whitchurch off the B3400

Chawton is now Jane Austen's chief shrine but this scatter of well-kept cottages is where she was born, grew up and wrote

Sense and Sensibility, *Pride and Prejudice* and *Northanger Abbey*. The parish notice-board outside the village hall proudly informs the visitor that Jane fainted on the spot when told that the family was moving away to Bath.

Church of St Nicholas. The small, isolated 13th-century church, where Jane Austen's father was rector for forty years, is tucked away up a by-road. Within can be seen several memorials to members of the Austen family as well as extensive traces of a floral-patterned wall painting and a 9th-century Saxon cross-shaft incised with dragons. The visitors' book records the delight of a steady stream of pilgrims to this peaceful place.

STOCKBRIDGE

Map p.148, D4 * *
8 miles S of Andover on the A3057

Driving down along Stockbridge's main street you seem to be driving along the high street of a busy country town. The street is not only unusually broad and dead straight in a manner more characteristic of Wiltshire (where high streets are also markets) but both sides are solidly built up with a fascinating range of decidedly urban architecture, mostly Tudor and Georgian. Viewed from above, however, Stockbridge looks remarkably like a stage set for there is virtually nothing on either side of the buildings except open water meadows. There are two churches of which Old Church, at the east end of the street, is worth a visit even though it consists simply of a 13th-century chancel. The rest was demolished in 1863. The parish church, St Peter's, dates from 1866 and contains some of the windows salvaged from the Old Church.

This little village actually has a Town Hall, built in 1810 and unmistakeable in its livery of yellow brick. There are a remakable number of excellent inns and restaurants, among them the elegant White Hart, by the Old Church, and the Grosvenor Arms, both dating from the early 19th century. The Grosvenor Arms is the headquarters of the exclusive Houghton Club, the club of fisherman which, founded in 1822, rigorously controls the fishing of the River Test – and much of the access to its banks.

STOKE CHARITY

Map p.149, C4
10 miles N of Winchester off the A34

Church of St Mary and St Michael.*
The Norman church, surrounded by meadows and watercress beds, is a veritable treasure-house. There are medieval floor-tiles and glass, massive columns and spectacular arches, a Jacobean altar-table and half a dozen major tombs, several with brasses, others with their heraldic decoration gaily repainted. In 1849 a rare carved altar-piece of *c.*1500, showing St.Gregory at Mass, was uncovered by chance and as recently as 1966 another lost treasure, a sizeable chunk of 13th-century wall-painting, was also rediscovered. A visit is well worth the hazards of an entrance-path much visited by grazing cows.

STRATFIELD SAYE

Map p.156, B2 * *
9 miles N of Basingstoke off the A33

Stratfield Saye and its neighbour Stratfield Turgis are dominated by the influence of successive Dukes of Wellington. Stratfield Saye House (see p.15) was given to Arthur Wellesley, the first Duke of Wellington, in recognition of his defeat of Napoleon in 1815. The splendid house is set among parkland through which flows the River Loddon. The Iron Duke's gallant horse, Copenhagen, who carried him for 18 hours during the Battle of Waterloo, was buried in the park and a gravestone marking the spot reads: 'God's humbler instrument, though meaner clay, shall share the glory of the glorious day.'

The Church of Our Lady, built in 1784, was described in Victorian times as a monster of ecclesiastical ugliness. That is a matter of opinion, but it is certainly an interesting building. On the A33 Basingstoke to Reading road at Stratfield

Turgis is the Wellington Arms pub and All Saints church. The church is unused and redundant but the pub remains busy.

SWAY

Map p.135, C3 *

12 miles SW of Southampton off the B3055

Sway marks the edge of the built-up area between the south coast and the New Forest. It grew up when the railway arrived, and road names like Manchester Rd recall the armies of navvies who built the line in 1888.

St Luke's Church, a little brick building of 1839, established the settlement; previously, the parish church had been many miles away at Boldre. Only a few of the old cob-built forest cottages survive among the modern housing.

Peterson's Tower* is a prominent landmark to the south of Sway, a 218ft folly built around 1880 in the revolutionary material, concrete, apparently according to spirit messages received from Sir Christopher Wren. Andrew Peterson, a retired Indian judge, built other concrete buildings and towers on his estate at Arnewood Court. The estate and tower are private, and can only be glimpsed from Barrows Rd which runs alongside. The tower is now a hotel.

Tiptoe, to the west, was the more important settlement before Sway grew up; its charming name derives from a 13th-century family, Typetot, and it has more thatch and cob cottages as well as newer housing.

The New Forest opens up beyond these wooded villages, with parking places provided to enjoy the wide views over the moors and woods to the north.

THRUXTON

Map p.148, A2 *

5 miles W of Andover on the A303

Most of Thruxton's neighbouring villages are safely tucked away among lanes which have scarcely changed over the past century. Thruxton is unfortunate in that the greatly widened A303 brutally slices its way through it, creating such an ugly scar on the Andover side that one is tempted to pass it by if approaching from that end. It is, however, well worth exploring, not least for its remarkable church. There is some good modern housing in the village, which does not intrude on the older part, and an excellent inn with a pleasant garden. The motor-racing circuit is reached from the A303 just west of the village.

The **Church of St Andrew**** is not only some little way out of the village but is in a cul-de-sac with only the elegant 18th-century rectory for company. Much of the church dates back to the 13th century but it fell into the hands of an unknown Victorian restorer in 1869 who went to work with such a will as to entirely alter its appearance. He did, however, have considerable panache so that the effect of the exterior, though startling, is also dramatic. There are some interesting monuments in the interior, among them a knight of the early 13th century and a beautifully carved limestone monument of the Lisle family, sculpted about 1510.

TICHBORNE

Map p.150, F2

2 miles SWNew of Alresford off the A31

Tichborne, now a declining agricultural village at the head of the Itchen valley, is best known for the dole ceremony when every Lady Day, 25 March, flour is distributed to residents. The ceremony dates from the days of King Henry II when Lady Mabella Tichborne, on her deathbed, begged her husband, Sir Roger, to distribute the value of a small portion of land annually among the villagers. Hard-hearted Sir Roger told her he would allocate as much land as she could encompass while carrying a burning brand. Lady Mabella hauled herself from her bed and managed to crawl around 23 acres of land which is known to this day as The Crawls.

Many years later the Tichborne family was involved in another notable controversy when in 1872 Arthur Orton arrived from Australia claiming he was the Sir Roger Tichborne who had been presumed lost at sea 18 years earlier. The ensuing Tichborne Claimant Case was until recently the longest-running in British legal history and ended with Orton being jailed for 14 years.

TITCHFIELD

Map p.137, B4 *

2 miles W of Fareham on the A27

Titchfield is a real mixture of ancient and modern. The well-preserved village centre has some of the oldest buildings in Hampshire, while on the outskirts are some of the newest factories, producing high-tech aerospace equipment. Although facing all the pressures of a growing urban and industrial area, Titchfield has managed to make the most of its dual role.

It was an important port and market town in the Middle Ages, thanks largely to its situation at the mouth of the River Meon and the influence of the Abbey (see p.37) which was founded in 1232. It continued to be a busy commercial centre for the next 400 years when, ironically, a subsequent owner of the Abbey, the Earl of Southampton, had a dam constructed across the mouth of the river to irrigate his fields and built a canal instead. The canal was unable to take boats of any size and the decline of Titchfield began. Nowadays an effigy of the Earl is burned annually at a ceremony organized by the Bonfire Boys.

The **Church of St Peter*** is the prominent feature of the village and although it has been enlarged several times, it dates from before the Norman Conquest. Inside is the tomb of the Earls of Southampton and in the crypt are the remains of other members of the family, said to be pickled in honey in lead coffins.

Most of the modern development has fortunately taken place well away from the attractive village centre with its wealth of 16th- and 17th-century cottages.

As well as aerospace industry, Titchfield also has the headquarters of the Office of Population, Censuses and Surveys which employs large numbers of computer operators sieving through information supplied by the ten-yearly national census.

TUFTON

Map p.149, A3 *

1 mile SW of Whitchurch off the A34

It is only too easy to miss this survival from the past for it lies at the end of a narrow lane which itself runs off a small country road leading off the A34. The lane ends in what appears to be, at first sight, a private estate or farmyard. There are two immense barns, evidently of great age but still part of a working farm, sheltering highly advanced agricultural machinery. There is also an estate office and a number of trimly thatched houses looking out on to a narrow green. The River Test runs through this idyllic spot, so wide and calm that it resembles a lake. High above it towards the west soars the elegant brick arch of the now disused railway.

The **Church of St Mary**** sits so modestly and snugly among its rural companions that one might almost take it for a barn were it not for its small graveyard. But though it is small in size and modest in appearance, its interior is of great interest. The chancel arch and two of the small windows are early Norman and a there is a dramatic 15th-century wall painting of St Christopher in its customary place on the north wall.

UPPER CLATFORD

Map p.148, B4 * *

1 mile S of Andover off the A3057

From the hill just behind the village you can get a plain view of Andover, ominously sprawling closer and closer so that it seems as though the village must be engulfed. Astonishingly, however, although there is some modern housing, Upper Clatford is completely unspoiled and could be in remote countryside. One of the reasons for this is that the little river Anna coils protectingly around it, the watermeadows and small lakes and subsidiary streams protecting it from development.

The village is built on a ridge rising gently to the north with the Iron Age fort of Bury Hill (see p.35) above it. A road junction at the upper, northern, end of the village, creates a sense of depth but most of the very mixed historic development follows the High Street. An iron works was established here in the early 19th century and the ironmaster's house (now known as Clatford Lodge) still survives.

The **Church of All Saints**** is in a rural setting on the far banks of the river, some considerable distance from the village itself. There are Saxon and Norman remains in the church and some eccentric restorations of the 17th century when a double arch to the chancel was created by adding a Norman arch taken from another part of the church. The purpose of this was probably to improve preaching facilities in accordance with the new doctrines of the Anglican Church.

UPTON GREY

Map p.156, F2 * *
7 miles N of Alton off the B3349

Upton Grey is one of the most attractive villages in Hampshire. Its focal point is the church of St Mary, with its unusual wooden exterior stairway to the tower. It is built at the top of a slope, close to the old Roman road which linked Chichester and Silchester. At the foot of the slope is the village pond where the ducks thrive thanks to the attentions of the villagers.

The houses are typical country cottages, likely to feature on calendars and chocolate boxes and Christmas cards, but Upton Grey retains its village atmosphere, thanks largely to the church, the pub and a village hall. Sadly the school has closed and names of properties like The Old Post House, The Old School House and The Forge are a reminder of busier times gone by when most residents worked on the land.

The Pond House is where the village tailor used to live and during Dickensian winter evenings when the pond froze over people would skate on it in the light from the tailor's lamp.

WARBLINGTON

Map p.139, B2
1 mile S of Havant off the A27

The peace of residential Warblington has been shattered in recent times by the construction of the new A27 dual carriageway and has resulted in several successful claims for compensation against the Department of Transport..

The **Church of St Thomas à Becket** has for centuries been the cornerstone of the village, set in a pleasant, isolated position overlooking Chichester harbour. So isolated, in fact, that near the main gate in the churchyard are two watchmen's huts built at a time when it was necessary to prevent unscrupulous medical men from stealing fresh corpses. Several gravestones reflect tragedies at sea. One shows a man about to be swallowed by a fish while another portrays a sailor desperately clinging to an upturned ship.

A single turret is all that remains of **Warblington Castle** and that is on private land. The castle was a fortified manor house built between 1513 and 1526 by the Countess of Salisbury. It was destroyed during the Civil War.

WEST MEON

Map p.145, A2 *
13 miles N of Fareham on the A32

The traffic which hurries through West Meon on the Alton to Fareham road is an unfortunate irritation to a seemingly idyllic way of life. West Meon is one of those villages removed from the hustle and bustle of modern life but which still retains the

The Bargate, Southampton.

services and amenities which make up an active community.

It has a school, a village hall, a post office, a grocer and a butcher, a doctor's surgery, a church and two pubs. Unfortunately it lost its rail service in 1955 with the closure of the Meon Valley Railway and the speedy dismantling of a steel viaduct effectively ruled out any possibility of restoration at some later stage.

The Thomas Lord, one of the local pubs, is named after the founder of Lord's cricket ground. He retired to the village in 1830 and is buried in St John's churchyard. More infamously, the ashes of the Russian spy Guy Burgess, the former British diplomat who died in Moscow, are scattered there. St John's church itself, built of flint in 1846, has a fine peal of eight bells.

WEST TYTHERLEY

Map p.148, F1 *

13 miles NW of Southampton off the B3084

This compact little village below the rolling hills of the Wiltshire border has a mixture of older timber-framed cottages and newer houses in brick.

Parish Church. The plain brick and flint church, at the southern end of the main street, was built in 1833. Inside, the Purbeck marble font came from the medieval church, while the west gallery, with its central part theatrically breaking forward, is less restrained than the rest of the building. The memorial to members of the Baring family, with its large, gesturing angel, just by the entrance porch, is another uncharacteristically flamboyant feature.

The Barings lived at Norman Court, now a school to the north-west; the Edwardian neo-Georgian exterior can be seen from the footpaths which pass nearby.

West Tytherley was also, curiously, the place where Robert Owen, the early socialist, established his short-lived rationalist community of Harmony Hall in 1841–2. The building, designed to accommodate 140, was demolished in 1903. Queenwood Farm, to the north of the village, was the hall's laundry, and Harmony Hall stood in the woods opposite.

WESTON PATRICK

Map p.156, F2

5 miles SE of Basingstoke off the A339

The twin villages of Weston Patrick and Weston Corbett are in an unspoilt corner of the county where little happens apart from the coming and going of the seasons. Agriculture has long dominated this area, though like everywhere else, modern farming techniques have decimated the labour force.

The Green family were important landowners for many years and many of them have their graves in St Lawrence churchyard, marked with ageing tombstones.

Weston Corbett House was the family home, built in the 17th century, and when the line died out in the 19th century it was left to the Wyatt family who lived there until the 1920s.

The kitchen was reputed to be one of the finest around, packed with the best equipment of the day including many beautiful copper vessels. In Victorian times it was used to prepare food for the many estate workers who had their meals with the family in the 'houseplace'. The kitchen and much of its contents has since been removed and reassembled at Sulgrave Manor, the George Washington Memorial Home near Banbury, in Oxfordshire.

WHITCHURCH

Map p.149, A3 * *

11 miles N of Winchester on the B3400

Incorporated as a borough and market in the 13th century, Whitchurch sent two members to Parliament from the reign of Elizabeth I until 1832. Charles I spent the night here before the second battle of Newbury. The White Hart, a former coaching-inn, confirms the strategic importance of this location where six roads meet.

Whitchurch Silk Mill. Standing on the River Test, Whitchurch already had four mills at the time of the Domesday survey. In 1815 this imposing brick building with pediment and cupola was opened as a brush-factory. By 1830 it had switched to making silk. The water-wheels have been replaced by electricity but silk is still produced for the legal profession, the fashion trade and a theatrical costumier. On display are historic looms and waterwheel powering machinery, and there is a gift shop selling silk items.

The **Church of All Hallows**, restored in 1866, includes among its treasures the fine brass of Richard Brooke and family (1603) complete with rhyming epitaph, a 15th-century solid wood-block flight of belfry steps and an 18th-century painted panel complementing the Ten Commandments with biblical scenes. Pride of place, however, goes to a 9th-century sculpture with a figure (of Christ?) holding a book and a Latin inscription,'Here lies the body of Frithburga, buried in peace.' Her Saxon name means 'Pledge of Peace' and she was probably a nun at Wherwell. Generations of bell-ringers used her memorial as a convenient platform until it was recognized for what it was.
Whitchurch Silk Mill: *All year, Tues–Sun and BHs 10.30am–5pm. Looms do not operate on Sundays. Tel: (0256) 893882.*

WHITSBURY

Map p.141, C2 *
4 miles NW of Fordingbridge off the A338

Like its neighbours on the chalk downs, Martin and Damerham, Whitsbury was transferred from Wiltshire in 1895. The brick and timber village houses are arranged along one main street, and the most conspicuous industry is keeping horses. There are paddocks and stables throughout the parish; even the sign on the steep pathway to the church directs visitors to 'visiting mares, stud office and church'.

St Leonard's Church was built in 1878, in brick with a curious, waisted brick tower and, just as oddly, nautical memorials inside.

Whitsbury Down★★ just to the north has a number of prominent prehistoric earthworks, and paths lead over the ridge to Breamore and its Mizmaze (see p.36).

WICKHAM

Map p.138, A1 *
3 miles N of Fareham on the A32

Apart from its magnificent Georgian square, which unfortunately now serves as a monster car park, Wickham is known for its annual fair. It is recorded that Henry III granted a charter for the fair in 1268 and it is supposed to have been held every year without exception since then, including the war years. Nowadays it tends to be mainly a funfair with state-of-the-art mechanical rides, but a certain amount of horse trading still goes on and there is a time-honoured ceremony which involves taking a pony into a pub and giving it a pint of beer.

Wickham was an important crossing place on the River Meon centuries ago and there is evidence of Roman activity in the area. It was here that William of Wykeham, Bishop of Winchester and founder of Winchester College, was born in the 14th century.

The **Church of St Nicholas** was originally built by the Normans in 1120 but it has been altered many times since then. The major change was in the 1870s when the tower, belfry and spire were added. Unfortunately the construction of the Meon Valley Railway at the turn of the century cut between the church and the village which now appears rather isolated.

Various industries have harnessed the power of the River Meon over the years, not least **Chesapeake Mill**. That was rebuilt by John Prior in 1820 using timbers from the American man-o-war, *Chesapeake*, which was captured by *HMS Shannon* off Boston in 1813. Close by is the place known to villagers as the dip hole where steps down to the river enabled people to get their water in bygone days.

The river also provided power for a tannery and a brewery, both of which are now part of history. The long row of timbered buildings, known as **The Barracks**, are among the oldest in the village, being based on a previous 15th-century building.

WINCHESTER

Map p.149, F3 * * *
17 miles SW of Basingstoke off the M3

Winchester is a small country town which a reasonably energetic person can explore comfortably in a day. But it also represents a segment of European history worthy of a lifetime of study. We know more about it today than at any previous time in its 2000 years. In the 1960s an immense archaeological programme was triggered by the threat of commercial development in the city centre which began when foundations for the immense Wessex Hotel were dug on the very edge of the cathedral close. In a city as small as Winchester, with a continuous history stretching from the Iron Age down to our own time, the shallowest excavation will peel back the centuries. Fortunately this was realized from the beginning. In 1962 an Excavation Committee came into being, independent of the City Council but strongly supported by it. Six years later the Winchester Research Unit was set up to supervise publication of the enormous mass of material which now unfolds the story of England's ancient capital.

There are relatively few visible Roman remains but there is no equal in England for visual evidence of the period when Dane, Saxon and Norman, fighting with and against each other, brought 'England' into being. Apppropriately, the statue which dominates the High St is that of our greatest monarch, Alfred, the king who almost single-handedly gave England an identity.

Winchester is an easy city to explore as, with the exception of Holy Cross Hospital, all the historic buildings are within a few minutes' stroll of the High St and Broadway. These form, in effect, one continuous highway with other streets running off them at right angles. An energetic City Council has effectively tamed traffic in the centre so this is pre-eminently a city in which to ramble at leisure.

High Street.***

The Broadway. At the east end is the first national statue, erected in 1901, to King Alfred the Great, designed by Hamo Thorneycroft (who also designed the statue of Boadicea on Westminster Bridge). Towards the river is the City Mill, built in 1774 and now a youth hostel.

Abbey House and Gardens. Originally a Benedictine nunnery founded by King Alfred's wife, it fell into ruins in the 16th century and was turned into a public garden in 1890.

The Old Guildhall, now Lloyds Bank, was largely rebuilt in 1713. The curfew bell is still rung from the turret at 8pm each day. The statue is that of Queen Anne. This, with the distinctive clock, commemorates the Treaty of Utrecht (1713).

The Pentice is a 16th-century colonnade, adjoining the site of the palace of William the Conqueror who used Winchester as his capital city instead of the uncertain City of London.

The City Cross. Locally known as the 'Butter Cross', it was erected in the early 15th century and restored in 1865. It is still a popular meeting place.

Godbegot House. The distinctive 'Tudor' front is a modern restoration but the rest of the house is genuinely 16th-century. It owes its curious name to the fact that it stands on the site of the manor of Godbegot, owned by Queen Emma, wife of Canute.

The Westgate dates from the 13th century and is one of the two surviving gatehouses of the city, now housing a museum. For many years this was used as the city's prison for debtors and other offenders. The inscriptions carved by these unfortunate people to while away the time are still visible: the earliest is dated 1597. After being a wine merchant's and then a repository for city archives, the Westgate was turned into a museum of local history in 1898. It possesses the finest collection of civic weights and measures in the country.

Castle Hall was built between 1222 and 1235. Among the many famous trials that took place here was that of Sir Walter Raleigh. The building was used as an

Assize Court for many years but has now been splendidly restored to its original appearance. The enormous round table that hangs on a wall was made about 1250 although it is traditionally supposed to be the famous Round Table of King Arthur. Henry VIII had it embellished with the Tudor rose in order to bolster his royal status during the visit of the Emperor Charles V. The names of Arthur's knights are written in Tudor script around the edge of the Table.

Hyde Abbey.** About ten minutes' walk from the city centre and just outside the ancient city walls are the remains of the Abbey of Hyde. This was the burial place of Alfred the Great whose bones were shamefully dispersed in the 19th century. The area deteriorated until the 1960s when a residential development was incorporated into the ruins and the remains of the Abbey restored and used as the Historic Resources Centre. This is not simply a museum but a single centre to house all the historical and archaeological material in the city's care.

Cathedral of the Holy Trinity.*** A visit to the cathedral must take precedence over everything else, for it sums up not simply the history of Winchester but of England itself. On the north side of the cathedral, just by the great West Door, are the foundations of the original Saxon cathedral, uncovered in the 1950s, which dramatically point up the contrast between Saxon and Norman architecture. Although this was the royal Saxon cathedral, burial place of kings and site of one of the most popular shrines in England, that of St Swithun, it is a modest little building which could be tucked comfortably into a about a third of its giant neighbour. The Norman cathedral was begun in 1079 and finished barely fourteen years later although, of course, there have been many later additions. The crypt is one of the oldest in the country, and bears an odd notice indicating that entry is possible only when the water level permits: this is because the cathedral, in fact, sits in an underground lake. In 1905 a deep-sea diver, William Walker, spent five years working under water during the course of vital restoration work. Single-handed and working in complete darkness, he placed 25,800 bags of cement and 114,900 concrete blocks in position. He received the Royal Victorian Order from the hands of King George V and a statue was raised to his memory in the cathedral in 1964.

An indispensable guide book is on sale in the cathedral, drawing attention to its wealth of historic treasures. Among them are the six funerary chests which contain the remains of Saxon and Danish monarchs, including Queen Emma and Canute. The tomb of William Rufus, 'accidentally' killed in the New Forest in 1100, is in the south transept. The cathedral is famous for its splendid series of chantry chapels, among them that of Bishop Richard Fox, founder of Corpus Christi College, Oxford. In the chantry chapel of Bishop Stephen Gardiner is the chair upon which Queen Mary sat during her wedding with Philip of Spain. Behind the choir is the shrine of St Swithun. According to legend he showed his displeasure at being moved from the Saxon to the Norman cathedral by causing it to rain on the day of the removal, July 15; ever since, legend says it will rain 40 days and nights if it rains on that day, 'St Swithun's Day'. The cathedral also shelters the splendid tomb of William of Wykeham, bishop of Winchester and founder of Winchester College (where the scholars are known as Wykehamists). In the north aisle of the nave is an elegant memorial to Jane Austen who spent her last days in a house just outside the Close next door to the College.

Cathedral Close.*** This is a city within a city, every one of whose buildings is of architectural and historic interest. Among them are the Deanery; the 13th-century Pilgrims' Cloister where pilgrims gathered for meals; the Pilgrims' Hall where they were lodged; and the 16th-century Priory Stables. Most intriguing of all, perhaps,is the tiny Church of St Swithun. This is situated above Kingsgate, one of the original city gates and very probably of Roman origin. The garden beside it was laid out by Richard Gleadow, who designed the Stalingrad Sword presented to Stalin in World War II.

College environs.*** The road leading directly out of Kingsgate is the ancient Kingsgate St, a medley of architectural styles which leads to the Hospital of St Cross.To the left off Kingsgate is College St, on which is Jane Austen's house. Winchester College is one of the oldest public schools in the country, founded in 1382. It still maintains its tradition of providing education for '70 poor scholars', though these places are now open to competition. There are guided tours to the older part of the College from April to September.

Wolvesey Castle is further along College St. Originally built in 1137, it was 'slighted' (substantially demolished) after the siege of Winchester by Parliament during the Civil war of 1645. It was substantially rebuilt as the Bishop's Palace, probably by Christopher Wren. Remains of the old castle are visible on the public walk known as The Weirs.

Museums and Galleries***. For such a small city, Winchester is extremely well supplied with exhibition areas, reflecting both its history and sense of culture. **City Museum** in The Square is the oldest museum in Hampshire, opened in 1903. Its exhibits tell the story of Winchester and its locality going back 100,000 years. **Royal Greenjackets Museum**, near the Great Hall, illustrates the history of the regiment and the three regiments out of which it was formed. The **Royal Hampshire Regiment Museum and Memorial Garden**, Southgate St, is notable both for its regimental interest and for the splendid baroque building it occupies, known as Serle's House. Almost next door are the **Royal Hussars Museum** with its display of cavalry past and present and the **Gurkha Museum**. The **Guildhall Gallery** on the High St has a changing programme of exhibits by local artists. The **Winchester Gallery** in the School of Art just off Park Avenue also has changing exhibitions but of a national and international nature. The **Winchester Heritage Centre**, Brook St, mostly relates to local history.

Riverside walks.*** The little river Itchen has created a network of tributaries on the east side of the city, alongside which are a number of delightful walks. The Weirs Walk starts from the City Mill and not only follows the course of the river but also that of the Roman and medieval city walls around the grounds of Wolvesey Palace back to College St and the Close.There is a way-marked walk from College St across the watermeadow to St Cross Hospital. For the more energetic, a walk up St Giles Hill provides a panoramic view of the city. Catherine's Hill, with its distinctive clump of trees, is on the other side of the bypass. The trees were planted in 1762 to mark the site of a medieval chapel dedicated to St Catherine. Even older than the chapel is a hill fort of the Iron Age and what is probably a medieval maze still visible in the turf.

Hospital of St Cross.***.Winchester possesses no less than five hospitals or almshouses,four of which are within the city walls: St Mary Magdelene, by the Weirs; St John Baptist, north of Broadway; Christes Hospital in Symonde St; and Morley College near the Cathedral. Although all are of ancient foundations most have been restored or rebuilt. Most famous of them all, however, is St Cross, just outside the city, which can be reached by a pleasant walk over the watermeadows or along Kingsgate St. Founded in 1136, it is probably the oldest almshouse in England and still provides a home for elderly men. It even still provides the famous 'Wayfarers Dole' which you must ask for at the Porter's Lodge in the gatehouse. Originally the Dole was a massive horn of ale and hunk of bread but it is now simply a token – a thimbleful of ale and small piece of bread and limited in quantity on a first come, first served basis. There are guided tours to the public rooms of St Cross on weekdays.

Westgate Museum: *April–Sept, Mon–Sat 10am–5pm, Sun 2–5pm; Oct–March Tues–Sat 10am–5pm, Sun 2–4pm. Tel: (0962) 869864.*

Winchester Cathedral: *Daily 7.15am–6.30pm. Access restricted during services. Tel: (0962) 853137.*
Winchester College: *April–Sept, Mon–Sat 10am–6pm. Tours at 11am, 2pm and 3.15pm.*
Wolvesey Castle: *Easter–Sept, daily 10am–6pm. Tel: (0962) 854766.*
City Museum: *April–Sept, Mon-Sat 10am–5pm, Sun 2–5pm; Oct–Mar, Tues–Sat 10am–5pm, Sun 2–4pm. Tel: (0962) 863064.*
Royal Greenjackets Museum: *All year (exc. 14 days at Christmas), Mon–Sat 10am–5pm, Sun 12am–4pm.*
Royal Hamsphire Regiment Museum and Memorial Garden: *April–Oct, Mon-Fri 10am–12.30pm and 2–4pm, Sat–Sun and BHs 12am–4pm.*
Winchester Gallery: *All year, Tues–Fri 10am–4.30pm. Tel: (0962) 842500.*
Royal Hussars Museum: *All year, Mon–Fri 10am–4pm, Sat–Sun and BHs 12am–4pm.*
Guildhall Gallery: *All year, Tues–Sat 10am–5pm, Sun–Mon 2–5pm. Closed Mons Oct–Mar. Tel: (0962) 848269.*
Winchester Heritage Centre: *March–Oct, Tues–Sat 10.30am–12.30pm and 2–4pm, Sun 2–4pm.*
Hospital of St Cross: *All year, Mon–Sat: Summer 9.30am–12.30pm and 2–5pm; winter 10.30am–12.30pm and 2–3.30pm.*
Gurkha Museum: *Tues–Sat and BH Mons 10am–5pm, Sun 12am–5pm.*
Tourist Information Centre: *Guildhall, The Broadway. Tel: (0962) 840500.*

WINCHFIELD

Map p.156, D4 *
9 miles E of Basingstoke off the A30

The restoration of the Basingstoke Canal has breathed new life into Winchfield in the past twenty years. It was here, at Barley Bow Bridge in 1973, that the restoration project began. Since then 32 miles of waterway and towpath have been cleared. Winchfield remains important since it is the turning point for the John Pinkerton pleasure barge which operates from Odiham. There is a car park and a launching area for small boats.

Ironically it was the coming of the railway 150 years ago, leading to the demise of the canal, which first gave Winchfield some importance. Before the line through to Basingstoke and Southampton was completed, Winchfield was a temporary terminus and the mail brought by train from London would be transferred to horse-drawn coaches for wider distribution.

There is the site of a Stone Age settlement at Bagwell Green, a few hundred yards past the church in the direction of Odiham Common. The church itself was built in the 12th century and is regarded as an outstanding example of Norman architecture.

WOLVERTON

Map p.155, C2
5 miles NW of Basingstoke on the A339

Lanes bordered by high hedges connect Wolverton's scattered hamlets, commons, farms, and inns. Many of the farms are picturesque, with thatched buildings and duck ponds. The big house and church stand somewhat apart; a footpath from the overgrown churchyard leads down past the rendered late Georgian Wolverton House – the only substantial mansion in this once less fashionable part of the county – into the park and woods.

St Catherine's Church** is probably the best early Georgian church in Hampshire. The classically inspired brick west tower stands proudly over the church, whose odd proportions derive from its being a medieval building which was encased in red brick with unusual blue brick dressings. Stepped gables with round-headed niches on the transepts and east end give an 18th-century gloss to a 15th-century shape; of the original church, the charming braced timber roof survives inside. Otherwise, almost all the fittings – the box pews, the chancel panelling and reredos, the communion rail, and the curious arches which give access to the delicately carved matching pulpit and lectern – are of 1716, the date of the new church.

WONSTON

Map p.149, C3
9 miles N of Winchester off the A34

The **Church of Holy Trinity** claims to be the earliest recorded church in the county (901). It retains its 16th-century tower but has been repeatedly gutted by fire, most recently in 1908 when the Winchester fire engine, still horse-drawn, arrived too late to save the roof. In his rebuilding Sir Thomas Jackson incorporated the original chancel and chancel-arch and aumbry (a closed recess in the church wall), all of 1225, and south doorway (1170), and added an elegant arcade of fluted columns. Painted panels record the generosity of four founders of local charities but are outdone by another memorable (if inelegantly worded) claim to the regard of posterity: 'The best Benefactor to this church (burnt by fire) Was (10 guineas, a gift by) John Wallop Esquire.'

The Royal Arms above the south doorway are those of George IV and unusually incorporate those of Hanover.

Old House, to the west of the church, looks like a stuccoed Georgian building, but a glance at the roof-line shows that it merits its name; within there remains the skeleton of a 14th-century hall house.

WOODGREEN

Map p.141, C3 *
3 miles NE of Fordingbridge off the A338

The **village hall**** is the focus of life in Woodgreen, for inside its white-rendered walls is an extraordinary series of murals, painted in 1932 and celebrating all aspects of village life. The whole village is there, at the flower show or in Sunday school, morris dancing, picking apples or milking cows, and the individuals are named on plaques below each painting. The artists themselves, then newly qualified, portrayed themselves above the stage. The key to the hall is available from number 10, opposite the pub (a donation is appreciated). The pub also features in the mural, as do the cows and ponies which still roam the village lanes, as well as the panoramic viewpoint over the Avon Valley from the great Iron Age fortification of Castle Hill just to the south.

WOOTTON ST LAWRENCE

Map p.155, D3 *
3 miles W of Basingstoke off the B3400

St Lawrence's Church* by the green in the main village centre is a large flint building, which was extensively rebuilt in 1864 but still retains fine late Norman features like the south doorway and north arcade. The south arcade, by contrast, has exuberantly carved foliage and marble pillars which shout its Victorian date. The memorials inside deserve most attention, with many tablets to the Wither family and a remarkable tomb in the chancel by Roubiliac, executed in the 1750s but in the spirit of the 1670s to commemorate the young Sir Thomas Hooke who died in 1677. A glass window of 1953 to Charles Butler, a 17th-century rector who was a pioneering authority on bees, incorporates an image of the pre-1864 church; modern engraved glass memorials windows in the south aisle by Lawrence Whistler (whose distinctive and pretty work is found elsewhere in Hampshire) depict Manydown and Wootton Houses, two of the three large houses in the parish.

There is still considerable woodland in the parish, especially between the fields to the west, while most houses are concentrated in the main village or the hamlet of Upper Wootton on higher ground to the north. The older brick and flint houses, sitting on large plots, have been interspersed with newer housing; otherwise there are very few signs of Basingstoke's close proximity.

The nave, Winchester Cathedral.

Road Map Symbols

A20	Primary route
A286	Other A road
B270	B road
	Minor road
	Ring road
	Dual carriageway
	Road under construction
	Narrow road with passing places
	Drive or track
3	Distance in miles
BUXTON	Primary route destination
Toll	Steep gradient, Toll
BATTLE	Railway, Station and Level crossing
	County boundary
Sand Shingle	Beach

	Car ferry
(V)	Internal car ferry
(P)	Passenger only ferry
(H)	Hovercraft
R. SEVERN	Navigable river or canal
6	Lock, Flight of locks
	National Park, Forest Park or Area of Outstanding Natural Beauty
	Wooded area
	Principal airport
	Airfield
▲965	Principal height (in feet)
⚔ 1066	Site of battle and date
T	RAC/AA Telephone Box
	Caravan & camping sites

Recognised by the Countryside Commission

NORTH DOWNS WAY	Long distance footpath
	Picnic area
LIGHTWATER	Country park

Scale 1:100,000 (approximately 1½ miles to 1 inch)

0 1 2 3 4 5 **miles**

0 1 2 3 4 5 6 7 8 **kilometres**

Cartography: George Philip Ltd

© 1991 George Philip Ltd

The representation in these maps of any road, drive or track is not evidence of the existence of a right of way. Based upon the Ordnance Survey maps with the sanction of the Controller of Her Majesty's Stationery Office, © Crown Copyright.

Tourist Symbols

Tourist Information Centre	Art collection	Historic ship
Tourist Information Centre Summer only	Art collection/museum	Zoo
House (N.T. if National Trust)	Ancient monument	Safari park
Garden	Earthwork	Farm park
House & Garden	Windmill/Watermill	Aquarium/Dolphinarium
Castle	Other places of interest	Bird sanctuary/Aviary
Cathedral	Roman antiquities	Viewpoint
Abbey/Priory	Steam/miniature railway	Golf Course
Church	Transport collection	BRANDS HATCH Motor racing circuit
Museum	Military museum	NEWBURY Race course
Local museum	Maritime museum	JORDANS Youth hostel

Key Map

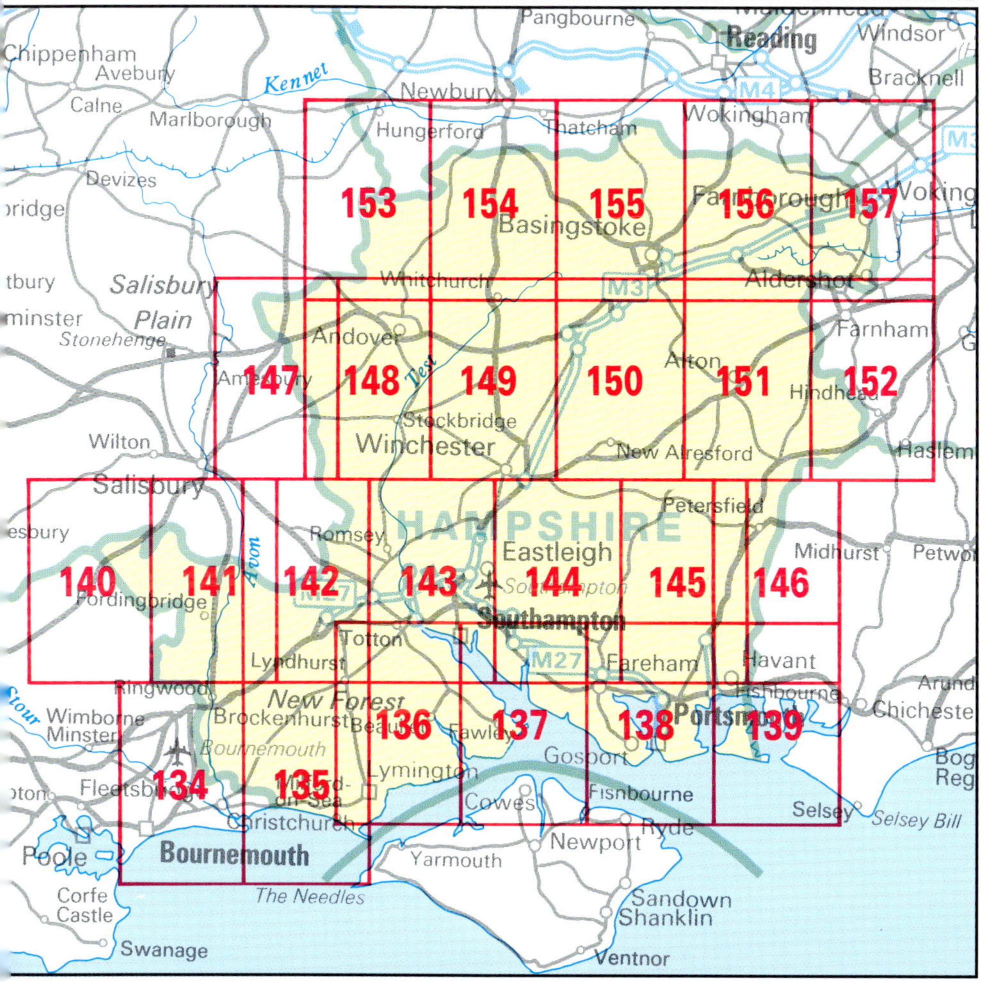

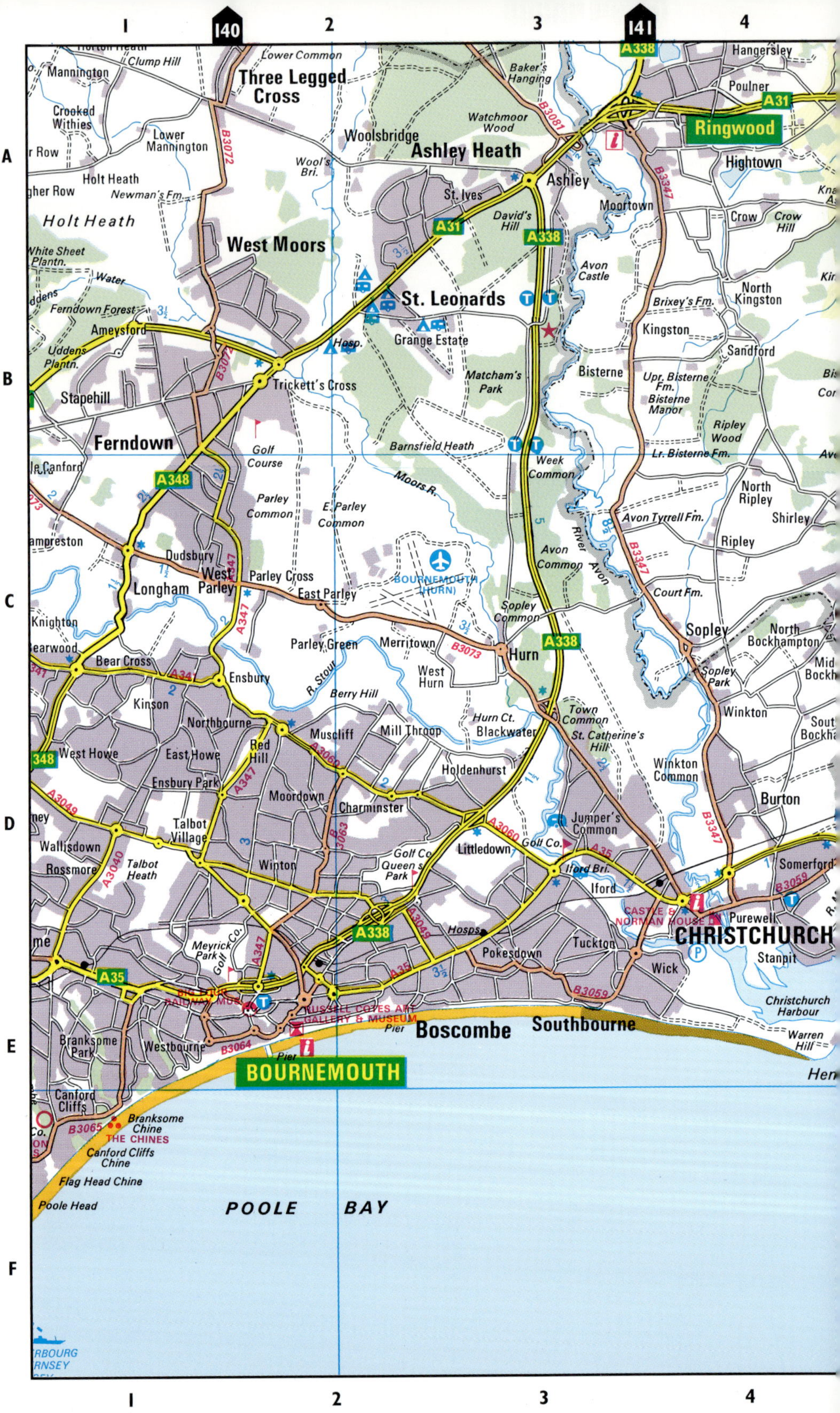
140
141
Three Legged Cross
Lower Common
Clump Hill
Mannington
Crooked Withies
Lower Mannington
Holt Heath
Newman's Fm.
Woolsbridge
Wool's Bri.
Ashley Heath
Baker's Hanging
Watchmoor Wood
Ringwood
Hangersley
Poulner
Hightown
Ashley
St. Ives
David's Hill
Moortown
Crow
Crow Hill
West Moors
White Sheet Plantn.
Ferndown Forest
Ameysford
Uddens Plantn.
St. Leonards
Grange Estate
Hosp.
Avon Castle
North Kingston
Brixey's Fm.
Kingston
Sandford
Bisterne
Upr. Bisterne Fm.
Bisterne Manor
Ripley Wood
Lr. Bisterne Fm.
Trickett's Cross
Matcham's Park
Stapehill
Ferndown
Golf Course
Barnsfield Heath
Week Common
Moors R.
Parley Common
E. Parley Common
North Ripley
Shirley
Avon Tyrrell Fm.
Ripley
Dudsbury
West Parley
Parley Cross
Longham
East Parley
BOURNEMOUTH (HURN)
Avon Common
River Avon
Court Fm.
Sopley Common
Sopley
North Bockhampton
Sopley Park
Knighton
Bear Cross
Parley Green
Merritown
Hurn
West Hurn
Ensbury
Kinson
R. Stour
Berry Hill
Town Common
St. Catherine's Hill
Winkton
Northbourne
Muscliff
Mill Throop
Hurn Ct.
Blackwater
West Howe
East Howe
Red Hill
Holdenhurst
Winkton Common
Ensbury Park
Moordown
Charminster
Burton
Wallisdown
Talbot Village
Littledown
Jumper's Common
Golf Co.
Rossmore
Talbot Heath
Winton
Queen's Park
Iford Bri.
Iford
Somerford
CASTLE & NORMAN HOUSE
Purewell
CHRISTCHURCH
Stanpit
Hosps.
Meyrick Park
Pokesdown
Tuckton
Wick
BIG FOUR RAILWAY MUSEUM
RUSSELL COTES ART GALLERY & MUSEUM
Pier
Boscombe
Southbourne
Christchurch Harbour
Warren Hill
Branksome Park
Westbourne
BOURNEMOUTH
Canford Cliffs
Branksome Chine
THE CHINES
Canford Cliffs Chine
Flag Head Chine
Poole Head
POOLE BAY
A338
A31
A348
A347
A341
A3049
A3040
A3060
A35
B3081
B3072
B3347
B3073
B3063
B3064
B3065
B3059
A, B, C, D, E, F
1, 2, 3, 4

141
142
136
Picket Post
Picket Plain
Old Ho.
Anderwood Inclosure
Inclosure
Gritnam Wood
Hursthill Inclosure
Berry Wood
Burley Lo.
Dames Slough Inclosure
Vinney Ridge Inclosure
Whitley Wood
Parkhill Inclosure
Verely Hill
Burley Moor
South Oakley Inclosure
Poundhill Inclosure
Hollands Wood
Burley Street
Burley New Inclosure
N
E
W
F
Black Water
Vales Moor
Rhinefield Sandy's Inclosure
Poundhill Heath
New Park
Castle Hill
Burley Old Inclosure
Ober Heath
Pignal Inclosure
Burley Hill
Burley Lawn
Rhinefield Ho.
Cranes Moor
Ober Water
Aldridgehill Inclosure
Burley
BURLEY Golf Course
Bisterne Close
Black Knowl
Great
Butts Lawn
Balmerlawn
Markway Hill
Slap
Clay Hill
North Weirs
Brockenhurst
Goatspen Plain
Wilverley Plain
Hinchelsea Moor
South Weirs
Brockenhurst Park
A35
B3055
A337
Dur Hill Down
Holmsley Lo.
Blackhamsley
Hinchelsea Ho.
Golf Co.
Wilverley Inclosure
Setley
Long Slade Bottom
Thorney Hill Holms
Holmsley Inclosure
Thorney Hill
Setley Plain
Setley Common
Brownhill Inclosure
Wootton Coppice Inclosure
Set Thorns Inclosure
Avon Water
Widden Bottom
Battramsley
Broadley Inclosure
Plain Heath
Boldre Grange
B3058
Wootton
Sway
Durns Town
Battramsley Cross
Poors Common
Heathfield
Mead End
Birchy Hill
St. Austins
Ossemsley
Bransgore
Arnewood Manor
Mount Pleasant
Nth. Hinton Fm.
Tiptoe
Bashley
Bashley Park
Neacroft
Ossemsley Manor Ho.
Arnewood Ct.
Buckland
Beckley
Godwinscroft
Hinton Park
Hordle Grange
Gordleton
Ramley
Bashley Manor Fm.
Hinton Admiral
Waterditch
Hordle
Upper Pennington
Lymington
Hinton Ho.
Cat & Fiddle Inn
Hinton
New Milton
Golden Hill
Arnewood Ho.
Batchley Fm.
Ashley
HINTON ADMIRAL
Walkford
Old Milton
Hooper's Hill
Yeatton Ho.
Pennington
Efford Ho.
Everton
A337
Ashley Manor Fm.
Ashley Clinton
Newlands Manor
Experimental Horticulture Station
Downton
Leagreen
Lower Pennington
Golf Co.
HIGHCLIFFE CASTLE
Lymore
Highcliffe
Barton on Sea
Golf Course
Hordle Ho.
Mudeford
Keyhaven Marshes
Hordle Cliff
Milford on Sea
Keyhaven
CHRISTCHURCH BAY
Sturt Pond
Salt Grass
Hurst Beach
HURST CASTLE
Totland Bay
Hatherwood Pt.
Headon Warren
B3322

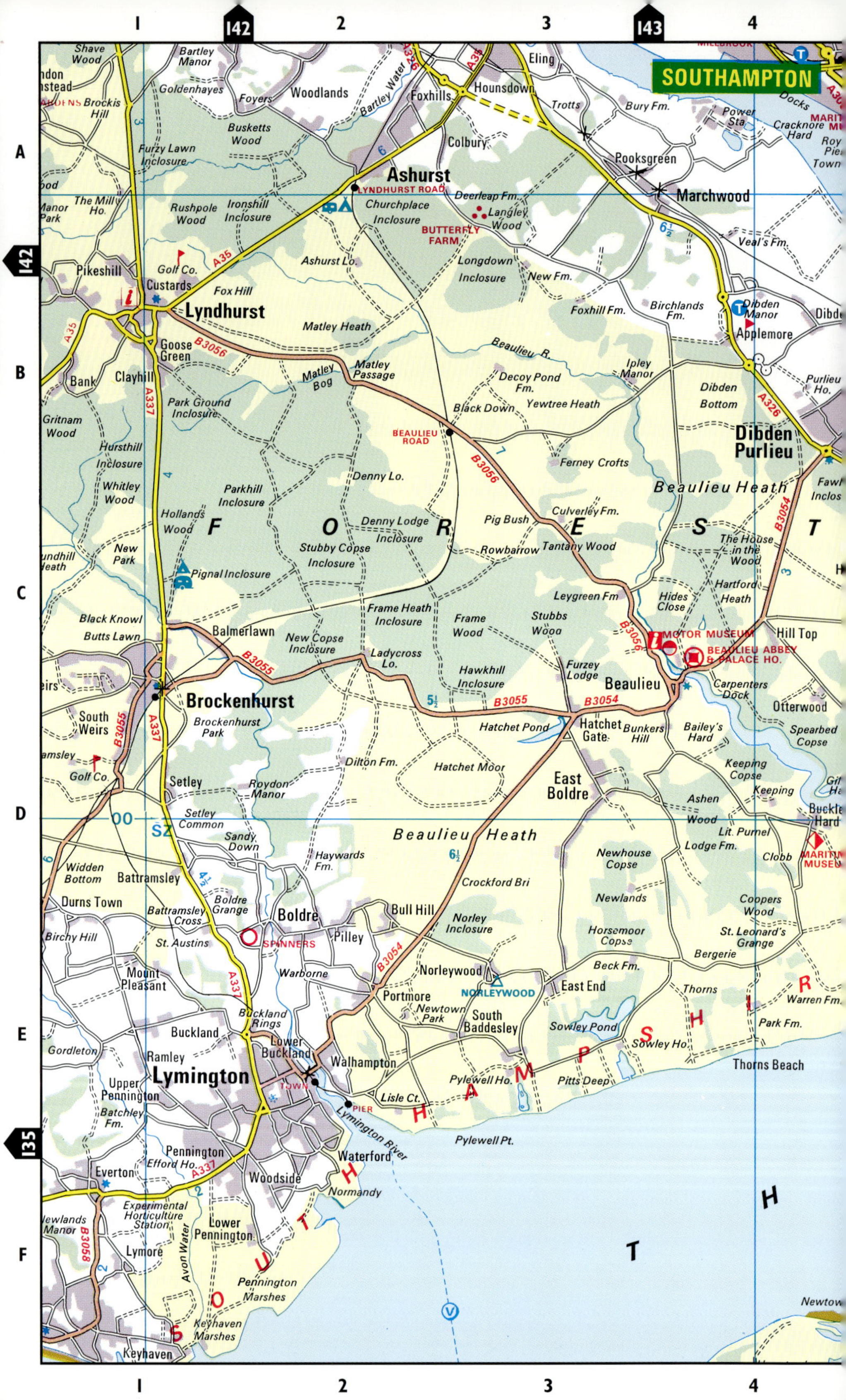
SOUTHAMPTON
Ashurst
Lyndhurst
Brockenhurst
Lymington
Beaulieu
Dibden Purlieu
Marchwood
F O R E S T
Beaulieu Heath
Eling
Hounsdown
Foxhills
Colbury
Woodlands
Trotts
Bury Fm.
Pooksgreen
Bartley Manor
Shave Wood
Goldenhayes
Foyers
Brockis Hill
Busketts Wood
Furzy Lawn Inclosure
The Mill Ho.
Rushpole Wood
Ironshill Inclosure
Churchplace Inclosure
LYNDHURST ROAD
BUTTERFLY FARM
Deerleap Fm.
Langley Wood
Longdown Inclosure
New Fm.
Foxhill Fm.
Birchlands Fm.
Dibden Manor
Applemore
Veal's Fm.
Pikeshill
Golf Co.
Custards
Fox Hill
Ashurst Lo.
Matley Heath
Goose Green
Bank
Clayhill
Matley Bog
Matley Passage
Beaulieu R.
Decoy Pond Fm.
Yewtree Heath
Ipley Manor
Dibden Bottom
Purlieu Ho.
Black Down
BEAULIEU ROAD
Gritnam Wood
Park Ground Inclosure
Hursthill Inclosure
Whitley Wood
Parkhill Inclosure
Denny Lo.
Ferney Crofts
Hollands Wood
Denny Lodge Inclosure
Pig Bush
Culverley Fm.
Stubby Copse Inclosure
Rowbarrow
Tantany Wood
The House in the Wood
Hartford Heath
New Park
Pignal Inclosure
Frame Heath Inclosure
Frame Wood
Stubbs Wood
Leygreen Fm
Hides Close
Black Knowl
Butts Lawn
Balmerlawn
New Copse Inclosure
Ladycross Lo.
Hawkhill Inclosure
Furzey Lodge
MOTOR MUSEUM
BEAULIEU ABBEY & PALACE HO.
Hill Top
Carpenters Dock
Otterwood
South Weirs
Brockenhurst Park
Hatchet Pond
Hatchet Gate
Bunkers Hill
Bailey's Hard
Spearbed Copse
Golf Co.
Setley
Roydon Manor
Dilton Fm.
Hatchet Moor
East Boldre
Keeping Copse
Keeping
Setley Common
Sandy Down
Ashen Wood
Lodge Fm.
Lit. Pumel
Clobb
Buckle Hard
Widden Bottom
Battramsley
Haywards Fm.
Crockford Bri
Newhouse Copse
Newlands
Coppers Wood
Durns Town
Battramsley Cross
Boldre Grange
Boldre
Bull Hill
Norley Inclosure
Horsemoor Copse
St. Leonard's Grange
Bergerie
Birchy Hill
St. Austins
SPINNERS
Pilley
Norleywood
NORLEYWOOD
Beck Fm.
Mount Pleasant
Warborne
Portmore
East End
Thorns
Warren Fm.
Buckland Rings
Newtown Park
South Baddesley
Sowley Pond
Park Fm.
Buckland
Lower Buckland
Sowley Ho.
Gordleton
Ramley
Walhampton
Thorns Beach
Upper Pennington
TOWN
Pylewell Ho.
Pitts Deep
Batchley Fm.
Lisle Ct.
PIER
Lymington River
Pylewell Pt.
Pennington
Efford Ho.
Waterford
Everton
Woodside
Normandy
Experimental Horticulture Station
Newlands Manor
Lower Pennington
Lymore
Avon Water
Pennington Marshes
Keyhaven Marshes
Keyhaven
S O U T H A M P T O N
H A M P S H I R E
A35
A337
A326
B3056
B3055
B3054
B3058
142
143
135
1
2
3
4
A
B
C
D
E
F

143
144
Hedge End
Hightown
Sholing
Weston Common
Sholing Common
Peartree Green
Itchen
Woolston
Newtown
Weston
Old Netley
Lowford
Bursledon
UPPER HAMBLE
Hoe Moor Ho.
Burridge Fm.
Burridge
Curbridge
Ridge Fm.
Ridge Copse
Botley Wood
Whiteley
Swanwick
Lower Swanwick
Sarisbury
SWANWICK
Park Gate
Lee Ground Coppice
Lee Ground
M27
Hythe
Pier
SOUTHAMPTON WATER
NETLEY ABBEY
Netley
Royal Victoria Hospital
ROYAL VICTORIA
Hamblecliff Ho.
Butlocks Heath
Hound
College
Hamble
Hamble Common
River Hamble
Locks Heath
TITCHFIELD ABBEY
Titchfield Common
Fleetend
Warsash
Newtown
Hook
Titchfield
Gt. Posbrook
Solent Ct.
Singledge Ho.
Lit. Posbrook
Solent Breezes
Brownwich Fm.
Langdown
Buttsash
Hardley
Little Holbury
Holbury Manor
Holbury
Fawley
Ashlett
Rollstone Fm.
Fields Heath
Fields Fm.
Power Sta.
CALSHOT CASTLE
Blackfield
Tom's Down
Badminston Common
Calshot
Blackwell Common
Sprat's Down
Langley
West Common
Stanswood Fm.
Nelson's Pl.
Exbury
Exbury Ho.
Stanswood Bay
Calshot Buoy
Titchfield Haven
Hill Head
138
Cadland Ho.
LEPE & CALSHOT FORESHORES
Stone Fm.
Lepe Fm.
Lower Exbury
Inchmery Ho.
Lepe
Stansore Pt.
Stone Pt.
HYDROFOIL
Needs Ore Pt.
SOLENT
Cowes Roads
Cowes
Castle
Egypt Pt.
Old Castle Pt.
Norris Castle
East Cowes
Golf Co.
MARITIME MUSEUM
Gurnard Bay
Osborne Bay
Gurnard
OSBORNE HOUSE
Barton Wood
Barton Manor
Gurnard Ledge
Rew Street
Gurnard Pines
Thorness Bay
King's Quay
Medham Ho.
Whippingham
Northwood
Woodhouse Fm.
Padmore Ho.
River Medina
Dallmores
Pilgrim's Park
Lit. Thorness
Great Thorness
Hillis Corner
Skinners Fm.
Werrar Fm.
Wootton
WOOTTON BRIDGE
Burnt Wood
Alverstone Fm.
Mark's Corner
Whitehouse Fm.
Binfield Fm.
Porchfield
Nature
Wootton Bridge
A B C D E F
1 2 3 4

144
145
137
Wickham
Meon Park
Cold Harbour Fm.
Webb's Land
R. Meon
Castle Fm.
Wickham Common
B2177
Hundred Acres
Goathouse Fm.
Little Forest
North Boarhunt
Corner
Worlds End
Hipley Copse
Ashlands
Staple Cross
Walton Heath
Lodge Fm.
Denmead
Eastland Gate
Bunkers Hill
Mead End
Anmore
FOREST OF
East or Creech Walk
Soake
Furzeley Corner
Creech Fm.
Closewood
Wanstead Fm.
Waterlooville
Southwick
Newlands Fm.
Purbrook
Hookheath Fm.
Crockerhill
Bere Fm.
Albany Fm.
Knowle Hosp.
Wallington R.
White Dell Fm.
Boarhunt
Funtley
Kneller Ct.
A32
Nth. Fareham Fm.
Ft. Nelson
Nelson's Mon.
Ports Down
Pigeon Ho. Fm.
Ft. Widley
Widley
Ft. Purbrook
FAREHAM
Wallington
M27
Catisfield
PORTCHESTER
Paulsgrove
Hosp.
Wymering
Drayton
A27
Lower Quay
Cams Hall
PORTSMOUTH
Cosham
West End
Ft. Fareham
Newlands Fm.
HMS Collingwood
B3385
Fleetlands
Foxbury Pt.
Portchester
PORTCHESTER CASTLE
Hilsea
Pewit I.
Stubbington
Peel Common
Bridgemary
PORTSMOUTH HARBOUR
Tipner
A3
M275
A2030
A288
A2047
B3334
LEE-ON-SOLENT
Chark Common
Ft. Brockhurst
Elson
Whale I
Stamshaw
North End
Golf Course
Hardway
PORTSMOUTH
Copnor
PORTSEA ISLAND
Golf Co.
Cherque Fm.
Rowner
Ft. Rowner
Brockhurst
Baffins
Burrow
MARY ROSE
Landport
B2752
Portsea
H.M.S. VICTORY
H.M.S. WARRIOR
HARBOUR
PORTSMOUTH & SOUTHSEA
Hosp.
Fratton
B3386
R. Alver
Ft. Grange
Annis Hill
GOSPORT
Lee-on-the-Solent
B3333
Privett
SUBMARINE MUS./H.M.S. ALLIANCE
Milton
Eastney
Browndown
Browndown Pt.
Alverstoke
H.M.S. Dolphin
Haslar Royal Naval Hosp.
Clarence Pier
B2151
B2154
West Winner
Stokes Bay
Clayhall
D-DAY MUS.
CASTLE MUSEUM
Pier
Southsea
Golf Co.
Gilkicker Pt.
Spit Sand Fort
SPITHEAD
Horse Sand Fort
No Man's Land Fort
Ryde Roads
PIER HEAD
Pier
Ryde
RYDE ESPLANADE
Ryde East Sands
Fishbourne
Golf Co.
A3054
Puckpool Pt.
Appley
Quarr Hill
Kite Hill
Binstead
ST JOHN'S ROAD
Weeks
Spring Vale
Nettlestone Pt.
Oakfield
B3330
Seaview
Mill
Newnham

145
146
1
2
3
4
A
B
C
D
E
F
BERE
Cowplain
The Queen's Inclosure
Golf Co
Havant Thicket
Bell's Copse
Dunsbury Hill Fm.
A3(M)
The Holt
Wellsworth
Golf Co.
Red Hill
Durrants
Rowland's Castle
Stansted Forest
Horsepasture Fm
STANSTED PARK
Stansted Ho.
Broadreed Fm.
Lumley Seat
B2146
Stoughton
Walderton
Walderton Down
Lordington
Stubbermere
Sindle's Fm.
Racton Monument
Adsdean Ho.
Downs Fm.
Racton Park Fm.
Funtington Down Ho.
Funtington
Southleigh Forest
Southleigh Park
R. Ems
Aldsworth
B2147
B2148
Stakes
West Leigh
Leigh Park
E. Leigh Ho.
Stockheath
B2149
Denvilles
HAVANT
New Brighton
Emsworth
Westbourne
A27
Woodmancote
Balsam's Fm.
Northbrook Fm.
Hambrook Ho
Hambrook
Breach
Inlands
Lumley
Hermitage
Southbourne
Ratham Mill
Bedhampton
Brockhampton
B2177
B2150
WARBLINGTON
A2030
A259
Warblington Castle
Langstone
A3023
Conigar Pt.
Prinsted
Nutbourne
Broadbridge
Bosham
North Binness I.
Long I.
Broad Lake
Langston Bri
Fowley I.
Great Deep
Eastfield Fm.
Chidham
Thorney Island
Thorney Airfield
Stanbury Pt.
Cobnor Fm
Southwood Fm.
Lowerhone Fm.
Baker's I.
South Binness I.
Russell's Lake
LANGSTONE HARBOUR
Northney
North Hayling
Tye
Stoke
Emsworth Channel
Marker Pt.
West Thorney
Cobnor Ho.
Cobnor Pt.
Bosham
Langstone Channel
Fleet
HAYLING ISLAND
Manor Ho.
Longmere Pt.
West Itchenor
Itchenor Ho.
Westlands Fm
Pilsey I.
SU
00
Gable Head
Tourner Bury
CHICHESTER HARBOUR
Stocker's Lake
Rookwood
Shipton Green
Holt Pl.
Golf Co
Ft Cumberland
Sinah Common
West Town
Westfield
Mengham
Selsmore
Eastoke
Black Pt.
East Head
Walnut Tree Ho.
Holme's Fm.
B2179
Somerley
East Winner
Hayling Bay
South Hayling
Eastoke Point
West Wittering
Cakeham Manor Ho.
East Wittering
B2198
Bracklesham
Bracklesham Bay

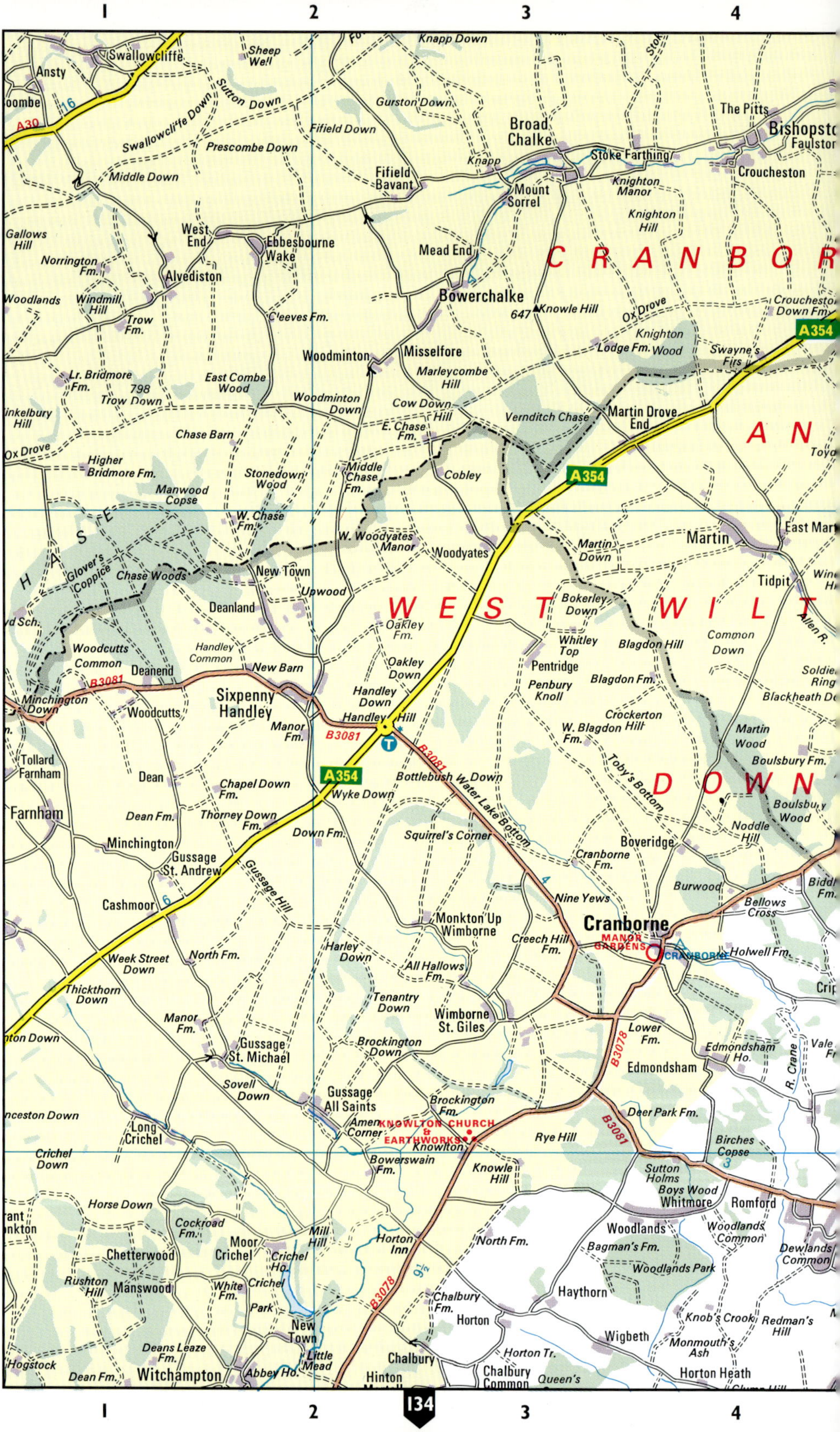

1
2
3
4
A
B
C
D
E
F
Swallowcliffe
Ansty
A30
Sheep Well
Sutton Down
Knapp Down
Gurston Down
Swallowcliffe Down
Fifield Down
Prescombe Down
Broad Chalke
The Pitts
Bishopstone
Faulston
Stoke Farthing
Knapp
Croucheston
Fifield Bavant
Mount Sorrel
Knighton Manor
Middle Down
Knighton Hill
Gallows Hill
West End
Ebbesbourne Wake
Mead End
Norrington Fm.
Alvediston
CRANBORNE
Bowerchalke
647
Knowle Hill
Ox Drove
Croucheston Down Fm.
Woodlands
Windmill Hill
Trow Fm.
Cleeves Fm.
Knighton Wood
Lodge Fm.
Swayne's Firs
A354
Woodminton
Misselfore
Marleycombe Hill
Lr. Bridmore Fm.
798
Trow Down
East Combe Wood
Woodminton Down
Cow Down Hill
Verditch Chase
Martin Drove End
E. Chase Fm.
Chase Barn
Ox Drove
Higher Bridmore Fm.
Middle Chase Fm.
Stonedown Wood
Cobley
CHASE
AND
Manwood Copse
W. Chase Fm.
W. Woodyates Manor
Woodyates
Martin Down
Martin
East Martin
Glover's Coppice
Chase Woods
New Town
Upwood
Tidpit
Deanland
WEST WILTS
Bokerley Down
Oakley Fm.
Whitley Top
Blagdon Hill
Common Down
Allen R.
Woodcutts Common
Handley Common
New Barn
Oakley Down
Pentridge
Deanend
B3081
Penbury Knoll
Blagdon Fm.
Soldiers Ring
Blackheath Down
Minchington Down
Sixpenny Handley
Handley Down
Handley Hill
Crockerton Hill
Woodcutts
Manor Fm.
W. Blagdon Fm.
Martin Wood
Tollard Farnham
Boulsbury Fm.
Toby's Bottom
Dean
Chapel Down Fm.
Bottlebush Down
Water Lake Bottom
DOWN
Wyke Down
Boulsbury Wood
Farnham
Dean Fm.
Thorney Down Fm.
Noddle Hill
Down Fm.
Squirrel's Corner
Cranborne Fm.
Boveridge
Minchington
Gussage St. Andrew
Gussage Hill
Burwood
Nine Yews
Cashmoor
Monkton Up Wimborne
Cranborne
Bellows Cross
MANOR GARDENS
CRANBORNE
Holwell Fm.
Creech Hill Fm.
Week Street Down
North Fm.
Harley Down
All Hallows Fm.
Thickthorn Down
Tenantry Down
Wimborne St. Giles
Manor Fm.
Lower Fm.
B3078
Edmondsham Ho.
Gussage St. Michael
Brockington Down
Edmondsham
R. Crane
Sovell Down
Gussage All Saints
Brockington Fm.
Deer Park Fm.
Long Crichel
Amen Corner
KNOWLTON CHURCH & EARTHWORKS
Knowlton
Rye Hill
Birches Copse
Crichel Down
Bowerswain Fm.
Knowle Hill
Sutton Holms
Boys Wood
Whitmore
Romford
Horse Down
Cockroad Fm.
Woodlands
Woodlands Common
Moor Crichel
Mill Hill
Horton Inn
North Fm.
Bagman's Fm.
Dewlands Common
Chetterwood
Crichel Ho.
Woodlands Park
Rushton Hill
Manswood
White Fm.
Crichel Park
Chalbury Fm.
Haythorn
Horton
Knob's Crook
Redman's Hill
New Town
Wigbeth
Monmouth's Ash
Deans Leaze Fm.
Little Mead
Chalbury
Horton Tr.
Hogstock
Dean Fm.
Witchampton
Abbey Ho.
Hinton
Chalbury Common
Queen's
Horton Heath
134

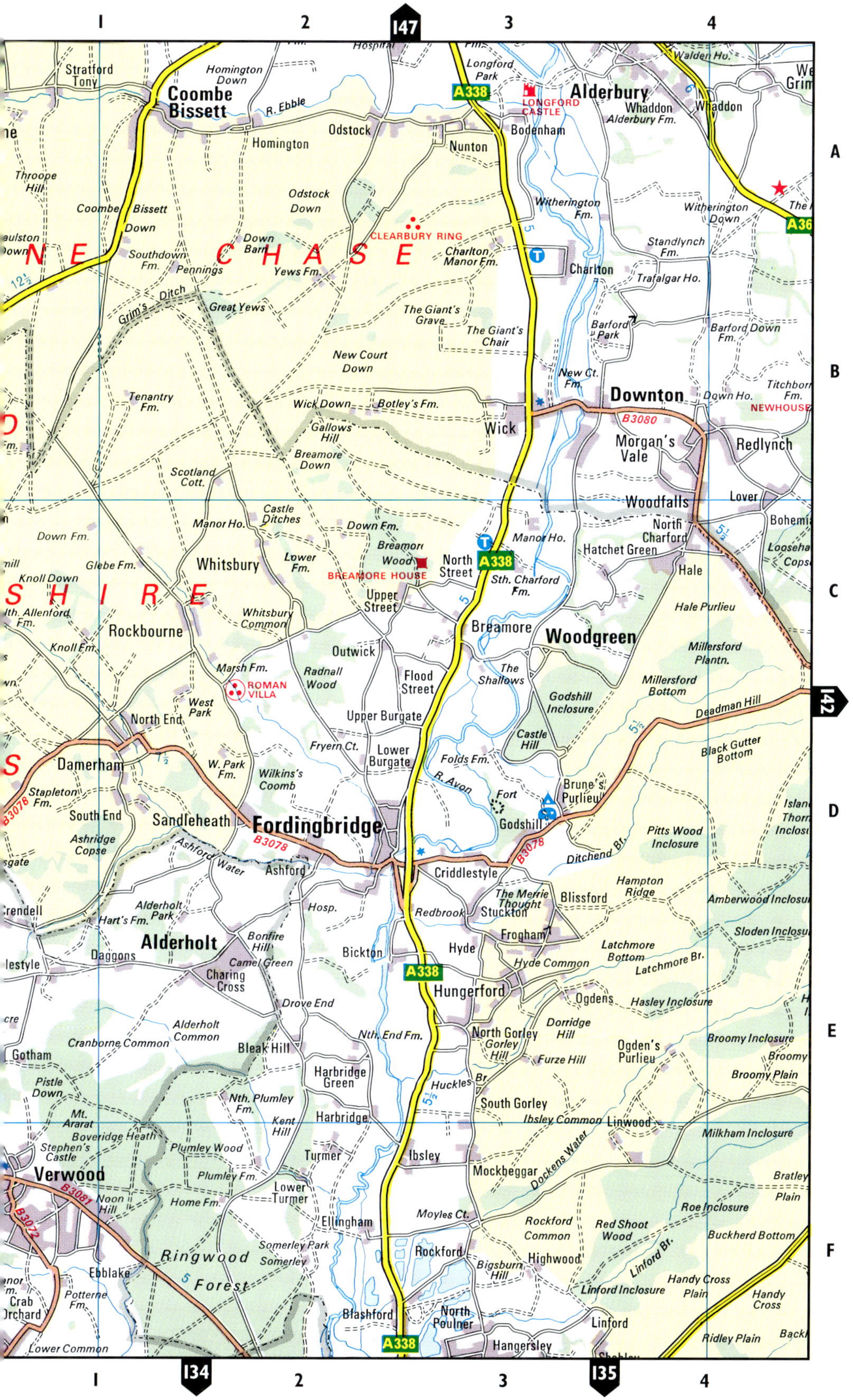

147
142
134
135
A338
B3080
B3078
B3081
B3072
Stratford Tony
Homington Down
Coombe Bissett
R. Ebble
Odstock
Homington
Nunton
Longford Park
LONGFORD CASTLE
Alderbury
Whaddon
Alderbury Fm.
Bodenham
Walden Ho.
Throope Hill
Coombe Bissett Down
Odstock Down
CLEARBURY RING
Witherington Fm.
Witherington Down
Southdown Fm.
Pennings
Down Barn
Yews Fm.
Charlton Manor Fm.
Charlton
Standlynch Fm.
Trafalgar Ho.
CHASE
Grim's Ditch
Great Yews
The Giant's Grave
The Giant's Chair
Barford Park
Barford Down Fm.
New Court Down
New Ct. Fm.
Downton
Down Ho.
Titchborne Fm.
NEWHOUSE
Tenantry Fm.
Wick Down
Botley's Fm.
Gallows Hill
Wick
Morgan's Vale
Redlynch
Breamore Down
Scotland Cott.
Woodfalls
Lover
Castle Ditches
Manor Ho.
Down Fm.
North Charford
Bohemia
Breamore Wood
BREAMORE HOUSE
Manor Ho.
Hatchet Green
Hale
Looseha... Copse
Down Fm.
Glebe Fm.
Whitsbury
Lower Fm.
North Street
Sth. Charford Fm.
Knoll Down
SHIRE
Nth. Allenford Fm.
Rockbourne
Whitsbury Common
Upper Street
Breamore
Woodgreen
Hale Purlieu
Knoll Fm.
Outwick
Millersford Plantn.
Marsh Fm.
Radnall Wood
Flood Street
The Shallows
Millersford Bottom
ROMAN VILLA
Godshill Inclosure
West Park
North End
Upper Burgate
Deadman Hill
Castle Hill
Damerham
Fryern Ct.
Lower Burgate
Folds Fm.
Black Gutter Bottom
W. Park Fm.
Wilkins's Coomb
R. Avon
Brune's Purlieu
Stapleton Fm.
South End
Fort
Godshill
Pitts Wood Inclosure
Sandleheath
Fordingbridge
Ashridge Copse
Ashford Water
Ashford
Criddlestyle
Ditchend Br.
Hampton Ridge
Alderholt Park
Hosp.
The Merrie Thought
Blissford
Amberwood Inclosure
Hart's Fm.
Redbrook
Stuckton
Frogham
Sloden Inclosure
Alderholt
Bonfire Hill
Daggons
Bickton
Hyde
Latchmore Bottom
Camel Green
Hyde Common
Latchmore Br.
Charing Cross
Hungerford
Ogdens
Hasley Inclosure
Drove End
Alderholt Common
Dorridge Hill
Nth. End Fm.
North Gorley
Gorley Hill
Ogden's Purlieu
Broomy Inclosure
Cranborne Common
Bleak Hill
Furze Hill
Broomy
Gotham
Harbridge Green
Huckles Br.
Broomy Plain
Pistle Down
Nth. Plumley Fm.
South Gorley
Mt. Ararat
Kent Hill
Harbridge
Ibsley Common
Linwood
Milkham Inclosure
Boveridge Heath
Plumley Wood
Stephen's Castle
Turmer
Ibsley
Verwood
Plumley Fm.
Mockbeggar
Dockens Water
Bratley Plain
Noon Hill
Home Fm.
Lower Turmer
Roe Inclosure
Ellingham
Moyles Ct.
Rockford Common
Red Shoot Wood
Buckherd Bottom
Somerley Park
Ringwood
Somerley
Rockford
Highwood
Linford Br.
Ebblake
Bigsburn Hill
Forest
Handy Cross Plain
Crab Orchard
Potterne Fm.
Linford Inclosure
Handy Cross
Blashford
North Poulner
Linford
Lower Common
Hangersley
Ridley Plain

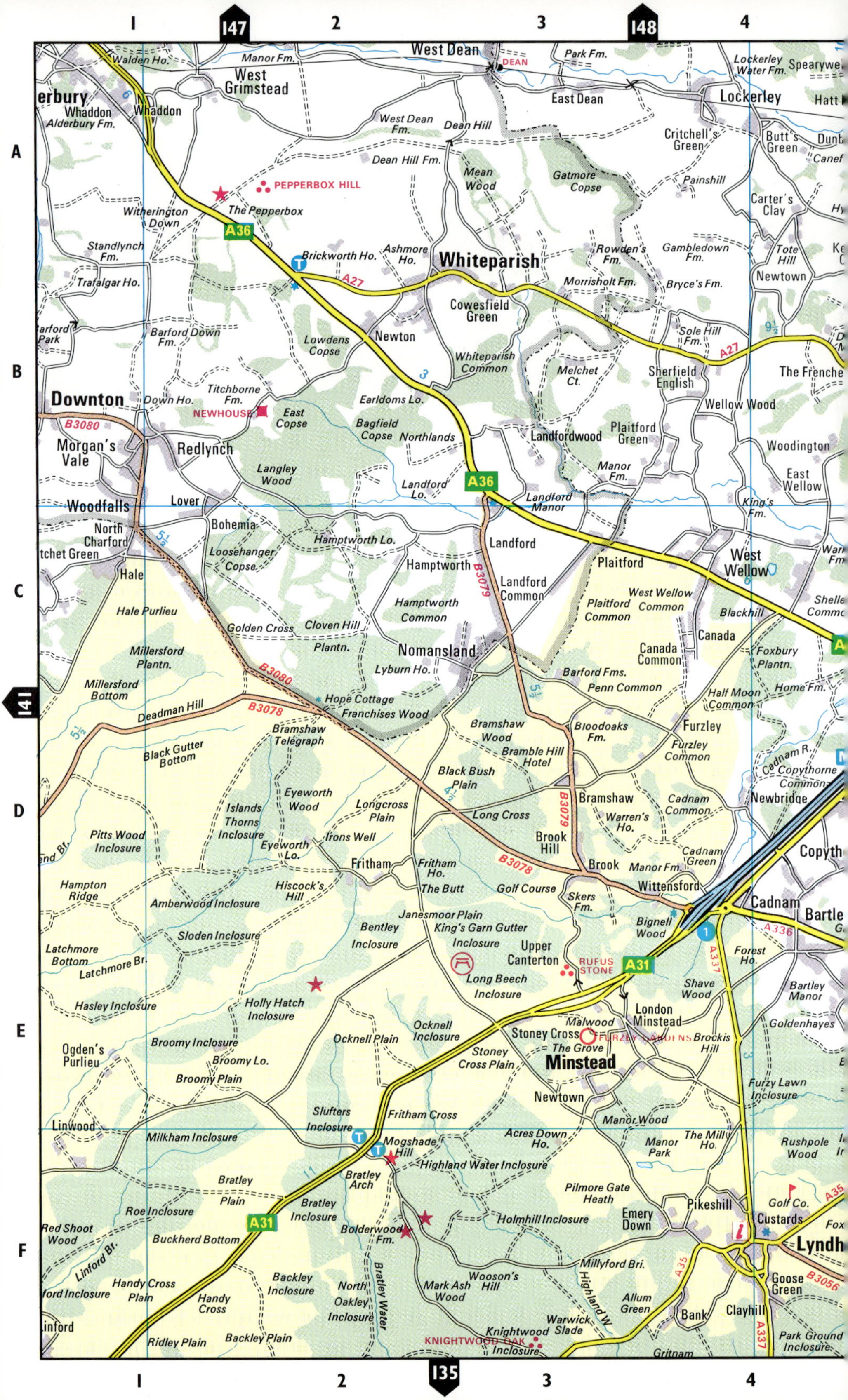
West Dean
DEAN
West Grimstead
Manor Fm.
Park Fm.
Lockerley Water Fm.
East Dean
Lockerley
Whaddon
Alderbury Fm.
West Dean Fm.
Dean Hill
Dean Hill Fm.
Critchell's Green
Butt's Green
PEPPERBOX HILL
The Pepperbox
Mean Wood
Gatmore Copse
Painshill
Carter's Clay
Witherington Down
A36
Standlynch Fm.
Brickworth Ho.
Ashmore Ho.
Whiteparish
Rowden's Fm.
Gambledown Fm.
Tote Hill
Newtown
Trafalgar Ho.
A27
Morrisholt Fm.
Bryce's Fm.
Cowesfield Green
Barford Down Fm.
Lowdens Copse
Newton
Sole Hill Fm.
Whiteparish Common
Melchet Ct.
Sherfield English
The Frenche
Downton
Down Ho.
Titchborne Fm.
NEWHOUSE
East Copse
Earldoms Lo.
Wellow Wood
B3080
Bagfield Copse
Northlands
Landfordwood
Plaitford Green
Woodington
Morgan's Vale
Redlynch
Langley Wood
Manor Fm.
East Wellow
Landford Lo.
Landford Manor
King's Fm.
Woodfalls
Lover
North Charford
Bohemia
Hamptworth Lo.
Landford
Plaitford
West Wellow
Hale
Loosehanger Copse
Hamptworth
B3079
Landford Common
West Wellow Common
Plaitford Common
Blackhill
Hale Purlieu
Hamptworth Common
Golden Cross
Cloven Hill Plantn.
Nomansland
Canada
Canada Common
Foxbury Plantn.
Millersford Plantn.
Lyburn Ho.
Barford Fms.
Penn Common
Millersford Bottom
Half Moon Common
Home Fm.
Deadman Hill
B3078
Hope Cottage
Franchises Wood
Bramshaw Telegraph
Bramshaw Wood
Bloodoaks Fm.
Furzley
Furzley Common
Black Gutter Bottom
Bramble Hill Hotel
Black Bush Plain
Cadnam R.
Copythorne Common
Eyeworth Wood
Islands Thorns Inclosure
Longcross Plain
Long Cross
Bramshaw
Warren's Ho.
Cadnam Common
Newbridge
Pitts Wood Inclosure
Eyeworth Lo.
Irons Well
Brook Hill
Cadnam Green
Fritham
Fritham Ho.
Brook
Manor Fm.
Hampton Ridge
Hiscock's Hill
The Butt
Golf Course
Skers Fm.
Wittensford
Cadnam
Amberwood Inclosure
Janesmoor Plain
Bignell Wood
Bentley Inclosure
King's Garn Gutter Inclosure
Forest Ho.
Latchmore Bottom
Sloden Inclosure
Upper Canterton
A336
A337
Latchmore Br.
RUFUS STONE
A31
Long Beech Inclosure
Shave Wood
Bartley Manor
Hasley Inclosure
Holly Hatch Inclosure
London Minstead
Goldenhayes
Malwood
Ocknell Inclosure
Stoney Cross
FURZEY GARDENS
Brockis Hill
Ocknell Plain
Broomy Inclosure
Ogden's Purlieu
Stoney Cross Plain
The Grove
Minstead
Broomy Lo.
Broomy Plain
Furzy Lawn Inclosure
Newtown
Fritham Cross
Slufters Inclosure
Manor Wood
Linwood
Milkham Inclosure
Acres Down Ho.
Mogshade Hill
The Mill Ho.
Manor Park
Rushpole Wood
Highland Water Inclosure
Bratley Arch
Bratley Plain
Pilmore Gate Heath
Roe Inclosure
Bratley Inclosure
Pikeshill
Emery Down
Golf Co.
A35
Red Shoot Wood
Bolderwood Fm.
Holmhill Inclosure
Custards
Buckherd Bottom
Lyndh
Linford Br.
Millyford Bri.
Backley Inclosure
North Oakley Inclosure
Bratley Water
Mark Ash Wood
Wooson's Hill
Goose Green
B3056
Handy Cross Plain
Handy Cross
Highland W
Allum Green
Bank
Clayhill
Warwick Slade
Knightwood Inclosure
KNIGHTWOOD OAK
Park Ground Inclosure
Ridley Plain
Backley Plain
Gritnam
147
148
135
141

148
149
136
137
144
Mottisfont
MOTTISFONT ABBEY (N.T.)
MOTTISFONT DUNBRIDGE
Kimbridge
Stonymarsh
Bear & Ragged Staff
Michelmersh
Farley Ho.
Hall Place
Pitt Fm.
Upper Slackstead
Violet Hill
Merdon Manor Fm.
Merdon Castle
Nan Trodd's Hill
Standon
Hunt's Fm.
Casbrook Common
Braishfield
H
A
Pucknall
Lower Slackstead
Home Fm.
Hursley Park
Hursley
Shawlands Fm.
Timsbury Manor
Awbridge Ho.
Fairborne's Fm.
Ampfield Wood
Upper Ratley
Awbridge
R. Test
B3084
A3057
Abbotswood Fm.
Jermyns Ho.
Knapp
Ratlake
The Potters Heron
Ladwell
Home Fm.
Cranbury P.
Lower Ratley
Stanbridge Earls
Great Bri.
Abbotswood
Ampfield
Golf Co.
Gosport
Woodley
Crampmoor
B3043
Hiltingbury
Roke Manor
Shootash
Squabb Wood
Cupernham
Romsey
ROMSEY
ROMSEY ABBEY
Spursholt Ho.
A27
A31
Halterworth
Bucket Corner
Flexford
Baddesley Common
Chandler's Ford
Fryern Hill
Sch.
Hall Copse
Burnt Grove
BROADLANDS
Broadlands Ho.
Whitenap
North Baddesley
Nutburn
Great Covert
Zionshill Fm.
Kentford Lake
Ashfield
Embley Wood
R. Blackwater
Yewtree Copse
R. Test
Chilworth
Hut Wood
A33
Toothill
Rownhams Services
Chilworth Manor
Ridge
Lee
M27
Golf Co
Chilworth Common
Golf Course
Nth. Stoneham Park
Wigley
Upton
Rownhams
Moorcourt
Golf Courses
Ower
Nursling Ho.
Lord's Wood
Bassett
Bassett Green
Hillstreet
Nursling
M271
Sports Centre
A35
Swaythling
Stonyford
Mill
Lord's Hill
SOUTHAMPTON
Hampton Park
Testwood Ho.
Aldermoor
University
Barrow Hill
Ord Survey Offices
Coxford
Shirley Warren
Upper Shirley
Highfield
Winsor
Hosp.
Calmore
Testwood
Maybush
Old Shirley
Southampton Common
Bitterne Park
Tatchbury Manor Ho.
Hammond's Green
Redbridge
Wimpson
A30
Portswood
St. Denys
Hanger Fm.
Totton
Shirley
Netley Marsh
A336
REDBRIDGE
TOTTON
A3057
Bitterne
Millbrook
Ashurst Bridge
Brokenford
A3024
Freemantle
Northam Bri.
Northam
ART GALLERY
Civic Centre
A326
Eling
MILLBROOK
SOUTHAMPTON
Peartree Green
River Itchen
Woodlands
Bartley Water
Foxhills
Hounsdown
Docks
A3025
TUDOR HO. MUS.
Itchen
Trotts
Bury Fm.
Power Sta.
Cracknore Hard
MARITIME MUS.
Colbury
Royal Pier
Toll
Woolston
Town Quay
Rooksgreen
Ashurst
LYNDHURST ROAD
Deerleap Fm.
Marchwood
Churchplace Inclosure
Langley Wood
BUTTERFLY FARM
Veal's Fm.
Ashurst Lo.
Longdown Inclosure
New Fm.
NETLEY ABBEY
SOUTHAMPTON
Pier
Hythe
Foxhill Fm.
Birchlands Fm.
Dibden Manor
Dibden
Matley Heath
Applemore
Beaulieu R.
Matley Bog
Matley Passage
Decoy Pond Fm.
Ipley Manor
Purlieu Ho.
Dibden Bottom
Langdown
Black Down
Yewtree Heath
A326

1
149
2
3
150
4
A
B
C
D
E
F
143
137
138
Battery
Twyford Down
Golf Course
A33
B3057
Compton Down
Compton End
Compton
Shawford
SHAWFORD
Twyford
B3335
A335
R. Itchen
Otterbourne
Manor Ho.
Otterbourne Grange
Allbrook
Brambridge
Highbridge
Colden Common
Nob's Crook
Fisher's Pond
Stoke Common
Stoke Park Fm
Fish Pond
Hensting
Hensting Fm.
Marwell Hall
MARWELL ZOOLOGICAL GDNS.
B2177
Marwell Manor
Hurst Fm.
Roughay Fm.
Morestead Down
Morestead Fm.
Hazeley Down
Moresteadd
Hazeley Fm.
Fawley Down
Longwood Warren
Longwood Warren Ho.
Old Down
Warren Fm.
New Warren Fm.
Lane End Down
Lane End
Lane End Fm.
Holding Fm.
Beauworth
Hamilton Fm.
Longwood Ho.
Greendowns
Whiteflood Fm.
Longwood Dean Fm
Dur Wood
The Holt
Preshaw Ho.
Preshaw
Bottom Fm
Owslebury
Baybridge
Whaddon Fm.
Green Hill
Blackdown
Belmore Ho.
Woodcote
Bigpath Fm.
Stephen's Castle Down
Corhampton
Dean Fm.
Corhampton Down
Upham
West Hall
E A S T
S H
Park Hills Wood
Crowdhill
Hall Lands Ho.
Stroudwood
B3037
Lower Upham
Stakes Fm.
Dean
Galley Down
Dundridge
The Hangers
B3035
Woolstreet Fm.
Wintershill Hall
Cross Lanes Fm.
Northbrook
Wintershill
Newtown
PALACE
Bishop's Waltham
Hoe
Hill Top
Bishopstoke
Stoke Park Wood
EASTLEIGH
Fair Oak
Knowle Hill
Greenwood Fm.
Lake Fm.
SOUTHAMPTON PARKWAY
Horton Heath
Chalcroft Fm.
Durley
Durley Manor Fm.
Locks Fm.
Snakemoor
Brown Heath
Clewers Hill
Glebe
Moorgreen Fm.
Croft Ho.
Stapleford Fm.
M27
Hatch Bottom
Townhill Park
Berrywood Fm.
Moorgreen
Braxells Fm
Durley Mill
Harfields
Nation's Fm.
Waltham Chase
Long Common
Hosp.
B3035
Boorley Green
Curdridge
Row Ash
Shedfield Ho
B2177
Shirrell Heath
Midanbury
West End
Harefield
A334
Wildern
Broadoak
Botley
BOTLEY
Kitnocks
Hall Ct.
Shedfield
Turkey Island
Kingsmead
Frith Fm.
Thornhill Park
Thornhill
A27
B3033
Hedge End
Steeple Ct.
Fairthorne Manor
Biddenfield
Meon Park
Sholing Common
Weston Common
A3024
Hightown
Netley Hill
Manor Fm.
Curbridge
Cold Harbour Fm.
Sholing
UPPER HAMBLE
Ridge Fm.
Webb's Land
Hoe Moor Ho.
Ridge Copse
A3025
Newtown
Lowford
Burridge Fm.
A3051
Burridge
Botley Wood
R. Meon
Old Netley
Whiteley
Bursledon
Lower Swanwick
Swanwick
Lee Ground Coppice
Knowle Hosp.
Butlocks Heath
B3397
Sarisbury
SWANWICK
Gt. Funtley Fm.
Hound
NETLEY
Netley
A27
Park Gate
Lee Ground
Funtley
Kneller Ct.
Royal Victoria Hospital
HAMBLE
Hosp.
River Hamble
M27
ROYAL VICTORIA
Hamblecliff Ho.
Locks Heath
A32
College
TITCHFIELD ABBEY
Hamble
FAREHAM

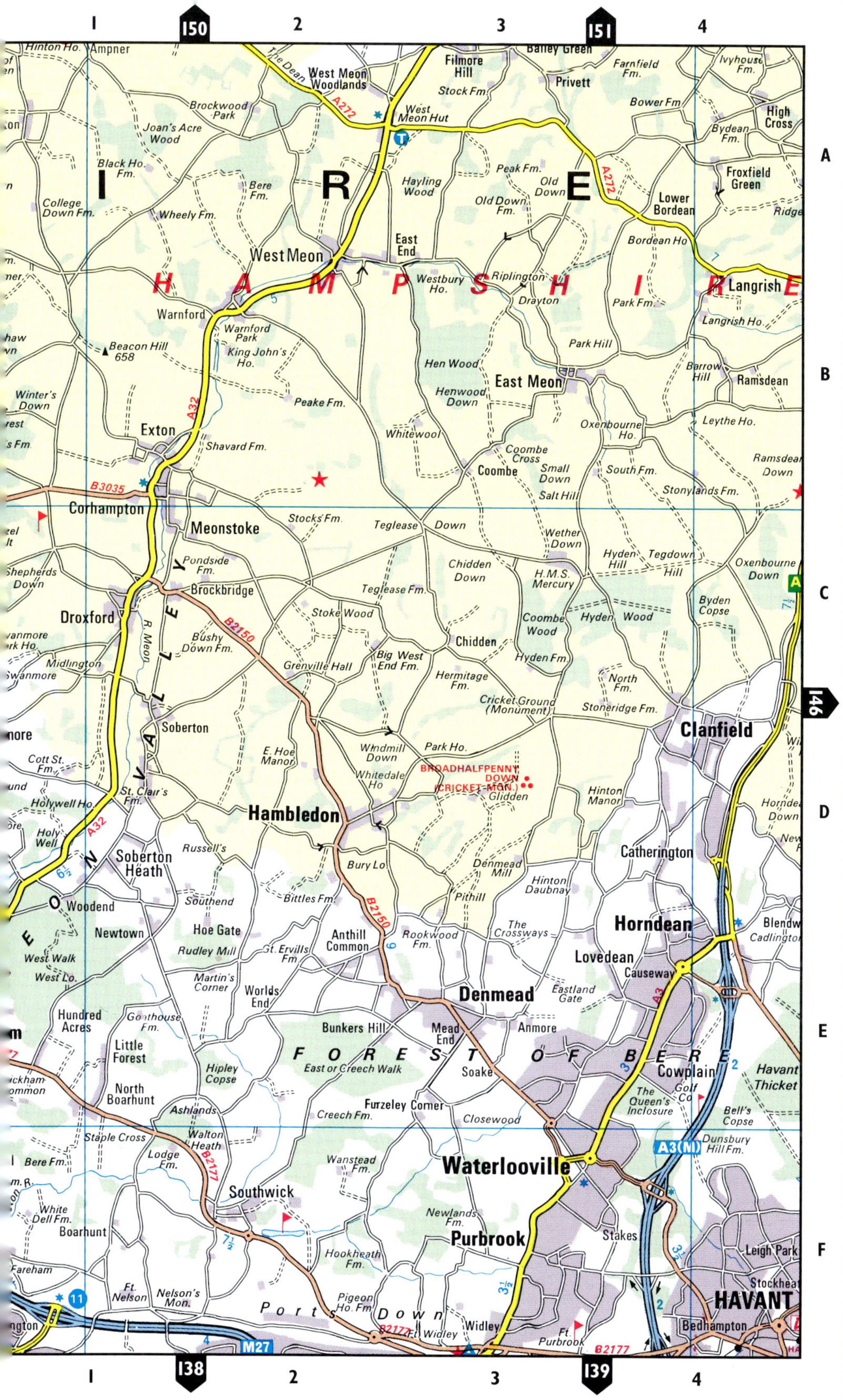
HAMPSHIRE
West Meon
Warnford
Exton
Corhampton
Meonstoke
Droxford
Soberton
Soberton Heath
Hambledon
East Meon
Langrish
Clanfield
Catherington
Horndean
Lovedean
Denmead
Cowplain
Waterlooville
Purbrook
Southwick
HAVANT
FOREST OF BERE
MEON VALLEY
Hinton Ampner
West Meon Woodlands
Filmore Hill
Stock Fm.
West Meon Hut
Privett
Farnfield Fm.
Ivyhouse Fm.
Bower Fm.
High Cross
Bydean Fm.
Froxfield Green
Lower Bordean
Bordean Ho.
Brockwood Park
Joan's Acre Wood
Black Ho. Fm.
Bere Fm.
Hayling Wood
Peak Fm.
Old Down
Old Down Fm.
College Down Fm.
Wheely Fm.
East End
Westbury Ho.
Riplington
Drayton
Park Fm.
Langrish Ho.
Warnford Park
King John's Ho.
Beacon Hill 658
Hen Wood
Park Hill
Barrow Hill
Ramsdean
Henwood Down
Winter's Down
Peake Fm.
Whitewool
Oxenbourne Ho.
Leythe Ho.
Coombe Cross
Coombe
Small Down
Salt Hill
South Fm.
Stonylands Fm.
Ramsdean Down
Shavard Fm.
Stocks Fm.
Teglease
Down
Wether Down
Hyden Hill
Tegdown Hill
Oxenbourne Down
Pondside Fm.
Brockbridge
Chidden Down
H.M.S. Mercury
Shepherds Down
Teglease Fm.
Byden Copse
Stoke Wood
Coombe Wood
Hyden Wood
Bushy Down Fm.
Chidden
Hyden Fm.
Midlington
Swanmore
Grenville Hall
Big West End Fm.
Hermitage Fm.
North Fm.
Cricket Ground (Monument)
Stoneridge Fm.
Windmill Down
Park Ho.
E. Hoe Manor
BROADHALFPENNY DOWN (CRICKET MON.)
Whitedale Ho
Glidden
Hinton Manor
Cott St. Fm.
St. Clair's Fm.
Holywell Ho.
Holy Well
Horndean Down
Russell's
Bury Lo.
Denmead Mill
Woodend
Southend
Bittles Fm.
Pithill
Hinton Daubnay
Newtown
Hoe Gate
Anthill Common
Rookwood Fm.
The Crossways
West Walk
Rudley Mill
St. Ervills Fm.
West Lo.
Martin's Corner
Worlds End
Eastland Gate
Causeway
Hundred Acres
Goathouse Fm.
Bunkers Hill
Mead End
Anmore
Little Forest
East or Creech Walk
Soake
Havant Thicket
Hipley Copse
Golf Co.
North Boarhunt
Furzeley Corner
The Queen's Inclosure
Bell's Copse
Ashlands
Creech Fm.
Closewood
Staple Cross
Walton Heath
Dunsbury Hill Fm.
Bere Fm.
Lodge Fm.
Wanstead Fm.
White Dell Fm.
Boarhunt
Newlands Fm.
Stakes
Leigh Park
Hookheath Fm.
Fareham
Ft. Nelson
Nelson's Mon.
Pigeon Ho. Fm.
Ports Down
Ft. Widley
Widley
Ft. Purbrook
Stockheath
Bedhampton
A272
A32
A3
A3(M)
B3035
B2150
B2177
M27
150
151
146
138
139
1
2
3
4
A
B
C
D
E
F

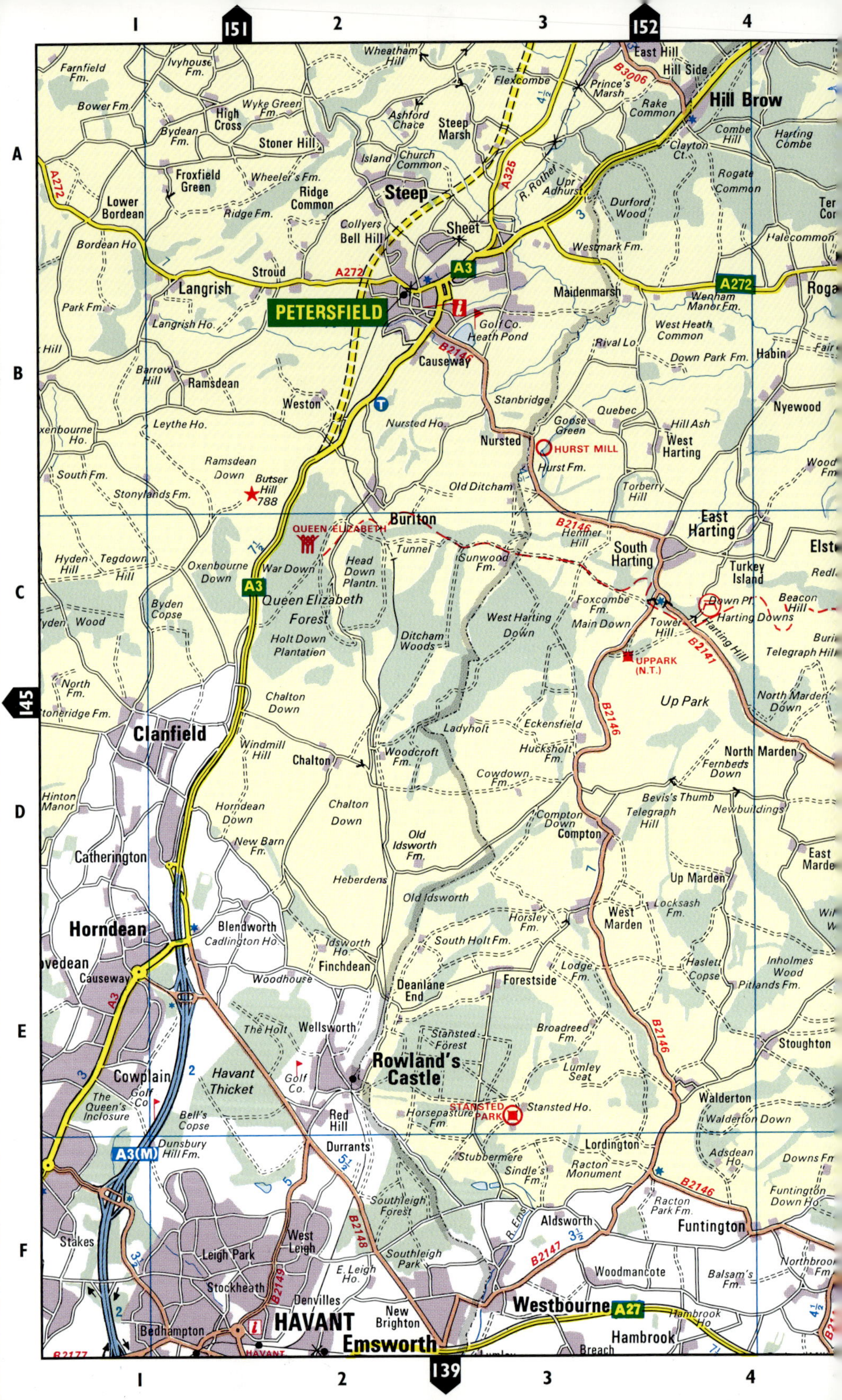

1
151
2
3
152
4
A
B
C
D
E
F
145
139
PETERSFIELD
A3
A272
A325
B3006
B2146
B2141
B2148
B2149
B2147
A27
A3(M)
B2177
Farnfield Fm.
Ivyhouse Fm.
Wheatham Hill
Flexcombe
East Hill
Hill Side
Hill Brow
Bower Fm
High Cross
Wyke Green Fm.
Ashford Chace
Steep Marsh
Prince's Marsh
Rake Common
Bydean Fm.
Stoner Hill
Combe Hill
Harting Combe
Island
Church Common
Clayton Ct.
Froxfield Green
Wheeler's Fm.
Rogate Common
Lower Bordean
Ridge Common
Steep
R. Rother
Upr Adhurst
Durford Wood
Ridge Fm.
Collyers
Bell Hill
Sheet
Bordean Ho
Westmark Fm.
Halecommon
Stroud
Langrish
Maidenmarsh
Wenham Manor Fm.
Park Fm.
Golf Co.
Heath Pond
Langrish Ho.
West Heath Common
Rival Lo
Causeway
Down Park Fm.
Habin
Barrow Hill
Ramsdean
Weston
Stanbridge
Quebec
Nyewood
Leythe Ho.
Nursted Ho.
Goose Green
Hill Ash
Nursted
HURST MILL
West Harting
Ramsdean Down
Hurst Fm.
South Fm.
Butser Hill 788
Old Ditcham
Torberry Hill
Stonylands Fm.
QUEEN ELIZABETH
Buriton
Hemner Hill
East Harting
Tunnel
South Harting
Hyden Hill
Tegdown Hill
Oxenbourne Down
War Down
Head Down Plantn.
Sunwood Fm.
Turkey Island
Queen Elizabeth Forest
Foxcombe Fm.
Down Pl.
Beacon Hill
West Harting Down
Main Down
Harting Downs
Tower Hill
Harting Hill
Byden Copse
Holt Down Plantation
Ditcham Woods
UPPARK (N.T.)
Telegraph Hill
North Fm.
Chalton Down
Up Park
North Marden Down
Clanfield
Ladyholt
Eckensfield
Windmill Hill
Chalton
Woodcroft Fm.
Hucksholt Fm.
North Marden
Fernbeds Down
Cowdown Fm.
Hinton Manor
Horndean Down
Chalton Down
Bevis's Thumb
Telegraph Hill
Newbuildings
Compton Down
Compton
New Barn Fm.
Old Idsworth Fm.
Catherington
East Marden
Heberdens
Up Marden
Old Idsworth
Horndean
Blendworth
Cadlington Ho.
Horsley Fm.
West Marden
Locksash Fm.
Idsworth Ho.
South Holt Fm.
Causeway
Finchdean
Haslett Copse
Inholmes Wood
Deanlane End
Forestside
Lodge Fm.
Pitlands Fm.
Woodhouse
Stansted Forest
Broadreed Fm.
The Holt
Wellsworth
Stoughton
Havant Thicket
Golf Co.
Rowland's Castle
Lumley Seat
Cowplain
The Queen's Inclosure
Walderton
Bell's Copse
Red Hill
STANSTED PARK
Stansted Ho.
Walderton Down
Horsepasture Fm.
Dunsbury Hill Fm.
Durrants
Stubbermere
Lordington
Adsdean Ho.
Downs Fm
Sindle's Fm.
Racton Monument
Southleigh Forest
Racton Park Fm.
Funtington Down Ho.
Stakes
West Leigh
Aldsworth
Funtington
R. Ems
Leigh Park
Southleigh Park
Woodmancote
Balsam's Fm.
E. Leigh Ho.
Stockheath
Denvilles
Westbourne
Hambrook Ho.
New Brighton
Bedhampton
HAVANT
Emsworth
Hambrook
Breach

153
148
141
142
South Tidworth
Tidworth Ho.
Ashdown Copse
Kimpton Down Fm.
Pickford Hill
Thruxton
Figheldean Field
Gallows Barrow
Ablington Down
Danger Area
Figheldean
Ablington
Silk Hill
Hare Warren
Home Fm.
Golf Course
Dunch Hill
Syrencot Ho.
Brigmerston Field
Milston Down
R. Avon
Brigmerston
Milston
Bulford Field
Carter Barracks
Durrington
Durrington Walls
Beacon Hill
Bulford
Bulford Camp
Shipton Bellinger
Snoddington Manor
Snoddington Down Fm.
Althorne
Lains Fm.
Middlecot
Thruxton Hill
Thruxton Fm.
Park Ho.
Home Fm.
Cholderton Hill
Quarley
Quarley Manor Fm.
Cholderton
Cholderton Lo.
A303
A338
A3028
Countess
Ratfyn
Amesbury
The Pennings
EARL'S FARM DOWN BARROWS
Beacon Hill Fm.
Ann's Fm.
R. Bourne
Wilbury Ho.
Quarley Down Fm.
Grateley
GRATELEY
B3084
Arundel Fm.
Newton Toney
Warren Fm.
Boar Knoll
Palestine
A345
Stockport
Boscombe Down Airfield
Allington
Boscombe
Sunnyside Fm.
Castle Fm.
Martin's Clump
Tower Hill
Croft Fm.
Allington Fm.
Idmiston
Boscombe Down East
Isle of Wight Hill
Sudden Hill
Jack's Bush
Cusse's Gorse
Birdlime Fm.
Porton
Idmiston Down
Roche Court Down
A343
Hollom Down Fm.
Downbarn West
Gomeldon
Porton Down
The Pheasant Hotel
Lopcombe Corner
A30
Hurdcott Fm.
Winterbourne Gunner
Winterbourne Dauntsey
Battery Hill
Ashley's Copse
Roche Ct.
Winterbourne Earls
Thorny Down
East Winterslow
Hurdcott
Figsbury Ring
The Haven
Firs Road
New Manor Fm.
Hill Fm.
Broughton
Bracknell Croft
Dunstable Fm.
Warren Fm.
Ford
Middle Winterslow
Stock Bottom
Bentleigh Fm.
The Common
Noad's Copse
St. Thomas's Bri.
West Winterslow
Hedgemoor Copse
Fussells Lodge Fm.
Picked Copse
Bishopdown
Queen Manor Fm.
Pitton
Savage's Fm.
Pitton Lo.
Hound Wood
Bentley Wood
Northaw School
Laverstock
SALISBURY
Beechy Dean Copse
The Livery
Coalpits Copse
West Tytherley
Clarendon Palace (remains)
Milford
Long Copse
Farley
Petersfinger
A36
Best's Fm.
Barnridge Copse
The Green
Tytherley Common
Nightwood Copse
Clarendon Ho.
Howe Fm.
Dean Copse
Britford
Shute End
Hawks Grove
Frenchmoor Fm.
Ivychurch Fm.
Common Plantn.
East Grimstead
Pilgrims Croft

153

1 2 3 4

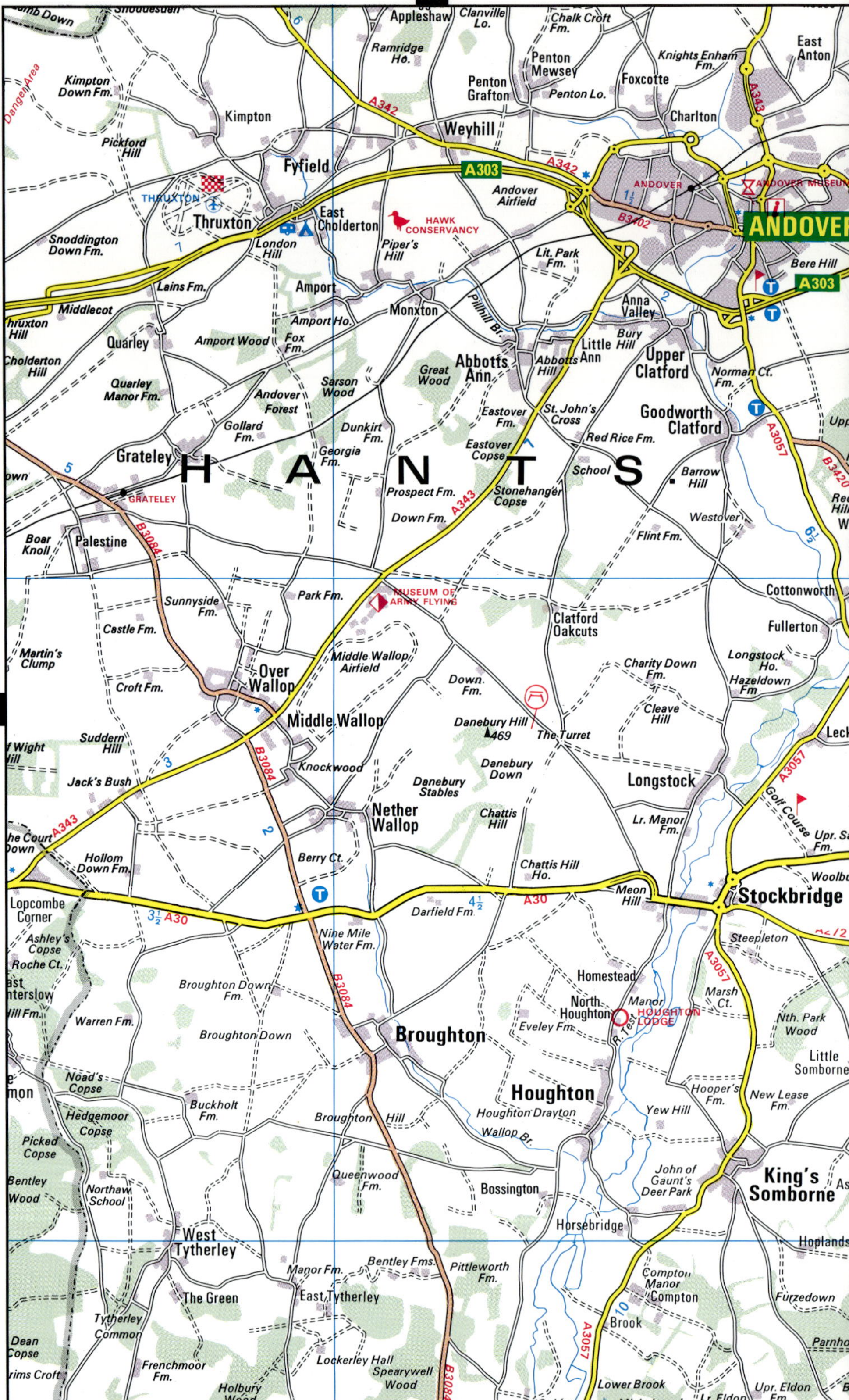

147

142

143

1 2 3 4

1
2
154
3
4
A
B
C
D
E
F
150
143
144
HAM
Laverstoke
Turrill Hill Fm.
Freefolk
Whitchurch
Lynch Hill
Southfield Fm.
Spring Pond Fm.
The Mansion
Hurstbourne Park
Finkley Manor Fm.
Faulkner's Down Fm.
Tinker's Hill
The Common
Picket Piece
Harewood Peak
Tufton
New Barn Cotts.
Laverstoke Grange Fm.
Upr. Whitehill Fm.
Laverstoke Wood
B3400
Budgett Fm.
Hurstbourne Priors
Testbourne
New Barn Fm.
Brickkiln Wood
Andover Down
Down Ho.
Forest
Tracy's Dell
East Aston
B3048
R. Test
Roundwood Fm.
Old Pound
Longparish
Longparish Ho.
Lr. Mill
Firgo Fm.
Tufton Warren Fm.
Freefolk Wood
Middleton
A34
Forton
South Side Fm.
Harewood
Cottage End
Drayton Camp
Tidbury Ring
Upr. Norton Fm.
Gavelacre
Bransbury
A303
Tidbury Fm.
Bullington Cross Inn
Warren Fm.
Park Fm.
Upr. Cranbourne Fm.
B3048
Bransbury Common
Tidbury Common
Dublin Fm.
Upr. Bullington
Norton Manor
Hunton Grange Fm.
Lwr. Bullington
Newton Stacey
Barton Stacey
Cranbourne Grange
Priory
B3420
Hill Barn
Norsebury Ring
Northbrook Ho.
Gravel Hill
Sutton Scotney
Chilbolton
Egypt
Hunton
Norsebury Ho.
Cocum Fm.
Newton Down Fm.
Wonston
Stoke Charity
Weston Colley
A30
Moody's Down Fm.
Middlebarn Fm.
Borough Fm.
Wonston Manor Fm.
Old Stoke
Hill Fm.
Sutton Down Fm.
West Stoke Fm.
Borough Down Fm.
The Leckford Hutt
Chilbolton Down
Brockley Warren
Newdown Fm.
Sth. Wonston Fm.
Crawley Down
Lunway's Inn
South Wonston
Tunnel
Crawley Forest
Burnt Wood
Crawley Warren
Heath Ho.
Dumper's Oak
New Barn
B3420
Crawley Ct.
Burntwood Fm.
Windmill Hill
Crawley
A33
Bull Fm.
Folly Fm.
Beeches Fm.
Littleton Ho.
Down Fm.
A272
Long Park
Abbots Worthy
B3047
Sombourne Ho.
Rookley Manor
Northwood Park
Up Somborne
Littleton
Headbourne Worthy
Kings Worthy
Coll. of Agriculture
Lainston Ho.
Harestock
A3090
M3
Easton
Gt. Up Somborne Wood
Moor Ct. Fm.
Ashley Wood
Ashley Castle
Sparsholt
Dean
A33
Weeke
B3044
Ham Green
SU
30
40
B3041
Teg Down
Fulflood
Forest of Bere Fm.
Farley Mount
Crab Wood
WINCHESTER
Prison
St. Giles's Hill
No Man's Land
B3404
City Museum
Hosp.
Cathedral
Wolvesey Castle
Magdalen Hill Down
Farley Mt. 572
Mount Down
Pitt Down
Bar End
Chilcomb
Farley Down
Enmill Fm.
Stanmore
South Lynch
St. Cross
Oliver's
A333
St Catherine's Hill

155

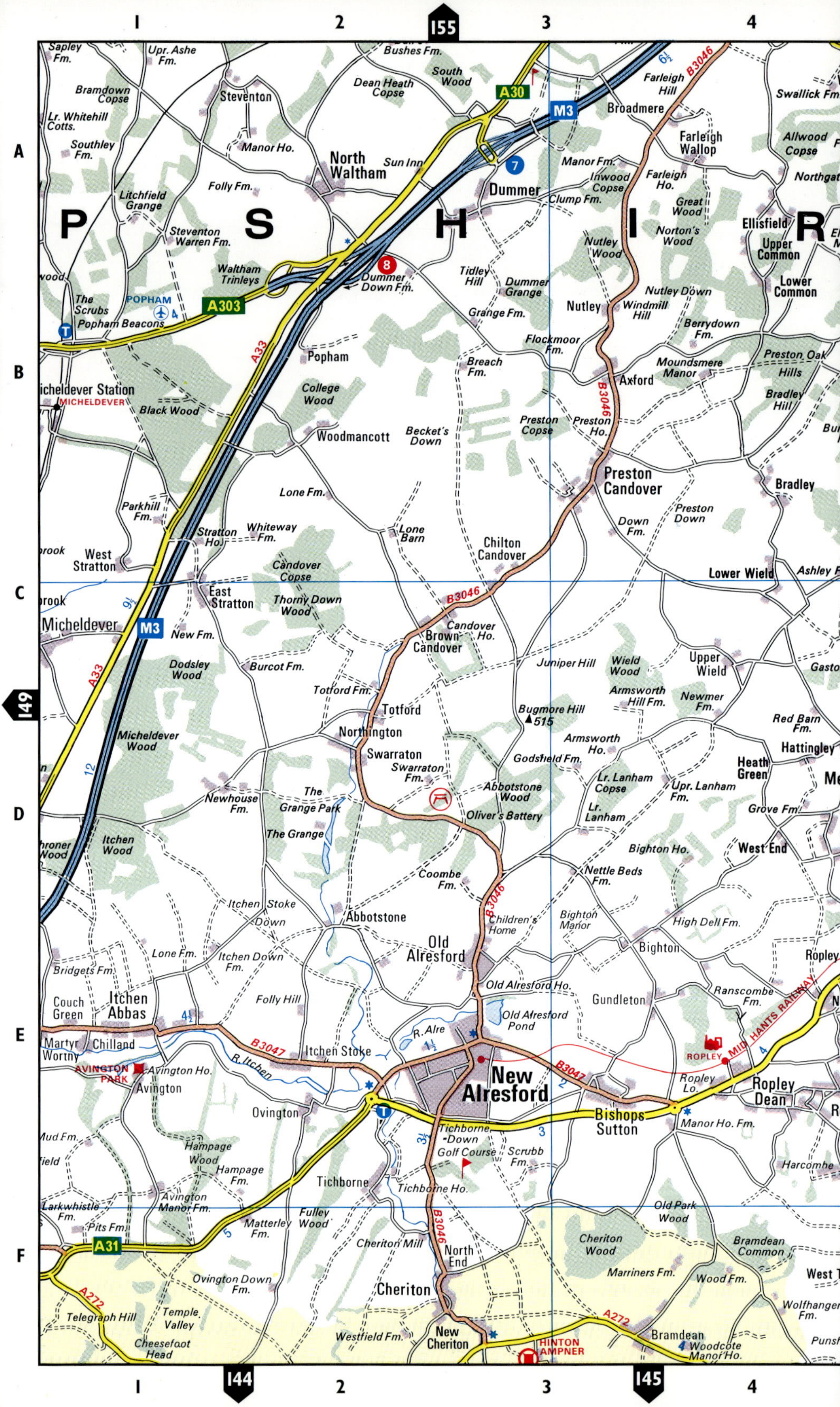

149

144

145

156
145
146
152
Tunworth
Weston Corbett Pl.
Upton Grey
Four Lanes End
Horsedown Common
Park Corner Fm.
Tile Barn Fm.
Stapely Fm.
Hen Wood
Weston Corbett
Hoddington Ho.
South Warnborough
Warnborough Park
Sutton Warblington
Hesters Copse
Long Sutton
Travers Fm.
Weston Patrick
Lit Park Copse
College
Long Sutton Ho.
Well
Herriard Park
Herriard Ho.
Herriard
Humbly Grove Copse
New Fm.
Vinney Copse
Sutton Common
Highnam Copse
Crest Hill Fm.
Isnage Fm.
E
Lee Fm.
Nash's Green
Herriard Grange
New Fm.
High Wood
Great Park
Weston Common
Powntley Copse
Bagmore
Southrope
Swaineshill Fm.
Yamhams Fm.
Hawkins Wood
Lower Froyle
JENKYN PLACE
Bentley
Coldrey
Herriard Common
LASHAM
Shalden Green
Golden Pot
Ham Wood
Upper Froyle
R. Wey
Lasham Hill
Lasham Wood
Shalden Park Wood
Brockham Hill Fm.
Holybourne Down
Isington
Lasham
Shalden
Golf Co.
Mill Ct.
A339
A31
B3349
Cuckoo's Corner
Binsted
Stean Fm.
West Ct.
Wadgett's Copse
Southwood Fm.
Amery Wood
Holybourne
Hay Pl.
Neatham
Bentworth
Bentworth Lo.
Warren Fm.
Anstey
Copt Hill
Childer Hill Fm.
Thedden Copse
ALTON
CURTIS MUSEUM
South Hay
Wyck
Wyck Pl.
Holt End
Thedden Grange
Bentworth Hall
Will Hall
Wilsom
Neatham Down
Clay's Fm.
The St
Beech
B3004
Wivelrod
Hosp.
Green Street
Medstead Grange
The Abbey
Bushy Leaze Wood
JANE AUSTEN'S HOME
East Worldham
B3006
King John's Hill
Chawton Pk. Fm.
Chawton
Alton Forest
West Worldham
Binswood
Chawton Park Wood
Shortheath Common
Barleywood Fm.
Hartley Mauditt
Shortheath
South Town
Roe Downs
MID-HANTS RAILWAY
A32
Woodside Fms.
Hartley Park Fm.
Candovers
Oakhanger
The Warren
MEDSTEAD & FOUR MARKS
Lower Farringdon
Upper Farringdon
Chapel Fm.
Wick Hill Fm.
Soldridge
Norton Fm.
Golf Co.
Pies Fm.
Four Marks
Priory Fm.
Annetts Fm.
New Barn Fm.
Inadown Fm.
Kitfield Fm.
Hawthorn
Newton Common
Pelham Pl.
Selborne Hanger
Temple Manor
Blackmoor
Newton Valence Pl.
Selborne
Old Down Wood
OATES MEMORIAL MUS. & GILBERT WHITE MUS.
Kitwood
Plash Wood
Shotters
Selborne Common
Newton Valence
Swelling Hill
Rotherfield Park
Bradshott Hall
Benhams Fm.
East Tisted
Heard's Fm.
Noar Hill
Plain Fm.
Charlwood
Le Court
Lyewood Ho.
Goleigh Wood
Empshott Green
Empshott
Greatham
EAST
Colemore
Monkwood
Vann Fm.
Hawkley Hurst
Merryfield Fm.
West Tisted Common
Slade Fm.
Field Fm.
Church Fm.
Manor Ho.
A325
Brickkiln Fm.
Colemore Common
Hawkley
HAMPSHIRE
Burgates
The Warren
West Liss
Basing Park
The Jumps
Barnet Side
Coles
Warren Corner
Oakshott
Liss Pl.
Liss

157
146
151
Dora's Green
Upper Hale
Hale
Farnham Park
Badshot Lea
A324
Runfold
A31
Pilgrim's Way
Sandy Cross
Seale
NORTH DOWNS
Lr. Old Park
FARNHAM CASTLE KEEP
Hosp.
FARNHAM
College
Upr. Clare Fm.
Powderham Castle
Dippenhall
A325
A287
FARNHAM
B3001
Compton
College
R. Wey
Binton Fm.
Golf Courses
The Sands
Crooksbury Hill
Littleworth Cross
Hampton
Glade Fm
Ridgway Ho.
Hill Fm.
Bury Ct.
Wrecclesham
The Bourne
Waverley
WAVERLEY ABBEY
Culverswell Hill
Crooksbury Common
Black Lake
Fullbrook Fm.
East Green
Shortheath
B3384
Lower Bourne
Sheephatch Schools
Charleshill
Elstead
Holt Pound
Boundstone
SURREY
Holt Pound Inclosure
Rowledge
BENTLEY
BIRDWORLD
Lodge Pond
Alice Holt Lo.
ALICE HOLT FOREST
Tilford Reeds
Tilford
Pot Common
Shortfield Common
Tilford Common
Yagden Hill
Woolford's Fm.
Elstead Common
Catham Copse
Bucks Horn Oak
West End
Millbridge Sch.
Golf Course
Spreakley
Lane End
The Moat
Blacknest
Willow's Green Inclosure
Frensham Lit. Pond
Abbot's Lo.
Hankley Common
Danger Area
Kettlebury Hill
Thursley Common
Binsted Pl.
Batt's Corner
Pitt Fm.
Frensham
Frensham Manor
FRENSHAM COMMON
Woodlands
Abbotts Wood Inclosure
Dockenfield
Frensham Gt. Pond
Rushmoor
Houndown
Truxford
Nature Reserve
Wheatley
Straits Inclosure
Frithend Ho.
Hoggatt
Frithend
Convent
Churt Ho.
Churt Common
The Devil's Jumps
Pitch Place
Thursley
Cosford Ho.
Bowlhead Green
Kingsley
Malthouse Fm.
R. Slea
Mellow Fm.
Stream Fm.
Churt
Green Cross
Hyde Fm.
Punch Bowl Fm.
Kingsley Common
Sleaford
Headley Park
Tignals
Stock Fm.
Emley Fm.
Barford
Broxhead Common
Hearn
Golf Co.
Beacon Hill
Highcomb Bottom
A3
Free Piece
R. Wey
Arford
Land of Nod
Headley Down
Whitmoor Vale
HINDHEAD
A287
Lindford
B3002
Hindhead
Devil's Punch Bowl
Gibbet Hill 894
High Bu
Bordon Camp
Deadwater
Headley
Grayshott Hall
Ludshott Common
Gentle's Copse
Common
Coombe Head
Bordon
Grayshott
Whitehill
Whitehill Chase
Standford
Passfield
Waggoners Wells
Mt. Alvernia
Weydown Common
Hollywater
Passfield Common
Bramshott Ct.
Ludshott Manor
Downlands
Bramshott Common
Round Hill
Fern Hill
B3004
Bramshott
HASLEMERE
Critchmere
Cranmer Bottom
WOOLMER FOREST
Conford
Bramshott Vale
Hammer Bottom
Shottermill
Holm Hills
Cold Ash Hill
Hosp.
Hammer
Woolmer Pond
Griggs Green
B2131
Camelsdale
A286
B2131
Holly Hills
Liphook
Linchmere Common
Marley Common
Bohunt
Newtown
Longmoor Camp
Foley Manor
Linchmere
Marley Ho.
Kingsley Green
Stanley Common
Cognor Wood
Palmer's Ball
Marley Heights
Friday Hill
Weavers Down
Forest Mere
Golf Course
Wheatsheaf Common
Greenhill Wood
Liss Forest
Langley
Hollycombe
HOLLYCOMBE STEAM COLLECTION
Parkgate Rough
Langley Ct.
Chapel Common
Lower Lodge Fm.
Fernhurst
The Mint
Milland Pl.
East Liss
Ciddy Hall
Milland
Elmers Copse
Minepit Copse
A3
Wardley
Rake

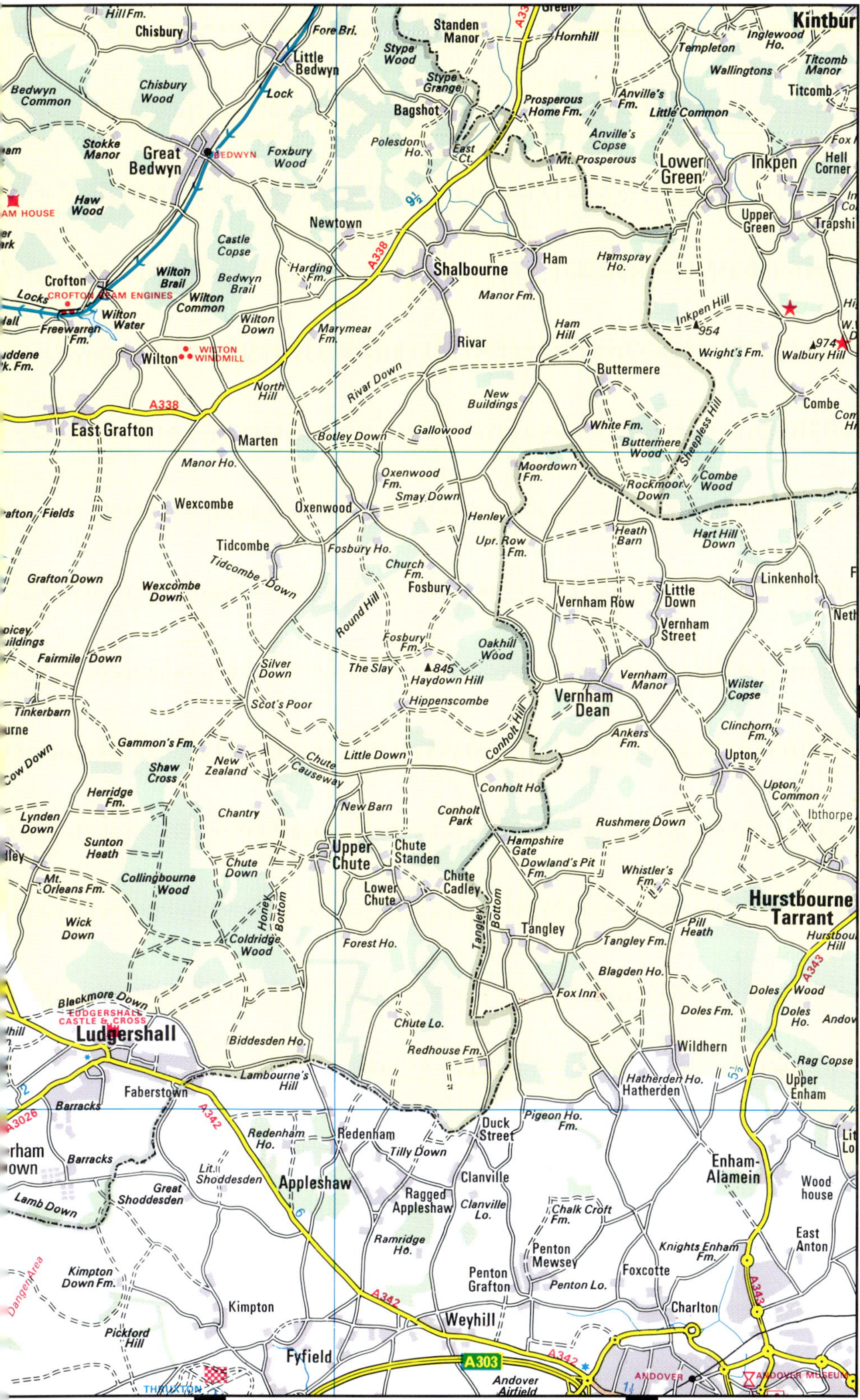
Hill Fm.
Chisbury
Fore Bri.
Little Bedwyn
Stype Wood
Standen Manor
Hornhill
Kintbury
Inglewood Ho.
Templeton
Wallingtons
Titcomb Manor
Titcomb
Bedwyn Common
Chisbury Wood
Lock
Stype Grange
Bagshot
Prosperous Home Fm.
Anville's Fm.
Little Common
Stokke Manor
Great Bedwyn
BEDWYN
Foxbury Wood
Polesdon Ho.
East Ct.
Anville's Copse
Mt. Prosperous
Lower Green
Inkpen
Hell Corner
Haw Wood
Newtown
Upper Green
Trapshill
Castle Copse
A338
Shalbourne
Ham
Hamspray Ho.
Crofton
Wilton Brail
Harding Fm.
Bedwyn Brail
Locks
CROFTON STEAM ENGINES
Wilton Common
Manor Fm.
Inkpen Hill
Wilton Water
Freewarren Fm.
Wilton Down
Marymear Fm.
Ham Hill
954
974
Wright's Fm.
Walbury Hill
Wilton
WILTON WINDMILL
Rivar
Buttermere
North Hill
River Down
New Buildings
Combe
East Grafton
Marten
Gallowood
Botley Down
White Fm.
Buttermere Wood
Sheepless Hill
Manor Ho.
Oxenwood Fm.
Moordown Fm.
Smay Down
Rockmoor Down
Combe Wood
Wexcombe
Oxenwood
Fields
Henley
Tidcombe
Fosbury Ho.
Upr. Row Fm.
Heath Barn
Hart Hill Down
Tidcombe Down
Church Fm.
Fosbury
Linkenholt
Grafton Down
Wexcombe Down
Little Down
Vernham Row
Round Hill
Vernham Street
Fosbury Fm.
Oakhill Wood
Fairmile Down
Silver Down
The Slay
845
Haydown Hill
Vernham Manor
Wilster Copse
Vernham Dean
Scot's Poor
Hippenscombe
Tinkerbarn
Conholt Hill
Ankers Fm.
Clinchorn Fm.
Gammon's Fm.
Little Down
Upton
Shaw Cross
New Zealand
Chute Causeway
Conholt Ho.
Upton Common
Herridge Fm.
New Barn
Conholt Park
Ibthorpe
Lynden Down
Chantry
Rushmere Down
Sunton Heath
Upper Chute
Chute Standen
Hampshire Gate
Dowland's Pit Fm.
Chute Down
Whistler's Fm.
Mt. Orleans Fm.
Collingbourne Wood
Lower Chute
Chute Cadley
Hurstbourne Tarrant
Honey Bottom
Tangley Bottom
Tangley
Pill Heath
Wick Down
Coldridge Wood
Forest Ho.
Tangley Fm.
Hurstbourne Hill
Blagden Ho.
A343
Blackmore Down
Fox Inn
Doles Wood
LUDGERSHALL CASTLE & CROSS
Chute Lo.
Doles Fm.
Doles Ho.
Ludgershall
Biddesden Ho.
Redhouse Fm.
Wildhern
Rag Copse
Lambourne's Hill
Hatherden Ho.
Hatherden
Upper Enham
Faberstown
A342
Barracks
A3026
Pigeon Ho. Fm.
Redenham Ho.
Redenham
Duck Street
Tilly Down
Enham-Alamein
Barracks
Lit. Shoddesden
Appleshaw
Clanville
Wood house
Great Shoddesden
Ragged Appleshaw
Clanville Lo.
Chalk Croft Fm.
Lamb Down
Ramridge Ho.
Penton Mewsey
Knights Enham Fm.
East Anton
Kimpton Down Fm.
Danger Area
Penton Grafton
Penton Lo.
Foxcotte
Kimpton
Charlton
Weyhill
Pickford Hill
Fyfield
A303
ANDOVER
ANDOVER MUSEUM
THRUXTON
Andover Airfield

147
148
154

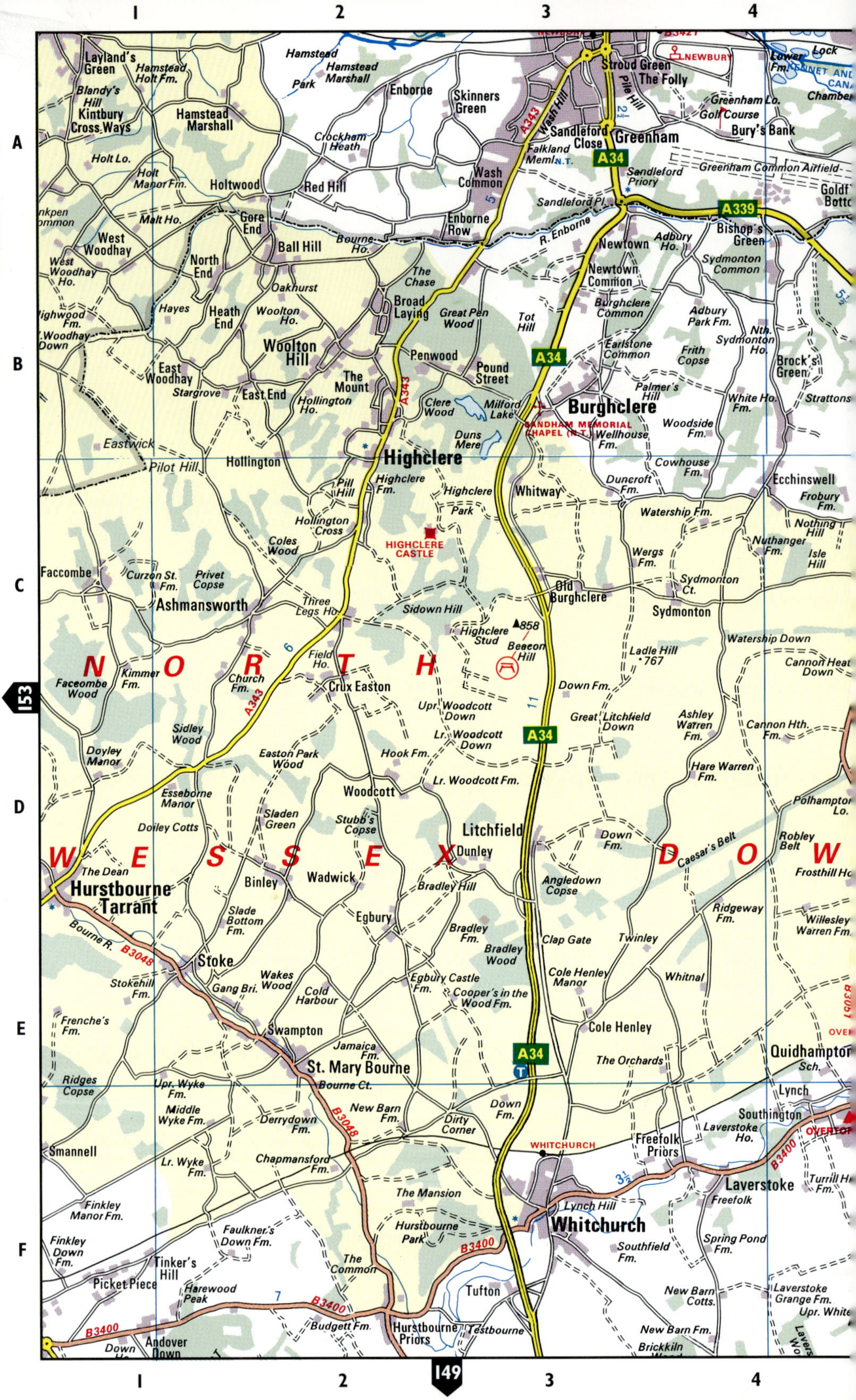

Layland's Green
Hamstead Holt Fm.
Blandy's Hill
Kintbury Cross Ways
Hamstead Marshall
Hamstead Park
Enborne
Skinners Green
Newbury
Stroud Green
The Folly
Pile Hill
Greenham Lo. Golf Course
Bury's Bank
Lower Fm.
Lock
Kennet and Avon Canal
Chamber
Crockham Heath
Wash Hill
Sandleford Close
Greenham
Falkland Meml. N.T.
A34
Greenham Common Airfield
Holt Lo.
Holt Manor Fm.
Holtwood
Red Hill
Wash Common
Sandleford Priory
Sandleford Pl.
A339
Goldf Botto
Gore End
Malt Ho.
Enborne Row
Bourne Ho.
R. Enborne
West Woodhay
Ball Hill
Newtown
Adbury Ho.
Bishop's Green
West Woodhay Ho.
North End
The Chase
Newtown Common
Sydmonton Common
Oakhurst
Burghclere Common
Adbury Park Fm.
Hayes
Heath End
Woolton Ho.
Broad Laying
Great Pen Wood
Tot Hill
Highwood Fm.
Woodhay Down
Woolton Hill
Earlstone Common
Frith Copse
Nth. Sydmonton Ho.
Penwood
Brock's Green
East Woodhay
The Mount
Pound Street
Palmer's Hill
Stargrove
East End
Hollington Ho.
Clere Wood
Milford Lake
Burghclere
White Ho. Fm.
Strattons
Sandham Memorial Chapel (N.T.)
Wellhouse Fm.
Woodside Fm.
Eastwick
Duns Mere
Highclere
Pilot Hill
Hollington
Cowhouse Fm.
Pill Hill
Highclere Fm.
Highclere Park
Whitway
Duncroft Fm.
Ecchinswell
Frobury Fm.
Watership Fm.
Nothing Hill
Hollington Cross
Highclere Castle
Nuthanger Fm.
Isle Hill
Coles Wood
Wergs Fm.
Faccombe
Curzon St. Fm.
Privet Copse
Old Burghclere
Sydmonton Ct.
Ashmansworth
Three Legs Ho.
Sidown Hill
Sydmonton
858
Highclere Stud
Watership Down
Beacon Hill
Ladle Hill 767
Cannon Heath Down
Field Ho.
N O R T H
Faccombe Wood
Kimmer Fm.
Church Fm.
Crux Easton
Down Fm.
Upr. Woodcott Down
Great Litchfield Down
Ashley Warren Fm.
Sidley Wood
Lr. Woodcott Down
Cannon Hth. Fm.
Doyley Manor
Easton Park Wood
Hook Fm.
Hare Warren Fm.
Lr. Woodcott Fm.
Esseborne Manor
Woodcott
Polhampton Lo.
Sladen Green
Stubb's Copse
Litchfield
Doiley Cotts
Down Fm.
Robley Belt
Caesar's Belt
W E S S E X
Dunley
D O W
The Dean
Hurstbourne Tarrant
Binley
Wadwick
Bradley Hill
Angledown Copse
Frosthill Ho
Slade Bottom Fm.
Egbury
Ridgeway Fm.
Willesley Warren Fm.
Bourne R.
B3048
Bradley Fm.
Clap Gate
Twinley
Bradley Wood
Stoke
Wakes Wood
Egbury Castle Fm.
Cole Henley Manor
Whitnal
Stokehill Fm.
Gang Bri.
Cold Harbour
Cooper's in the Wood Fm.
Frenche's Fm.
Swampton
Cole Henley
Jamaica Fm.
The Orchards
Quidhampton Sch.
St. Mary Bourne
Ridges Copse
Upr. Wyke Fm.
Bourne Ct.
Lynch
Middle Wyke Fm.
New Barn Fm.
Down Fm.
Southington
Derrydown Fm.
Dirty Corner
Laverstoke Ho.
Freefolk Priors
Smannell
Whitchurch
Overton
Chapmansford Fm.
B3400
Lr. Wyke Fm.
Laverstoke
Turrill Ho Fm.
The Mansion
Freefolk
Lynch Hill
Finkley Manor Fm.
Hurstbourne Park
Whitchurch
Faulkner's Down Fm.
Southfield Fm.
Spring Pond Fm.
Finkley Down Fm.
Tinker's Hill
The Common
Picket Piece
Harewood Peak
Tufton
New Barn Cotts.
Laverstoke Grange Fm.
Upr. White
B3400
Budgett Fm.
Hurstbourne Priors
Testbourne
New Barn Fm.
Andover Down
Brickkiln Wood
1
2
3
4
A
B
C
D
E
F
153
149

1
2
3
4
A
B
C
D
E
F
Colthrop
Midgham
Thatcham
Avon
Lock
Lock
Lock
Lock
Old Mill Ho.
Padworth Ho.
Church
Padworth
Ufton Court
Ufton Park
Burghfield Common
Cowpond Piece
Gibbet Piece
Round Oak
Crookham Manor
Brimpton Mill
Wasing Lr. Fm.
Aldermaston
Stone Ho.
Brimpton
Shalford Fm.
Aldermaston Ct.
Court Fm.
Padworth Common
Burnt Common
Crookham Common
Crookham
Lt. Park Ho.
R. Enborne
Wasing
Aldermaston Park
Benyon's Inclosure
Mortimer West End
Hyde End
Decoy Pond
Mill Green
Goose Hill
Brimpton Common
A340
Calleva Museum
Blacknest
Heath End
Tadley Common
Silchester Common
Calleva (Roman Town)
Headley
Huntsmoor Hill
Ashford Hill
B3051
Inhurst
Pamber Heath
Silchester
Woodlands
The Holt
Three Ash
Plastow Green
Tucker's Hill Fm.
Fair Oak
Axmansford
Pamber Forest
Waits Fm.
Hawley Ho.
Tadley
Dairy Ho. Fm.
Wheat Hold
Skate's Fm.
Haines Fm.
Pitchorn Fm.
Upr. House Fm.
Baughurst
Latchmere Green
Wolverton Common
Browninghill Green
Pamber Green
Little London
Bramley Corner
Gt. Knowl Hill
Frith Common Fm.
Baughurst Ho.
Pound Green
Wyeford Fm.
Court Corner
Sandford Wood
Stratton Manor
Pember Fm.
A339
Wolverton Ho.
Towns End
West Heath
Pamber End
Kingsclere
Stony Heath
Beaurepaire Ho.
The Old Ho.
Wolverton
Foscot Fm.
Charter Alley
Salters Heath
Park House
Ramsdell
Cufaude
Plantation Hill
Morgaston Wood
The Vyne (N.T.)
White Hill
Dorrel Wood
Skyer's Wood
Vyne Park
Cottington's Hill
Ewhurst Ho.
Kiln Green
Monk Sherborne
Freemantle Pk. Fm.
Sherborne St. John
Manor Fm.
Crock
For Down
Hannington
Spier's Copse
Basing Forest
Woodgarston Fm.
Balstone Fm.
Upper Wootton
Elm Bottom Cross
Popley Fields
Tidgrove Warren Fm.
North Oakley
Ibworth
Shothanger Fm.
Popley
Whitedown Cotts.
Warren Bottom Copse
Hosp.
N
S
Freemantle Fm.
Hay Wood
Tangier Ho.
Sheardown Fm.
Wootton St. Lawrence
Wortingwood Fm.
Winklebury
Houndmills
Oakridge
South View
Malshangar Ho.
Basingstoke
White Lane
Manydown Ho.
Basingstoke
Willis Museum
Gt. Deane Wood
Worting
B3400
Ashe Warren Ho.
Newfound
Summer Down Fm.
Kite Hill
Buckskin
South Ham
Kings Furlong
Deane Down Fm.
Clarken Green
Polhampton Fm.
Battledown Fm.
Deane
Ashe
Oakley
Kempshott
Down Grange
Overton
Source of the R. Test
College
East Oakley
Brighton Hill
Ashe Park
Cheesedown Fm.
Berrydown Ct.
Pardown
Cliddesden
Bull's Bushes Copse
Bull's Bushes Fm.
Hatch Warren Fm.
Sapley Fm.
Upr. Ashe Fm.
B3046
South Wood
Dean Heath Copse
Farleigh Hill
Swallick Fm.
Bramdown Copse
Steventon
A30
Broadmere
M3
Lr. Whitehill Cotts.
Allwood Copse
Farleigh Wallop
Southley Fm.
Manor Ho.
North Waltham
Sun Inn
Manor Fm.
Northgate
Inwood Copse
Farleigh Ho.
Folly Fm.
Dummer
Litchfield Grange
Clump Fm.
Great Wood
Ellisfield
156
150

1
2
3
4
A
B
C
D
E
F
Grazeley
Hyde End
Auclam
Culverlands
Pierce's Fm.
Highlands
Spencer's Wood
Arborfield Ct.
Langley Common
Goddard's Green
Sch.
Bloomfield Hatch
Kenney's Fm.
Lamb's Fm.
SWALLOWFIELD PARK
Swallowfield
Headlands Fm.
Wokefield Park
Mortimer Ho.
Crosslane Fm.
Loddon Ct.
Wyvols Ct.
Farley Castle (Sch.)
Arborfield Garrison
Long
Mortimer
Foudry Br.
Gt. Park Fm.
Trunkwell Ho.
The Priory
Farley Hill
Farleyhill Ct.
Hogwood Fm.
West Ct.
Stratfield Mortimer
MORTIMER
Perrins Fm.
Beech Hill
Blackwater R.
A327
Home Wood
Stanford End
Riseley
The Leas
Baniste
Fair Cross
Cordery's Fm.
Ford
New Mill
B3348
The Devil's Highway (Roman Road)
Park Corner
B3349
Bramshill
Plantation
Springwater Fm.
Stratfield Saye Park
Birchen Copse
Lower Common
Eversle
A33
Wellington Mon.
Heckfield Heath
Park Fm.
Warbrook
Stratfield Saye
West End Green
Lavell's Fm.
Kings Fm.
STRATFIELD SAYE HOUSE
WELLINGTON
Heckfield Pl.
Bramshill
Heath Warren
Park Pitham Copse
Heckfield
B3011
Fair Oak Green
Wellington Arms
Southend Fm.
Lawn Fm.
Highfield Ho.
New Inn
Stratfield Turgis
Police Coll.
Holly Cross
Folly Fm.
Bylands Sch.
Bramshill Park
Warren He
Turgis Green
Spanish Green
Bramley Green
Lillymill Fm.
Clay's Fm.
Hound Green
Hazeley
Hulford's Copse
Bramley
BRAMLEY
Flood's Fm.
Hartley Wespall
Thackham's Fm.
Mattingley
Hazeley Heath
Sherfield on Loddon
Baker's Fm.
Topford's Fm.
Dipley
Inholmes Ct.
Hare's Fm.
Hartf
Mill Fm.
Black Wood
R. Whitewater
Golf Co.
Nth. Foreland Lo.
Lyde Green
Hartley Wintney
Sherfield Ct.
Church End
Dutch Ho.
Street End
West Green
WEST GREEN HOUSE GARDEN (N.T.)
Rotherwick
Sherfield Hill
Wildmoor
R. Loddon
Lyde R.
The Old Ho.
Borough Ct.
Phoenix Green
Moulshay Fm.
A30
Four Lanes Fm.
Tylney Hall Sch.
Tylney Home Fm.
B3349
Scutts Fm.
Taplin's Fm.
Murrell Green
Four Lanes End
Hook Ho.
M3
Shapley Heath
Chineham
Blackland's Fm.
Hook
Holt
WINCHFIELD
Winchfield
Hurst
Basing Lo. Fm.
Pyott's Hill
Newnham
HOOK
B3016
Court Ho. Fm.
Daneshill
Gold's Fm.
Hook Common
Bartley Heath
Potbridge
Oliver's Battery
A30
Heather Row
Poland Mill
Odiham Common
Swan's Fm.
Dogmersf
Old Basing
Water End
Nately Scures
Lodge Fm.
BASING HO.
Andwell
Butter Wood
Whitehall
Basingstoke Canal
Tundry Pond
A30
Hatch
Up Nately
North Warnborough
Broad Oak
Dogmersfield Park Coll.
M3
Tunnel
Colt Hill
Huish Ho.
Mapledurwell
Greywell
A287
Dicken's La. Plantn.
Hungry Lo.
Odiham
Hill Side
Coxm Woo
Bullock's Fm.
Polecat Corner
Five Lanes End
Spring Head
Chosley Fm.
Lit. Rye Fm.
Hackwood Fm.
Down Fm.
Ford Fm.
Odiham Airfield
Roke Fm.
Hackwood Ho.
Hackwood Park
Bidden
B3349
Penn Cr
Gaston Copse
Stapely Down Fm.
Park Corner Fm.
Tunworth
Upton Grey
Four Lanes End
Horsedown Common
Weston Corbett Pl.
Winslade
Tile Barn Fm.
Stapely Fm.
Hoddington Ho.
Hen Wood
Swan Fm.
South Warnborough
Sutton Warblington
Long Sutton
Travers Fm.
Weston Corbett
Weston Patrick
Warnborough Park
Hesters Copse
Herriard Park
Lit. Park Copse
College
Well
Herriard Ho.
Long Sutton Ho.
Herriard
Humbly Grove
New Fm.

155

151

Crowthorne
Sandhurst
Finchampstead
Yateley
Frogmore
Blackwater
Hawley
Camberley
Bagshot
Frimley
Frimley Green
Mytchett
Cove
Farnborough
Farnborough Airfield
Fleet
Crookham Village
Church Crookham
Aldershot
Ash Vale
Ash
Tongham
Heath End
Weybourne
Hog Hatch
Crondall
Farnham
Bramshill Forest
Owlsmoor
College Town
Royal Military Academy
Wellington College
Broadmoor Hosp.
Eversley Cross
Up Green
Darby Green
Cricket Hill
Yateley Common
Hartford Bridge Flats
Hawley Common
Hornley Common
Minley Manor
Fleet Services
Fleet Pond
Southwood Camp
Farnborough Green
West Heath
Farnborough Park
Deepcut Barracks
Ash Common
Ash Green
North Town
Badshot Lea
Runfold
Upper Hale
Dippenhall
Compton
The Sands
Seale
Sandy Cross
Pilgrim's Way
North Downs
Lightwater
Heatherside
Chobham Ridges
Olddean Common
Gravel Hill 420
Surrey Hill 427
Beacon Hill 581
Long Valley
Rushmoor Arena
Airborne Forces Museum
Gurkha Museum
Farnham Castle Keep
M3
A30
A31
A287
A322
A3016
A325
A321
A323
A327
B3013
B3014
B3348
B3430
1
2
3
4
A
B
C
D
E
F

152

INDEX

Places with entries in the gazetteer are not necessarily included in the index, unless they are also mentioned elsewhere. Reference in *italic* are to illustrations.